JEWISH STATESMANSHIP

Lest Israel Fall

Paul Eidelberg

University Press of America,® Inc.
Lanham · New York · Oxford

Copyright © 2002 by
Paul Eidelberg

University Press of America,® Inc.
4720 Boston Way
Lanham, Maryland 20706
UPA Acquisitions Department (301) 459-3366

12 Hid's Copse Rd.
Cumnor Hill, Oxford OX2 9JJ

All rights reserved
Printed in the United States of America
British Library Cataloging in Publication Information Available

ISBN 0-7618-2380-8 (paperback : alk. ppr.)

∞™ The paper used in this publication meets the minimum
requirements of American National Standard for Information
Sciences—Permanence of Paper for Printed Library Materials,
ANSI Z39.48—1984

Dedicated to the Jewish People

They have allayed the [impending] disaster of My people by making light of it, saying, "Peace! Peace!" But there is no peace.

JEREMIAH 6:14

CONTENTS

Chapter 1: Introduction and Executive Summary 7

Chapter 2: Israel's Flawed Declaration of Independence:
A Partial Remedy 19

Chapter 3: Democracy Versus Judaism:
Beyond Spinoza 35

Chapter 4: Israel's Citizenship Problem:
Conceptual Therapy 55

Chapter 5: Israel's Flawed Parliamentary System:
A Jewish Remedy 83

Chapter 6: Jewish Statesmanship:
A Presidential Remedy 105

Chapter 7: Israel's Flawed Judicial System:
A Democratic Remedy 123

Chapter 8: The Nature of the Muslim-Jewish Conflict:
A Philosophical Analysis of the "Peace Process" . . 159

Chapter 9: Democratic Versus Martial Diplomacy:
A Jewish Alternative 177

Chapter 10: A Jewish Democratic Constitution for Israel 207

Epilogue 227

Endnotes 231

Bibliography 251

Index 257

The Ariel Center for Policy Research 260

The Foundation for Constitutional Democracy 261

ACKNOWLEDGMENTS

This book is very much the result my work as founder and President of the Foundation for Constitutional Democracy, an Israeli-American research institution based in Jerusalem. Hence, I am especially indebted to the Foundation's co-founder and Chairman, Dr. Mark I. Rozen. It is with pleasure that I also acknowledge the support of our Executive Director, Eleonora Shifrin, who has brought many of the teachings of this book to Israel's Russian-speaking community.

The publication of *Jewish Statesmanship* would not have been possible were it not for the Foundation's membership and the support of its friends, too numerous to mention. Here I can only express my profound gratitude to Mr. Abraham Aizenman, Mr. Bernard Dworkin, Mr. Jack Greenberg, Rabbi Herzl Kranz, Ms. Sylvia Mandelbaum, Dr. David Morrison, Mr. Joseph Orlow, Professor Zeev Pearlman, Rabbi Eliezer Perr, Mrs. Caral Fread-Perry, Dr. Richard Rolnick, Mrs. Sarah Schweig, Mr. Alan Silverstein, Dr. Joseph Wahl, and Dr. Robert Warren.

I owe special thanks to Mr. Arieh Stav, chairman of the Ariel Center for Policy Research. During the past thirteen years, Arieh Stav brought many of my writings to the attention of the Hebrew-reading public via Israel's premier journal, *Nativ: A Journal of Politics and the Arts*, of which he is the dauntless editor.

Jewish Statesmanship could not have been written, however, were it not for my two extraordinary teachers, of blessed memory, HaGaon Dr. Chaim Zimmerman and Professor Leo Strauss. From the latter I learned the nature of statesmanship articulated in the works of the greatest political philosophers; from the former I learned how to interface statesmanship with the Torah, the paradigm of wisdom and of how man should live.

May this book serve the sacred cause of the Jewish People to whom it is dedicated.

CHAPTER 1
Introduction and Executive Summary

[W]e ought not to forget that there is an incessant and ever-flowing current of human affairs towards the worse, consisting of all the follies, all the vices, all the negligences, indolences, and supinenesses of mankind; which is only controlled, and kept from sweeping all before it, by the exertions which some persons constantly, and others by fits, put forth in the direction of good and worthy objects.

John Stuart Mill
Representative Government

Introduction

Israel is disintegrating. The basic causes of this disintegration may be listed under four headings: (1) disunity resulting from a lack of Jewish statesmanship and Jewish national purpose; (2) disunity resulting from flawed political and judicial institutions; (3) disunity resulting from extreme cultural heterogeneity, and (4) disunity resulting from secular-religious discord. Underlying each of these causes is a more fundamental one: a normless or irrational conception of democracy that clashes with Judaism and renders it impossible for Israel to achieve the national unity required for its survival in a hostile Arab-Islamic environment.

From the moment of Israel's re-establishment, evident in its Declaration of Independence of May 14, 1948, this so-called Jewish state has been suffering from cognitive dissonance. By this I mean that the basic concepts of public discourse in Israel clash with traditional Judaism, and most Jews in this country are quite traditional. Such concepts as the "state", "religion", "politics", "democracy", "freedom", "equality", "citizenship", etc., need to be clarified and assimilated to Jewish thought and values. Otherwise, Jewish statesmanship is inconceivable and Israel will continue to disintegrate until it collapses.

Jewish statesmanship simply does not exist in Israel. Of course Jews become prime ministers, as did Benjamin Disraeli and Pierre Mendes France. But no sober person expected *Jewish* statesmanship from these remarkable English and French Jews. No one expected them to incorporate Jewish laws and principles into the legislation of their respective countries, or to pursue foreign policies inspired by distinctively Jewish goals. These Jews did not think like *Jews*, but like *Gentiles*. Much the same may be said of the prime ministers of Israel.

If statesmanship is defined as the application of philosophic wisdom to action, then *Jewish* statesmanship is the application of *Jewish* wisdom to action. Architectonic statesmen such as James Madison and Alexander Hamilton studied the great philosophers, those who addressed themselves to such questions as "How should man live?" and "What kind of government is most conducive to human excellence?" These philosophic statesmen employed ancient and modern wisdom in the process of designing a constitution appropriate to the character and circumstances of the American people.[1] Although Jewish statesmen ought to study the greatest philosophers, they will delve primarily into the wisdom of Judaism and ask, "How should Jews as *Jews* live?" and "What kind of government is appropriate to contemporary Israel and conducive to *Jewish* excellence?"

Statesmanship requires not only exemplary personalities, but well-designed political institutions. As we shall see, however, Israel's political institutions are utterly flawed, none more so than its parliamentary system of proportional representation with an electoral threshold low enough for taxi drivers to form a party in the hope of winning two seats in the Knesset! This system encourages what may be termed "egotistical pluralism". Twenty-two new parties registered for, and thirty participated in, the 1999 Knesset elections! No less than fifteen won Knesset seats, as a result of which the Government formed thereafter consisted of eight parties, each with its own priorities. Such a Government is simply incapable of formulating and pursuing a rational and resolute national strategy. Such a Government renders statesmanship of *any* kind is inconceivable. No wonder the concept of

Jewish statesmanship is unheard of in Israel, in consequence of which the pursuit of distinctively Jewish national goals is impossible.

Complicating the task of Jewish statesmanship in Israel is its cultural incongruity. Israel is a nation of immigrants. Jews from a hundred countries have returned to the land of their fathers. These immigrants were influenced by ethnic characteristics as diverse as the countries from which they originated. Most come from non-democratic and non-Western regimes. They harbored different conceptions of political and economic freedom, of the relationship between the individual and the state. They also differed in their attitude toward the Jewish heritage, especially as concerns the relationship between religion and the state.

But what renders this cultural melange explosive is the presence in Israel of a burgeoning population of 1.25 million Arabs. The Arabs are a proud people, and all efforts to assimilate them have failed.[2] Despite their enjoying a standard of living and a level of education unequaled in the Arab-Islamic world, and notwithstanding their political freedom and fair representation in Israel's parliament, they do not want to live under a Jewish government. In fact, while calling for the return of Arab refugees, they are developing institutions for the establishment of another "Palestinian" entity. Their commitment to Israel's demise is transparent. If this were not enough, anti-Semitism is also rife among some 350,000 gentiles who immigrated to Israel from Russia since 1989. A demographic time-bomb is ticking, threatening five million Jews.

Israel might be able to mitigate and perhaps overcome this cultural incongruity were it not for the fourth cause of disintegration, secular-religious discord. The Zionists who founded the Third Commonwealth were, for the most part, atheists from Eastern Europe. They disdained religious Jews, especially the Sephardim from North Africa. This disdain still animates Israel's left-wing elites, who regard Haredi Jews, be they Sephardi or Ashkenazi, with repugnance.

Let me not be misunderstood. All honor to the architects of modern Israel, who facilitated the in-gathering of a million and more Jews, and who developed the nation's economic and scientific-technological infrastructure. But we need to be candid about the malignant divisions in this country, for at stake is Israel's survival and therefore the well-being of all its people, be they religious or not.

Israel's first Prime Minister, David Ben-Gurion, was a self-professed Marxist. His Mapai Party – hereafter called the Labor Party – controlled virtually every lever of public power for the first twenty-nine years of the State's existence. Labor's ideological objective was to reduce Judaism to a "religion" as opposed to a nationality (precisely the goal of the nineteenth-century Reform movement). The Torah would then be relegated to the private domain; it would cease to have any affect on public law and national policy. Israel's world-historical purpose as a light unto the nations would be less than a dim memory.

Paradoxically, while Israel's secular Labor Party paraded under the banner of "democracy", the Jewish population over which it ruled was for the most part either orthodox or traditional, with a majority believing in the divine origin of the Torah! An ideological rift separated the rulers from most of the ruled – and still does. This cleavage would collapse the country were it not for Israel's external threat.

In the long run, however, the fear of war or of violent death, which no doubt impels many Israelis to sacrifice much of their heartland for peace, is hardly a sufficient basis for national unity and survival, especially vis-a-vis relentless foes whose attitude toward life and death differs profoundly from that of Jews. This religious and cultural asymmetry renders Israel's mundane policy of "territory for peace" more than dubious. But this policy, we shall see, is itself a manifestation of a culturally and politically divided nation.

How can the idea of Jewish statesmanship take root in Israel when its prime ministers are not well-versed in Judaism enough to couch their public pronouncements and policies in a language recognizably Jewish, hence linked to the Prophets and Sages of Israel? How can any Israeli government pursue a distinctively Jewish national goal when its cabinets consist of a hodgepodge of secularists and religionists, virtually all of whom are more concerned about their place on their party's electoral list than with the destiny of the Jewish people? And these cabinets have become increasingly discordant.

To be sure, Israeli cabinets have almost always consisted of secularists and religionists. But the atmosphere today is charged with fearful uncertainty, and for the following reason. Prior to the 1999 elections, the Labor and Likud parties each had more Knesset Members (MKs) than the combined number of MKs of the religious parties in Israel's 120-member parliament. No longer is this the case. In 1999, the ultra-orthodox Shas Party (Sephardi) alone won an astonishing 17 seats, while United Torah Judaism, another ultra-orthodox party, won 5 seats, to which add 5 won by the National Religious Party. In contrast, the Likud plummeted from a previous 32 seats to 19, while Labor, which had won 34 seats in 1996, could do no better than win 23. Bearing in mind that the ultra-secular Meretz and Shinui parties respectively won 10 and 6 seats, one may reasonably conclude that neither Labor nor the Likud, Israel's two major secular parties, has sufficient power to prevent the antagonism between the ultra-secular and the ultra-religious parties from tearing the country apart in the near future.

Of course, secular and religious Jews may combine to forestall the ascendancy of an Arab nationalist coalition. Perhaps they will eventually act on the recognition that Israel's Arab parties (as will be shown later) are surrogates of the PLO whose vaunted territorial objective is a Palestinian state extending from the Jordan to the Mediterranean. In the long run, however, an alliance of secular and religious Jews would be of no avail. For inasmuch as the birthrate of Israel's Arab citizens is twice that of Jews, then, given the democratic principle of one adult/one vote, Israel will eventually lose its reputation as a Jewish as well as a democratic state. But this means that democracy, *as understood and practiced in Israel*, is self-contradictory and self-destructive. (Which only indicates that a more rational conception of democracy is urgently needed.)

Unfortunately, even if Israel were not threatened by a demographic time-bomb, its long-term survival as a Jewish commonwealth would be doubtful given the anti-traditional agenda of its Supreme Court. This judicial body is the most powerful in the world, a veritable super legislature. Much the same may be said of the US Supreme Court, which has become the primary engine of social change in America, affecting even the moral values of American society. Unlike its American counterpart, however, which adjudicates less than 200 cases a year, Israel's Supreme Court and subsidiaries annually render thousands of decisions affecting the political, social, moral, religious, and even the ethnic character of the country – and this with only minute reference to the laws and principles of the Jewish heritage. No other Court in the world ignores the legal history of its own people.

Moreover, by relying increasingly on American jurisprudence, the Supreme Court imports into Israel's daily life the permissiveness and indiscriminate egalitarianism of American society. This cannot but further diminish Israel's Jewishness, on which the nation's unity and survival ultimately depend. We need only add here that the method of appointing Supreme Court judges in Israel is strikingly undemocratic. This enables the Court to pursue more systematically an ultra-secular agenda which cannot but erode Jewish national consciousness, a precondition of Jewish statesmanship and Jewish national unity.

If anything is capable of uniting the Jews of Israel, it is only the Torah (but not as simplistically perceived). After all, it was the laws and world-inspiring teachings of the Torah that unified and sustained the Jewish people during 2,500 years of dispersion, humiliation, and decimation. It was the Torah that imbued the Jewish people with national consciousness, indeed, with a loftiness of character and purpose that entitled them, in Nietzsche's words, to "despise their despisers".

Now, most remarkable is the fact that, despite Labor's control of Israel's economy, the mass media, and the country's educational and cultural institutions, an unprecedented "return" to Torah Judaism has occurred in recent decades, most notably by men trained in the rigorous sciences. During the 1990s alone more than 200,000 Israelis became observant. The 1999 elections saw no less than 33 orthodox Jews enter Israel's Knesset! In stark contrast, that decade witnessed the demise of secular Zionism. The Zionists who founded the State of Israel metamorphosed into "post-Zionists" even more alienated from the Jewish heritage. But this only renders secular-religious antagonism more conspicuous and ominous.

Israel's secular elites see that the revival of Torah Judaism and the high birthrate of religious Jews as leading to the latter's political ascendancy. These elites, whose fathers founded the State and developed its infrastructure, have become bitter and desperate, judging from their unprecedented public vilification of Haredi Jews, the most prolific of Israel's Jewish population. To compensate for its diminishing electoral base among Jews, the Labor Party must court Arab voters as never before. In fact, the Arabs can now determine who will be Israel's Prime Minister. It should be obvious, however, that Labor politicians can hardly win Arab voters without making concessions to the PLO with which most of Israel's Arab citizens identify. It is in this light that we are to understand post-Zionism and Labor's victory in the June 1992 elections, and perhaps even the Israel-PLO Declaration of Principles of September 13, 1993.

* * *

Summing up, Israel's cultural disunity will soon reach explosive proportions. So, too, will its secular-religious disunity. As for the disunity resulting from Israel's political and judicial institutions, this more tractable problem has already prompted some parties to advocate a constitutional remedy, but none equal to the task; indeed, the "remedy" may further divorce religion from the state.

Consequently, this book will prepare a comprehensive philosophical and constitutional framework for dealing with the basic causes of Israel's disintegration *before* the country collapses.

Executive Summary

Pessimists will say, "There is no time." The present writer has heard this response repeatedly over the last twenty years whenever he or someone else offered a remedy for Israel's malaise. This excuse for inaction leaves us to conclude that, short of a miracle or a profound revolution, Israel will not see much of the twenty-first century. The author nonetheless believes that the Israel's collapse can be avoided, but only by Jewish, constitutional means. Obstructing any remedial action is an irrational and self-destructive conception of democracy which clashes with Judaism. This problem will be elucidated in Chapter 2 in the process of discussing Israel's Declaration of Independence. Suffice to say here that while the Declaration proclaims Israel as a Jewish state, it also prescribes political equality for all its inhabitants irrespective of religion. Since political equality is a cardinal principle of democracy, and since this principle can lead to the political ascendancy of a non-Jewish majority, the Declaration harbors a contradiction noted but unresolved by various commentators.

Chapter 3 will resolve the contradiction between democracy and Judaism by showing that the contradiction only applies to *contemporary* democracy, and not to *classical* democracy. For whereas the former is *normless* and contrary to the Torah, the latter is *normative* and can be assimilated to the Torah. Analysis of these two types of democracy will reveal different conceptions of freedom and equality. These will be related to the Judaic understanding of freedom and equality as revealed in primary Jewish sources. Since these two principles involve Jewish law, and since Jewish law evokes in the minds of many the idea of "theocracy", Chapter 3 will show that, properly understood, the idea of theocracy, like that of democracy, obscures the true nature of Jewish governance.

Discussion of the meaning of equality within the context of the Declaration of Independence and the Torah raises the issue of citizenship in a Jewish commonwealth. This issue will be discussed in Chapter 4. The question will arise as to whether Israel is the "State of the Jews" or the "State of its citizens" (as post-Zionists avow). We shall transcend this issue by showing that the concept of citizenship is foreign to Jewish law. This will enable us to design a form of government that does not depend entirely on the concept of citizenship. We shall then be in a more advanced intellectual position to deal with the Arab demographic problem. However, dissolving the concept of citizenship as applied to Jews leads to the issue of "Who is a Jew?" We shall discuss this issue primarily from a philosophical and political perspective.

Clarification of the concept of the Jew and of citizenship provides background for discussing the flaws in Israel's parliamentary system, the subject of Chapter 5. There we shall reveal the undemocratic character of Israel's Knesset: how the system of fixed party lists insulates politicians from, and renders them unaccountable to, the voters. We shall also show that the system of fixed party lists tends to lower the quality of those elected to the Knesset. A Jewish remedy will require a bicameral parliament in which the upper branch is assigned the function of legislation, while the lower branch is assigned the function of administrative oversight. The latter function is beyond the capacity of the present Knesset, if only because of its members' subservience to their party leaders who head the cabinet ministries.

The current mode of electing the Knesset directly affects the composition of the Cabinet, which has hitherto consisted almost entirely of members of parliament. Since no party has ever gained a parliamentary majority, the Cabinet has of necessity consisted of several parties. The result, as indicated above, is fragmented Government, one may even say, a plural Executive. In place of coalition cabinet government, we shall propose, in Chapter 6, a presidential system – the appropriate context in which to enlarge on the subject of Jewish statesmanship. Presidential governm will be justified on Jewish as well as on secular grounds. Arguments against presidential government will be refuted and will be shown to have no relevance to Israel.

Chapter 7 will discuss Israel's flawed judicial system. As indicated above, Israel's Supreme Court resorts almost entirely to non-Jewish laws and principles in adjudicating countless cases affecting the daily life and character of Israeli society. Actually, this practice violates the Foundations of Law Act of 1980 which was intended to make Jewish law *primus inter pares* ("first among equals") vis-a-vis English, Continental, and American law. Chapter 7 will discuss the political and moral consequences of a Supreme Court that substitutes foreign legal systems for the legal heritage of the Jewish people. The chapter will also contrast English, Roman, and American law with Jewish civil law. It will provide prima facie evidence showing that Jewish civil law is more rational and more ethical than its gentile counterparts. We shall propose a very simple democratic remedy to the undemocratic and unJewish judicial system now operative in Israel.

Having discussed Israel's ideological and institutional flaws and how they may be remedied, we shall then turn, in Chapter 8, to a philosophical analysis of the Arab-Jewish conflict with special reference to the theoretical underpinning of the Israel-PLO agreements. The basic question raised in this chapter concerns the motives of Arab-Islamic rulers and whether economic prosperity can provide an adequate basis for peace in the Middle East. Empirical data will supplement our philosophical analysis of the Middle East peace process.

Chapter 9 will thus provide the foundation on which to examine Israeli diplomacy. There we shall discuss the theoretical flaws of democratic diplomacy and its inability to compete well with martial diplomacy. This will require analysis of the nature of democratic regimes and of Arab-Islamic culture. A brief "handbook" will be developed showing alternative ways of negotiating with dictatorships, both from a democratic and Jewish perspective. We shall then show how Israel can seize the initiative in foreign affairs.

Chapter 10 will provide a rationale for, as well as the general structure of, a Jewish democratic Constitution for Israel. This Constitution will make Jewish statesmanship possible, will galvanize the Jewish spirit required to overcome the causes of Israel's disintegration and thus prevent this country's impending collapse.

CHAPTER 2
Israel's Flawed Declaration of Independence: A Partial Remedy

We hold these Truths to be self-evident, that all men are created equal, that they are endowed by their Creator with certain inalienable Rights, that among these are Life, Liberty, and the pursuit of Happiness.
The (American) Declaration of Independence

The natural aristocracy I consider as the most precious gift of nature for the instruction, the trusts, and government of society... May we not even say that that form of government is best which provides the most effectually for a pure selection of these natural aristoi into the offices of government?
Thomas Jefferson

The most serious flaws in Israel's Declaration of Independence are hardly known even to the academic community, let alone the general public. These flaws are not remedial. They go to the roots of secular or political Zionism, whose death certificate, drafted in Oslo on August 20, 1993, was signed by Prime Minister Yitzhak Rabin the following month on the White House lawn. (It should not be forgotten that it was under Mr. Rabin's premiership that the words "Zionism" and "Eretz Yisrael" and even "Judaism" were stricken from the Soldiers Code of Ethics.) Nevertheless, the flaws in the Declaration need to be revealed, for they underlie the basic causes of Israel's disintegration. This means that the Declaration of Independence contains the seeds of this country's approaching collapse. These will be discussed in the first section of this chapter.

There is, however, one serious flaw in the Declaration that can be remedied, at least philosophically. Although this flaw is fairly well known to the intellectual community, it has yet to be properly addressed. I am alluding to the apparent contradiction between a Jewish state and democracy. This flaw will be remedied in the second section of this chapter in the hope that steps will be taken to translate the remedy into a program of public education.

The death of Zionism means nothing more than the death of a political movement whose primary goal was to establish a secular democratic state in the Land of Israel. This goal was accomplished in 1948. Israel is now floundering, however, in a post-Zionist era, and whether it can survive as a secular democratic state is more than dubious. Contrast between the old and the new will help elucidate the problem.

Because the generation of Ben-Gurion spoke first of "Eretz Israel" and secondly of "peace", it could take the *initiative* vis-a-vis Israel's adversaries. Today, however, precisely because Israel's political elites speak only of "peace", they can only *react* to the forward policy and unrelenting demands of Israel's adversaries. By signing and implementing various agreements with the PLO, i.e., the Palestine Liberation Organization, Israeli prime ministers not only renounced the Jewish people's claim to Judea, Samaria, and Gaza, but endowed a terrorist organization with responsibility for Israel's security – to be monitored, ostensibly, by the CIA and the American State Department! Strange as it may seem, this abandonment of the Israel's heartland and this partial surrender of Israel's sovereignty are inevitable consequences of the mode of thought underlying Israel's flawed Declaration of Independence.

A Critical Analysis

Officially known as the Proclamation of the Establishment of the State of Israel, the Declaration begins with this sentence: "The Land of Israel was the birthplace of the Jewish people." This sentence is pregnant with significance. It suggests that the Jews did not become a "people" until the conquest of the Land of Canaan by Joshua, and, therefore, only *after* the Law-giving at Mount Sinai. Yet the Children of Israel are repeatedly referred to as a people even *before* their exodus from Egypt, as well as during their wanderings in the Wilderness. In fact, they are also called a "nation". Thus: "What great *nation* has laws and social rules so righteous as this Torah?" (Deut. 4:8; also Exod. 1:9; Num. 23:9).

Admittedly, it was only after forty years of learning and applying the revolutionary new laws and teachings of the Torah that Moses could say to the descendants of Abraham: "Hear O Israel; this day you have become a *people* unto the Lord your God" (Deut. 27:9). But a people or a nation is not constituted by a single generation. Hence the Torah goes on to say: "Neither with you only do I make this covenant...but with him that is not here with us today," meaning posterity (Deut. 29:13). It is therefore profoundly misleading if not fallacious to say that the Land of Israel was the birthplace of the Jewish people. Let us try to understand this more deeply.

The Jewish people, like no other, was constituted a nation *before* they received a land of their own. This means that the physical possession of a country is not the condition for the Jewish people's existence as a nation. What made the Jews a people was not the Land of Israel so much as their "portable homeland", the Torah. It was only the Torah that preserved them as a nation despite their having been without a land of their own for nineteen centuries.

In positing the Land of Israel as the origin of Jewish nationhood, the political Zionists were simply imitating the *territorial nationalism* of the non-Jewish world. The French cannot be Frenchmen, or Poles cannot be Polish, without the existence of a territory called France or Poland. In contrast, Scripture declares: "Behold a people (an *Am*) that dwells alone and shall not consider itself [as merely one] among the nations (*Goyim*)" (Num. 23:9). As various commentators have noted, whereas an *Am* signifies a collectivity united by a religious heritage, *Goy* signifies a collectivity united only on the basis of a common territory or homeland. Scripture designates the Jews an *Am* as well as a *Goy*.

This distinction, in secular terms, corresponds to the difference between a people and a nation. A people is monocultural, united not only by language, but by endogamous patterns of marriage and by shared beliefs and values rooted in a common and immemorial past. Conversely, a nation can be multicultural as well as monocultural. For example, the Iraqi Kurds are Muslims but not Arabs. Like Iraq's ruling Sunni Arab majority, they are citizens of the state. Nevertheless, the Kurds' singular ethnic loyalty is far more meaningful and stronger than their political loyalty. Moreover, their ethnic identity is also stronger than their religious identity, else they would not seek separate nationhood vis-a-vis the Arab Muslims of Iraq. Much the same may be said of the Druzes in Lebanon and Syria, the Baluch of Pakistan, and the Berbers in Morocco and Algeria.[3]

Such tensions may also be seen in Eastern Europe, where nationalism based on ethnicity transcends Christianity. Historically, the Poles and Lithuanians have put their national interests ahead of their common religion, in this case Catholic Christianity. This subordination of religion to nationalism is to be attributed to the fact that both peoples had nationhood long before they were forced to accept Christianity. What distinguishes the Jews, however, is *religious* nationhood. The "Old Testament", unlike the "New", does not record the source of a religion, but rather the divine founding of a people-cum-nation, and prior to the establishment of its territorial domain.

To be sure, the Land of Israel is essential for the moral and intellectual perfection of the Jewish People. But the Land of Israel is only one of the three pillars of Jewish nationhood. The second is the Jewish People themselves, a designation that obviously excludes non-Jews (who, if they wish and qualify, may reside in the Land of Israel or even convert to Judaism). The third pillar of Jewish nationhood is, of course, the Torah itself. If Jewish nationhood means anything it means a distinctive way of life, namely that illuminated by the laws and teachings of the Bible of Israel.

For example, of the many laws that distinguish Jews from non-Jews, suffice to mention those pertaining to the Sabbath, the dietary laws, marriage and family purity, and such holy days as Rosh Hashana, Yom Kippur, Succot, Pesach, and Shevuot. These laws preserved the identity of the Jewish people down through the ages. They not only distinguished the Jewish nation from all other nations, but spared them from the fate of nations whose existence depended on having a land of their own. Some nations have been conquered and eradicated. Others have been amalgamated with their conquerors. Still other nations have undergone evolutions and revolutions that fundamentally altered their character. Only the Jews have preserved their 3,500 year-old national identity. This they could do because, in whichever country they lived, regardless of its beliefs and customs, they adhered to the laws of their Torah, such as those just mentioned.

Is it not ironic, therefore, that the political heirs of those who substituted territorial nationalism for the Torah nationalism created in the Wilderness should abandon Judea and Samaria, the heartland of the Jewish people? It were as if the Torah avenged itself against those who have forsaken it.

The denial of the Law-Giving at Mount Sinai is evident in other parts of the Declaration. After declaring that the Land of Israel was the birthplace of the Jewish people, the document continues:

Here their spiritual, religious, and political identity was shaped. Here they first attained to statehood, created cultural values of national and universal significance and gave to the world the eternal Book of Books.

Leaving aside for subsequent analysis the term "religious", which will not be found in the Book of Books, to say that the Jews "created" cultural values of national and universal significance is tacitly to deny that the Torah is God-given (and to genuflect before German "biblical criticism").[4] If it be said, for example, that the Jews created the Sabbath, then it may also be said they created monotheism, as David Ben-Gurion indicates in his *Memoirs*.[5] Monotheism, however, is the basis of the Torah's prohibitions against murder, stealing, adultery, false witness, coveting one's neighbor's wife, and the precept to honor one's father and mother. Morality may then be regarded as nothing but a human product. If so, it follows that what men can make at one time and place, others can alter or unmake at another time and place – a rather dangerous teaching, but one that conforms to the moral relativism of contemporary democracy. True, the authors of the Declaration refer to the Book of Books as "eternal," which suggests that the moral values "created" therein are eternal. This is paradoxical, for nothing created by man is eternal. Indeed, one may well argue that the moral values just mentioned will gradually cease to influence human behavior when severed from the rest of the Ten Commandments.

To avoid misunderstanding, it is not my purpose to expose the philosophical shallowness of Israel's Declaration of Independence, which, to be sure, does not stand comparison with its American counterpart.[6] Rather, and as previously indicated, we need to understand the logical relationship between the non-Jewish mode of thought underlying the Declaration – which was signed by four rabbis! – and the causes of Israel's disintegration. Israel desperately needs to engage in self-criticism if it is to be or become or endure as a Jewish commonwealth.

Before continuing this analysis, it should be noted that, in 1962, Israel's Supreme Court held that the Declaration of Independence "laid down the way of life of the citizens of the State, and its principles must guide every public authority of the State."[7] The Declaration, which is studied in the public schools, is exalted by politicians and jurists on Independence Day. Hence the document cannot simply be dismissed as a tract for the times. In fact, the Declaration has its critics. The most significant are post-Zionists or ultra-secularists who reject the Declaration's proclaiming Israel as a *Jewish* state! To appreciate this recent development, a brief historical digression is necessary.

Political Zionism originated as a liberal movement. Its founders, such as Herzl and Pinsker, reacted against the failure of Jewish assimilation to solve the Jewish problem, i.e., anti-Semitism. However, although Herzl and Pinsker started from the failure of liberalism to solve the Jewish problem, they continued to see the solution in liberal terms, as a merely human problem. As Professor Leo Strauss has written:

The terrible fate of the Jews was in no sense to be understood any longer as connected with divine punishment for the sins of our fathers or with the providential mission of the chosen people and hence to be borne with the meek fortitude of martyrs. It was to be understood in merely human terms: as constituting a purely political problem which as such cannot be solved by appealing to the justice or generosity of the nations... Accordingly, political Zionism was concerned primarily with nothing but the cleansing of the Jews from millennial degradation or with the recovery of Jewish dignity, honor, or pride. The failure of the liberal solution meant that Jews could not regain their honor by assimilating themselves as individuals to the nations among which they lived or becoming citizens like all the other citizens of the liberal states: the liberal solution brought at best legal equality, but not social equality; as a demand of reason it had no effect on the feelings of the non-Jews... Only through securing the honor of the Jewish nation could the individual Jew's honor be secured. The true solution of the Jewish problem requires that the Jews become "like all the nations" (I Sam. 8:20), that the Jewish nation assimilate itself to the nations of the world or that it establish a modern, liberal, secular...state.[8]

The political elite that led this movement succeeded in establishing a secular and reputedly democratic state, but have yet to solve the Jewish problem or restore the honor of the Jewish people. Political Zionism could not solve the Jewish problem because of the narrowness of its original conception. This was understood by cultural Zionism, which saw that political Zionism lacks historical and cultural perspective. The community of descent "must also be a community of the mind, of the national mind; the Jewish state will be an empty shell without a Jewish culture which has its roots in the Jewish heritage." But as Strauss adds:

One could not have taken this step unless one had previously interpreted the Jewish heritage itself as a culture, that is, as a product of a national mind, of the national genius. Yet the foundation, the authoritative layer, of the Jewish heritage presents itself, not as the product of the human mind, but as a divine gift, as divine revelation. Did not one completely distort the meaning of the heritage to which one claimed to be loyal by interpreting it as a culture like any other high culture? Cultural Zionism believed to have found a safe middle ground between politics (power politics) and divine revelation...but it lacked the sternness of the two extremes. When cultural Zionism understands itself, it turns into religious Zionism.[9]

It is in this historical light that we are to understand the flawed foundations of Israel's Declaration of Independence. We need to ask: "Can Israel endure on these foundations?"

The Declaration refers to Theodor Herzl – the only name mentioned in the text – as "the spiritual father of the Jewish State". The document recalls Herzl's summoning the First Zionist

Congress in 1897, which proclaimed the "right of the Jewish people to national rebirth in its own country". On what grounds did the signers of the Declaration base this "right"? Three are stated: "historic right", "national right", and international law. We need to explore these grounds, if only because Israel's policy of "territory for peace" may be attributed to the inadequacy of these grounds. It may well be that the abandonment of Judea, Samaria, and Gaza has less to do with the quest for peace than with the flawed mode of thought underlying the Declaration of Independence.

Do Jews have an historic right to Eretz Israel? Fortunately for the peace of mankind, there are no historic rights to land, neither in reason nor in international law, else Native Americans might initiate enormous territorial claims before the World Court against the United States! Or perhaps some surviving Canaanites would claim legal title to the "Land of Israel". Nor is this so fanciful. To justify their claim to "Palestine", the Arab Palestinians have recently found it convenient to trace their ancestry to the Philistines! Never mind that the Philistines were pagans, or that their name derives from a word meaning "trespassers", or that the kinsmen of Goliath are as extinct as the dodo. This does not deter the minions of Yasser Arafat, who, by the way is an Egyptian. In any event, the notion of "historic right" provides no solid ground for the Jewish people's right to their ancient homeland.

The claim to Eretz Israel on the basis of "natural right" fares no better. No political philosopher, ancient or modern, ever maintained that a people have a "natural right" to a homeland, let alone to a land already occupied by another population. The Arabs can with equal reason or unreason claim a "natural right" to Palestine. Which leaves us with international law as the basis of the Jewish people's right to the Land of Israel:

This right [says the Declaration of Independence] was recognized in the Balfour Declaration of November 2, 1917, and re-affirmed in the Mandate of the League of Nations which, in particular, gave international sanction to the historic connection between the Jewish people and the Land of Israel and to the right of the Jewish people to rebuild its National

Home. [Moreover,] On November 29, 1947, the United Nations General Assembly passed a resolution calling for the establishment of a Jewish State in the Land of Israel.

Let us see whether these statements can stand the test of critical analysis.

On November 2, 1917, Arthur James Balfour, British Foreign Minister, sent the following written communication to Lord Rothschild, which stated, in part:

I have much pleasure in conveying to you, on behalf of His Majesty's Government, the following declaration of sympathy with Jewish Zionist aspirations which has been submitted to the Cabinet.

His Majesty's Government views with favour the establishment in Palestine of a national home for the Jewish people, and will use their best endeavours to facilitate the achievement of this object.

Although the Balfour Declaration was approved by the British Cabinet, the English House of Lords opposed its incorporation in the Palestine Mandate. In fact, on June 21, 1922, a motion declaring the mandate to be unacceptable in its present form was carried by a vote of 60 to 29. In a subsequent debate in the House of Commons, a motion asking that the mandate for Palestine be submitted for the approval of Parliament was defeated. Hence it may be said that the Balfour Declaration was never approved by the House of Commons or by the House of Lords.[10] Besides, according to the American Jewish lawyer, Mr. Sol Linowitz,

The most significant and incontrovertible fact is...that by itself the [Balfour] Declaration was legally impotent. For Great Britain had no sovereign rights over Palestine; it had no proprietary interest; it had no authority to dispose of the land. The Declaration was merely a statement of British intentions and no more.[11]

Moreover, the inclusion of the Balfour Declaration in the Mandate of the League of Nations did not cure its invalidity, if only because Great Britain, as just noted, possessed no sovereignty over Palestine. Furthermore, it can also be argued that the League of Nations did not possess the power to grant the Jews any political or territorial rights in that country. One legal scholar has written:

The grant of the Palestine mandate to Great Britain also violated the Covenant [of the League of Nations] in that it ignored the wishes of the inhabitants, contrary to the provision in Article 22 which required that the wishes of the communities concerned must be a principal consideration in the selection of the Mandatory. The wishes of the Arab communities in this regard ... were that no mandate was desired, but if any mandate were to be given, their first choice was the United States, while Great Britain came second.[12]

As for the United Nations resolution for the partition of Palestine, various legal scholars agree that the United Nations possessed no sovereignty over Palestine and thus had no right to partition the country.[13]

Finally, neither Israel's admission to membership in the United Nations, nor its recognition (either *de jure* or *de facto*) by various nations, endows Israel with more than a political title over any part of the land that it now claims as its own – something which, in the last analysis, can be said of any other state as well. For the truth is – and this will offend moralists – *the conquest of territory is the basis of possession, and the power to maintain such possession is the only solid title to land in the present world.* Indeed, according to the doctrine of legal positivism, which dominates virtually every law school in the West, a law is such only if it is enforceable. This means that law is ultimately based on the primacy of force.[14]

It follows from this last consideration that Israel should never have felt any moral qualms or reservations about its control of Judea, Samaria, and Gaza. International law is but a fig leaf that renders respectable the once naked conquests of men. There is probably no nation on the face of the earth that did not acquire its land by means of conquest. To be sure, it is argued that conquest, as a claim to possession or rule, is no longer acceptable since the Fourteen Points and the UN Charter. But no one with a stitch of intellectual integrity can take this sort of thing seriously in an era when legal positivism is the reigning philosophy of law, or when moral relativism dominates every level of education in the democratic world, and when the democracies of this world have truck with tyrants and terrorists.

Consider, therefore, the words of Golda Meir in an interview published in *Le Monde* on October 15, 1971. Israel's Prime Minister confided that she felt no concern over the non-recognition of Israel by the Arabs. "This country," she unabashedly declared, "exists as a result of a promise made by God Himself. It would be ridiculous to ask for the recognition of its legitimacy." A remarkable statement from an avowed atheist. That statement, however, constitutes the only solid foundation of the Jewish people's right to the Land of Israel!

The authors of the Declaration of Independence, however, do not even allude to God's covenant with the Patriarchs of the Jewish people, which millions of Evangelical Christians acknowledge. To be sure, the authors must have felt constrained by the pressure of events when the Declaration was promulgated on May 14, 1948. But this was more than five months after the UN partition resolution. Besides, the architects of the Third Commonwealth had years to reflect upon the appropriate ideological foundations of a Jewish state. Alienated, however, from the Jewish heritage, they disregarded the Torah and, by so doing, they abandoned the only non-negotiable grounds on which to justify and maintain Jewish sovereignty over *any* part of the Promised Land. Is it any wonder that their political heirs have repeatedly said of this land, "everything is negotiable"?

Contemplate the biblical and world-historical significance of the Land of Israel. Consider, too, the countless millions of Jews who, down through the ages, have yearned to return to this land. Then ponder the mentality of Israeli prime ministers who trivialize this land and this people's yearning by saying "everything is negotiable". This lack of faith, this infirmity, cannot but disarm one's own people and encourage the designs of Israel's enemies, whose faith in Allah renders them all the more contemptuous of Jewish "infidels".

Notice that not one of Israel's religious parties, however "politically correct" or hypocritical they may be, would dare say, in relation to the Land of Israel, "everything is negotiable." Such a statement can only issue from those for whom the Law-Giving at

Sinai has no significance in the domain of statecraft. Which brings us back to the opening sentence of the Declaration of Independence and its tacit denial of Sinai. Such imperceptible flaws are beyond repair.

A Remedial Flaw

Turning to the one conspicuous flaw that can be remedied, the Declaration proclaims the establishment of Israel as a *Jewish* state, yet prescribes "complete equality of... political rights to all its inhabitants irrespective of religion..." Although various commentators have noted this rather obvious contradiction, none, to my knowledge, have resolved it. How, indeed, can Israel remain a Jewish state should its non-Jewish inhabitants become a majority?

As indicated in the Introduction, if Israel's Arab inhabitants, as a result of their prolific birthrate, were to become the majority, then, given the egalitarian principle of "one adult/one vote", Muslims would eventually dominate the Knesset and put an end to the Jewish state prescribed in the Declaration. In addition, not only would the Arabs establish an Islamic state, but, consistent with 1,300 years of Islamic history and the character of every existing Islamic or Arab regime, that state would not be a democratic one. As a matter of fact, had not 500,000 Arabs fled Israel during the 1948 War of Independence, it is difficult to see how the State of Israel, which then had only 650,000 Jews, could have survived, pinioned by the political equality solemnly promised by its Declaration of Independence.[15]

Today the Arabs comprise almost 20% of Israel's population (as compared to their 2% in the United States). The 1999 elections gave three Arab parties ten Knesset seats. Three other Arabs won seats by virtue of their inclusion in the Labor and Meretz party lists. Even in 1988, two Arab parties with only five seats cast the deciding votes on the "Who is a Jew?" issue! Perhaps this absurdity was a forerunner of things to come: Since the Arabs can now determine who will be Israel's Prime Minister, they can very much determine the character of the supposed-to-be Jewish state.

Israel's political and intellectual elites have studiously avoided this dilemma. They fear that any attempt to limit the political equality of Arab citizens will be denounced as "racism". Nevertheless, on May 6, 1976, the year after the UN General Assembly equated Zionism with racism, then Prime Minister Yitzhak Rabin said to high school graduates about to enter the army:

The majority of the people living in a Jewish State must be Jewish. We must prevent a situation of an *insufficient* Jewish majority and we dare not have a Jewish minority… There is room for a non-Jewish minority *on condition that it accept the destiny of the State vis-a-vis the Jewish people, culture, tradition, and belief.* The minority is entitled to equal rights as individuals with respect to their distinct religion and culture, *but not more than that.* (See note number 211 regarding Denmark, Holland, Japan, etc.)

Rabin's last sentence obviously refers to Israel's Arab inhabitants. It clearly implies that their equal rights as individuals do not include equal *political* rights! This remarkable statement contradicts Israel's Declaration of Independence. Let us try to dissolve this contradiction, or at least provide a philosophical rationale for Rabin's thus far unheeded warning.

Israel's Declaration of Independence not only refers repeatedly to the State of Israel as a "Jewish" state; it also calls for the "Ingathering of the Exiles". By so doing the authors acknowledge the one and only reason or justification for Israel's re-establishment, namely, that it be a *Jewish* state. This and this alone is Israel's *raison d'être*, which even the UN Resolution of November 29, 1947 acknowledges.

Now, by designating the State as "Jewish", that designation becomes the State's *paramount* principle, in relation to which any other principle may be limited lest it lead to the negation of the State's Jewish character. Accordingly, Israeli law prohibits any party that negates the Jewish character of the State – clearly a limitation of the principle of political equality prescribed in the

Declaration. This limitation of political equality is a logical as well as necessary limitation given the State's *raison d'être*. Let me formulate this another way.

By acknowledging Israel as a Jewish state, such that its being "Jewish" is the State's *raison d'être* and *paramount* principle, the "political equality" mentioned in the Declaration must then be construed not as an absolute, but as a logically subordinate principle. Hence, just as the law prohibits any party that negates the Jewish character of the State, so the law must limit citizenship to those who are loyal to the State. This is precisely the intention of the Citizenship Law of 1952, to be discussed in Chapter 4. It were as if the Citizenship Law recognized and resolved the contradiction between a Jewish state and the principle of political equality prescribed in the Declaration. It so happens, however, that the Citizenship Law has never been enforced against any disloyal Arab citizen, even against those who are members of terrorist organizations such as Hamas. This is one reason why an explicit and philosophically sound resolution of the contradiction in question is urgently required.

The Declaration needs to be construed in terms of a hierarchy of principles. The first and paramount principle is of course the *Jewish* principle (to be elucidated later). Second and subordinate is the *democratic* principle. Democracy, however, has two cardinal principles: in addition to equality, freedom. The question arises as to which of these two principles takes precedence. The Declaration first mentions freedom: "The State of Israel...will be based on freedom...as envisioned by the prophets of Israel; it will ensure complete equality of...political rights to all its inhabitants irrespective of religion..." Any intelligent and honest person, even if not religious, will admit that the prophets' understanding of freedom differs from the permissive freedom of what I call *normless* or *contemporary* in contradistinction to *normative* or *classical* democracy (discussed in Chapter 3). The prophets were not libertarians or moral pluralists. They did not regard "freedom", as do the vulgar, as "living as you like", which makes all "lifestyles" morally equal.

That freedom, as a concept, takes precedence over equality follows from the fact that freedom, rather than equality, distinguishes the human from the subhuman. Indeed, freedom is a faculty or power of the mind, something that cannot be said of equality. We may therefore ascribe to the Declaration the following hierarchy of principles: (1) the Jewish principle, followed by (2) freedom and then by (3) equality. Our problem, in the next chapter, will be to assimilate democracy and its two basic principles to Judaism. Before doing so, however, let us briefly contrast Israel's Declaration of Independence with its American counterpart.

Strange as it may seem, the term "democracy" appears neither in Israel's nor in the America's Declaration of Independence. Yet both are generally deemed unqualifiedly democratic. However democratic the American Declaration may be – and I have elsewhere questioned this prejudice – it was incorporated in the constitutions of several of the original thirteen states of the American Union, some of which had property and even religious qualifications for office.[16] Also, unlike Israel's Declaration, which mentions, rather obscurely, the "Rock of Israel", the American Declaration unabashedly refers to "God", the "Creator", the "Supreme Judge", and "Divine Providence". This is profoundly significant for what I call "classical" as opposed to "contemporary" democracy.

Unlike contemporary democracy, which will be discussed at length in the next chapter, classical democracy provides freedom and equality with ethical and rational constraints. Thus, when the American Declaration proclaims that "all men are created equal", it obviously means equal in their "inalienable rights", and then only because all men are created in the image of God (the meaning of which will be clarified later). But inasmuch as the Declaration refers to God as the "Supreme Judge", all men are obligated to obey the laws of their Creator (say the Seven Noahide Laws of Morality). Such laws obviously entail ethical and rational constraints on freedom and equality. Admittedly, the Declaration emphasizes "rights", whereas the Torah emphasizes "obligations".

Nevertheless, a person can only expect and demand those rights as he is ready to grant to others. In other words, rights and obligations are correlative: Your rights are my obligations, and vice-versa. Freedom and equality, democracies two cardinal principles, thus become part of a larger framework of ideas and considerations, which modulates these principles and hinders them from becoming immoral or irrational (as they would become if construed as absolutes).

Returning to Israel's Declaration of Independence, no difficulty arises when it proclaims that "The State of Israel...will be based on freedom...as envisioned by the prophets of Israel." For the freedom envisioned by the prophets of Israel will have the ethical and rational constraints derived from the Torah. The difficulty arises when the Declaration goes on to proclaim that the State "will ensure complete equality of...political rights to all its inhabitants irrespective of religion," for this equality has no rational or ethical constraints. This is why it was necessary to develop a hierarchy of principles, subordinating political equality to the paramount principle of the Jewish state. In fact, but indirectly, it is because the political equality prescribed in the Declaration lacks rational and ethical constraints that Yitzhak Rabin was compelled to say, "There is room [in the State of Israel] for a non-Jewish minority *on condition that it accept the destiny of the State vis-a-vis the Jewish people, culture, tradition, and belief.*" This is precisely the intention of the Citizenship Law to be discussed in Chapter 4. One may indeed say, therefore, that the Citizenship Law was intended to remedy a basic flaw in the Declaration. That it has not done so is largely because Israel's political and judicial elites are more solicitous of democracy than of Judaism, the subject of our next chapter.

CHAPTER 3
Democracy Versus Judaism: Beyond Spinoza

That which comes into your mind shall not be at all; in that you say, "We shall be as the nations..."

Ezekiel 20:32

We have said that the most basic and pervasive problem confronting Israel, one that affects the four causes of its disintegration, is the tension between Judaism and democracy. This tension prevents Israel from dealing effectively with its demographic dilemma, its secular-religious discord, its divisive political and judicial institutions, and even its deplorable lack of Jewish statesmanship and Jewish national purpose. The problem is very much a conceptual one, for in Israel, the language of public discourse, which obviously affects public policy, is thoroughly confused and incommensurate with the way of life of an authentic and confident Jewish commonwealth.

Consider the headnote: "That which comes into your mind shall not be at all; in that you say, 'We shall be as the nations...'" While the prophet Ezekiel is obviously referring to assimilation, he is also suggesting that Israel is metaphysically incapable of becoming like the nations. Let us try to understand this.

If we examine the language of public discourse, the one term that dominates all others, and less subject to questioning than any religious dogma, is Democracy. This term permeates the intellect and arouses the emotions of the educated perhaps even more than the uneducated. It endows individuals and groups with respectability and legitimacy, so much so that terrorists and tyrannies parade in the name of Democracy. God Himself has been made a Democrat, has made all individuals and all nations equal, regardless of their accomplishments, their goals, their ways of life, or whether they recognize Him or not. Only consider the moral equivalence manifested in the UN General Assembly, where the principle of one nation/one vote dignifies scores of tyrannies and so often results in the condemnation of minuscule Israel. Thus the prophet could say again: "That which comes into your mind shall not be at all; in that you say, 'We shall be as the nations...'"

Still, what would be Israel's character when it is neither true to itself nor simply assimilated? Surely its leaders, without being subjectively gentile, will not only employ gentile concepts (as Jews may in the Diaspora), but these concepts will clash with Jewish life in the Land of Israel, from which the Law is supposed to go forth and enlighten mankind. This land is no ordinary land. Is it not passing strange that, despite its extraordinary fertility, the Land of Israel remained desolate no matter which foreign nation occupied or controlled it, as many did over the course of 2,500 years? Perhaps a land that has flourished only under Jews cannot long tolerate being controlled by Jews who think and speak in non-Jewish terms and who therefore suffer from cognitive dissonance.

Cognitive Dissonance

Modern Israel is referred to as a "state" as well as a "democracy"; and of course public life in this so-called democratic state is dominated by "politics". But to practice "politics" in Israel, or to conceive of Israel as a "state" or as a "democracy", is to enter a world of thought, action, and passion utterly foreign to the Torah and out of place in the Holy Land.

Alfred North Whitehead, the great gentile philosopher and mathematician, wisely discerned that, "The Jews are the first example of [a] refusal to worship the state."[17] Perhaps the reason is this. The state, like the city of Babel, manifests the self-glorification of man. The state is wholly a human product, based on the autonomy of human will. Hence there is no essential difference in proclaiming *L'état c'est moi* and saying *Vox populi, vox Dei*. In both cases the laws of the state depend solely on the will of the sovereign, be it the One, the Few, or the Many. Obviously this idea of the state is fundamentally opposed to the Torah's conception of Israel. From a Torah perspective, Israel is supposed to be a *non-sovereign* state created by God to be the teacher of mankind. Perhaps this explains, ironically, why Israel today, by using foreign concepts, often fails to act like a sovereign state. Notice how Israel relies on Washington to mediate its conflicts with its Arab neighbors. This may not seem unreasonable, until we recall that Israel's Government invested the

American State Department with the power to supervise PLO compliance with the October 1998 Wye River Memorandum. To this add the Government's agreement to construct "free passages" across Israel's supposedly sovereign territory to facilitate Arab Palestinian travel between Gaza and what used to be called Judea and Samaria.

It would seem that Israel cannot but act awkwardly as a sovereign state, as the words of the prophet Ezekiel seem to suggest. Superficial observers will attribute this to "American pressure". Let us probe more deeply.

The state is ever seeking to concentrate all power to itself, and this is usually at war with family life and loyalties. Indeed, one may see in history a fundamental conflict between the impersonal state and the family. Israel, however, is supposed to be, more than any other, a nation of families with a godly mission. Unlike the state, which exalts power, wealth, and glory, the family, the nucleus of a God-oriented community, honors wisdom, virtue, and friendship. Consider America, a most benevolent state. The permissiveness fostered by the judicial and legislative organs of this liberal democratic state is a constant assault on family values. *But this permissiveness is actually a consequence of the state's arrogating to itself the power to decide the question of morality even while insisting that it is not the function of government to legislate morality!* The state's *laissez-faire* attitude toward morality is itself a decision *not to support traditional morality*, and therefore to grant a license to a *new morality*, which, from the traditional perspective, is nothing but immorality. That decision was a subtle but tremendous exercise of power, for it subverted the long-established morality of the Bible, a precondition of family life and of what families most cherish.

This deceptive war against family morality is occurring in the Land of Israel. As will be seen in Chapter 7, Israel's Supreme Court, influenced by American jurisprudence, has rendered decisions conducive to adultery and sodomy. What enables the Court to issue rulings that violate 3,500 years of Jewish history and morality is not simply the Court's ultra-secular agenda, but its being an organ of that all-powerful and impersonal entity, the "state".

When we utter the word "state", we have in mind an entity possessing a monopoly of power. But one can hardly find a state – certainly not a democratic state – whose power vis-a-vis its own people equals that of the so-called Jewish state of Israel. Not only can this state ignore with impunity its people's 3,500 year heritage. It is the only state in history that has voluntarily surrendered land its people won in a war of self-defense in exchange for an ill-defined peace, and with terrorists and tyrants who not only hate Jews but publically deny their right to statehood![18] Surely this power of the state is absurd, beyond reason or law. And what compounds the absurdity is that the word "state" is a misleading translation of the Hebrew word *medina*, whose root, *din*, means *law*, which unites reason and justice. Here is an example of how the mongrelized language of public discourse in Israel leads to irrational, lawless, and even suicidal behavior. Yet such behavior is occurring in a supposedly Jewish state whose political and intellectual elites boastfully describe as a "democracy"!

* * *

Before turning to a systematic analysis of the term "democracy", it should be noted that the claim of various apologists that Judaism is democratic would have amused or astonished Benedict de Spinoza. I mention Spinoza because he is not only the father of liberal democracy, but also of modern "biblical criticism" which so much influenced the founders of the Jewish state. As may be seen in the sixteenth and twentieth chapter of his *Theological-political Treatise*, Spinoza was the first philosopher who was both a democrat and a liberal.[19] His *Treatise* disdains Judaism as a tribal religion and exalts democracy as "the most natural form of government", for there "every man may think what he likes, and say what he thinks."[20] This statement lends itself to moral relativism. Consistent therewith, Spinoza's pantheistic God is beyond good and evil.[21] His liberalism therefore prepared the philosophical grounds for normless or contemporary democracy, which obviously contradicts the ethical monotheism of Judaism. It follows that those who contend that democracy is consistent with Judaism will not only have to formulate another type of democracy, but they will have to render it compatible with a view of the Torah that refutes Spinoza's egregious portrayal of Judaism as a tribal religion. Let us do this beginning with the concept of "religion".

Is Judaism a Religion?

Rabbi Samson Raphael Hirsch (1808-1888), an outstanding philologist, has said that the term "religion" is the greatest obstacle to an understanding of Judaism. The word "religion" has no Hebrew equivalent in the Torah. The Hebrew word *dat*, now commonly translated as "religion", does not appear in the Five Books of Moses. In the twenty-four books of the Hebrew Bible, the word *dat* will be found only in the Book of Esther, where it means *law*, not religion. Hence, to classify Judaism as a religion is to impose on Judaism a concept extrinsic to the Torah. Let us try to examine the Torah within its own conceptual framework.

Accordingly, inasmuch as the Torah records the creation of heaven and earth, the subject of cosmology, and since the laws of the Torah encompass not only morality, but anthropology, psychology, medicine, sociology, government, economics, agriculture, and universal history, surely the term "religion" is too narrow to describe Judaism. Professor Henri Baruk, a biologist, psychopharmacologist, psychologist, and sociologist, characterized the Torah as "the most complete science of man." He writes:

Though this extensive science has been vulgarized by the religions which have sprung from [the Torah], it still remains little known and even misunderstood. The[se] religions... took mainly from its moral principles with, moreover, various modifications which left out Hebraic Law, Hebraic biology, Hebraic sociology, etc., in a word, the concrete and material parts of the Torah... Then again the Torah forms an indivisible whole, and one cannot study it in borrowed versions or excerpts without completely falsifying its meaning and spirit.[22]

We may now return to Rabbi Hirsch:

Every European language speaks of religion. We, the People of Religion par excellence, have no expression for it. As soon as anything is used to designate some special relationship to our life as religious, it specializes just this, and implies that there are phases in life which have no relation to it. It makes it a separate realm. But where everything from birth to death belongs to religion, this conception cannot exist inasmuch as every phase of life is penetrated with it and nothing at all is left out. [Moreover,] the word religion, if it comes from the Latin "religare", to bind, is even contrary to the Jewish point of view. Our relation to God makes us free...[23]

More simply stated,

Judaism is no religion, the synagogue no church, and the rabbi no clergyman. Judaism is no appendage of one kind or another to life, nor is it part of man's vocation in life. Judaism embraces all the spheres of our life, being the sum of our life's vocation.[24]

Consistent with Henri Baruk, a twentieth-century scientist, classical Jewish philosophers, such as Maimonides (1135-1204) and Judah Halevi (1095-1150), deemed Judaism the most comprehensive truth-system. And it was only because they so regarded the Torah that they could regard the Jews as the educators of mankind – as indeed have gentile philosophers, historians, and statesmen, even though these gentiles were not privy to the esoteric wisdom contained in the Torah.

This said, let us now try to clarify the term democracy, the religion of our times.

Democracy: Conceptual Therapy

Like the word "religion", the word "democracy" is foreign to the Torah. Democracy literally means the "rule of the people" or popular sovereignty. Stated as such, and without qualification, the notion of popular sovereignty, and therefore democracy, clashes with the Torah which proclaims the sovereignty of God, the Creator of heaven and earth.

Etymology aside, judging from the prevailing ideas and behavior of Western societies, *contemporary* democracy is little more than a *random* aggregation of individuals and groups pursuing their own aims and interests. The result is egocentric pluralism and multiculturalism, fortified by the doctrine of moral and cultural relativism that dominates every level of education in the West. Lacking in contemporary democracy are not only unifying norms of human conduct, but any rational basis for *national loyalty*. Being normless, contemporary democracy denies the existence of universally valid standards by which to determine whether the way of life of one individual, group, or nation is intrinsically superior to that of another – superior in the sense of being more conducive to human excellence or to domestic and international harmony.

Stated another way, contemporary democracy – which is not to be confused with Athenian democracy – does not entail any particular ethnic or religious character. This is why there are no ethnic or religious qualifications for voting or holding office in contemporary democratic regimes, with the (ethnic) exception of Japan. In fact, political scientists define democracy as a "process" or the "rules of the game" by which individuals pursue their private interests and lifestyles. In contrast, Judaism is a *nationality*, a prescribed way of life. To be more precise, Judaism has endogamous marriage laws and ethical precepts, its own distinctive jurisprudence and economy, its own system of education and national literature. All this is quite foreign to contemporary democracy.

Also, democracies separate religion from the state or public law. But since "religion" and "state" are non-Torah concepts, their separation is meaningless in a Torah context! Actually, the idea of separating religion and state originated in the Christian doctrine, "Render unto Caesar the things that are Caesar's and unto God the things that are God's." This doctrine severed Christianity from *nationality* and eventually made religion a private matter Applied to Israel, this Christian doctrine would marginalize the Torah, as indeed it has. Only a few instances of Jewish civil law have been incorporated into Israel's legal system. Consequently, Jewish civil law hardly influences the daily life of the Jewish people, as it did throughout the Diaspora, wherever Jews, prior to the eighteenth century, enjoyed juridical autonomy and creatively applied Jewish law to the most diverse social and economic conditions.

Incidentally, these communities, generally speaking, had democratic constitutions in the sense that communal decisions were made by a representative body. Majority rule was accepted by most *halakhic* authorities, although it was a common practice to consult a Torah scholar.

Apropos of the democratic principle of majority rule, it should be noted that this principle is ethically neutral. By itself the principle would enable any majority to determine the laws and therefore the character of a regime. The majority could elect a party and condone the establishment of a totalitarian state, as happened in Weimar Germany and as almost certainly will happen in an Arabized "Palestine". How does the Torah avoid this democratic oxymoron?

While majority rule is an important Torah principle (see Exod. 23:2 and *Sanhedrin* 3b), its operation is constrained by higher principles, such as the Ten Commandments.[25] What is more, in Jewish law the meaning of majority rule is *rational* rather than *volitional*. Let us examine the relevant Hebrew concept.

Although the Hebrew word *rov* can be translated literally as "majority", the term "probability" better conveys its meaning.[26] What is decisive is not the *will* of the majority so much as the *judgment* of the majority. It is the judgment of the majority, reached by thorough examination of diverse evidence and opinions, that carries moral authority, for it is more likely to be in accord with truth on matters of law.

To clinch the point, because Jewish law aims at truth, the majority principle in Torah jurisprudence is only applicable among equals in scholarship. (See *Yevamot* 14a.) Consistent therewith, there are numerous cases in Jewish law when the conclusion of an outstanding individual jurist or scholar was accepted against the rest of his colleagues.[27] In contemporary democracies, however, what is decisive is not truth but the will of the majority, which is why opinion polls today play an important role in policy-making. A democracy would cease to be a democracy if the majority were to defer to the wisdom of some superlative individual. Deference to wisdom, however, is distinctive of a Torah community. This cannot be said of any regime dominated by "politics". How is this term understood nowadays?

Modern political scientists define politics as a struggle for power. What this really means is that those engaged in politics are animated by different degrees of individual or collective egoism, often couched, to be sure, in altruistic language such as "justice" or the "common good", or "peace" and "pluralism". In this age of television, however, it is obvious to people of the meanest intellect that politics is based on flim-flam. That candidates for public office should boast of their own virtues while besmirching the character of their rivals is evidence enough that politics is infinitely removed from the Torah's conception of Israel.

The cognitive dissonance produced by the use of non-Torah concepts in the Land of Israel has now been made sufficiently clear. The ground has thus been prepared for a remedy. Since democracy is the most important concept – it underlies Israel's malaise – the remedy will have to address democracy's two basic principles, freedom and equality, from a Torah perspective. The remedy will then yield a new conception or type of democracy, which, I dare say, will refute Spinoza's view of Judaism and transcend the democracy of which he is the father.

Freedom

Freedom is one of the most precious jewels of the Torah, so precious that kidnapping and depriving a man of his freedom is a capital offense (Exod. 21:16). Why this exaltation of freedom?

To begin with, the Torah's conception of freedom is rooted in the Genesis account of man's creation in the image of God. Therein is the ultimate source of free will and rationality, of human dignity and creativity, of human rights and duties. Freedom is a gift with which all men are endowed, be they Jewish or non-Jewish. For the Jews, moreover, freedom also has a *national* dimension, emphasized repeatedly in the Torah and in Jewish prayer books, namely, the deliverance of the Children of Israel from Egyptian bondage. The freedom attained in the Exodus, however, was not merely freedom from Egyptian servitude, which is negative, so much as the positive freedom to serve God. (See Exod. 7:16; 8:16, 21-22.) Jewish freedom therefore involves dependence on God and on God alone, and it is this dependence that has made Jews the most independent and creative of men, despite their having been reviled and ravished by the gentile world. But to better appreciate the Torah's conception of freedom, let us pause and consider various definitions of freedom advanced by modern democratic thinkers.

If freedom is to be consistent with man's creation in the image of God it cannot be defined, as did Bertrand Russell, as "the absence of obstacles to the realization of one's desires". Translated by the vulgar into "living as one likes", this is the prevalent view of freedom in the most "progressive" democratic societies. Nor will true freedom be found, as Montesquieu believed, in the interstices of the law, such that one may do whatever the law does not forbid. This view of freedom, like the former, can justify the Canaanite or sexual perversions decriminalized by the American and Israeli Supreme Courts. Nor does freedom consist in obedience to laws in whose formulation one has merged his will with the will of others, that is, in Rousseau's "general will". The general will can be as frivolous or as unjust as the will of a tyrant. Finally, freedom will not be found in Kant's "autonomous moral will", which posits universal principles of conduct. There is no *will* of man, but only the different wills of countless human beings more or less steeped in egoism and subjectivity. Hence obedience to one's own will, even if couched in universal terms, can be as arbitrary or as foolish and dangerous in their consequences as obedience to the will of a multitude. Quite the contrary, to be consistent with man's creation in the image of God, *freedom must be the voluntary and rational observance of laws which are independent of human volition.*

Philosophically speaking, freedom is a pure potentiality, whose actualization can be good or bad, noble or base. If freedom is to result in good, it must conform to the dictates of right reasoning. As Plato and Alfred North Whitehead saw, genuine freedom is action consistent with truth. This view may be assimilated to the Torah concept that God, Who alone is absolutely free, is the ultimate source of human freedom. Accordingly, to understand His laws and willingly obey them is to achieve the height of human freedom, for only those laws are wholly just and rational. This is why it has been said, "Where justice and reason reign, 'tis freedom to obey."

In contrast to Kant's "autonomous ethics", which deifies the "Good Will", Judaism maintains that "One who performs a good action because it is commanded by God stands higher than he who does it because he himself considers it good, and [then] acts in consequence of moral self-legislation instead of Divine legislation" (*Kiddushin* 31a; *Baba Kamma*, 38a, 87a). In other words, "He who is commanded and does stands higher than he who is not commanded and does" (*Avoda Zara* 3a). It requires a more powerful will and intellect to obey intelligently the Will of God than to obey one's own will, which is but to follow one's natural inclinations or pleasure. Contrary to modernity, the Torah does not exalt the "autonomous" man. "Do God's Will as you would do your own will, so that He may do your will as if it were His" (*Avot* 2:4). God's Will, of course, is crystallized in the Torah, and "you can have no freer man than one who engages in the study of the Torah" (*Avot* 6:2).

The Torah regards each individual as a unique creation, endowed with a unique combination of characteristics and capacities. Hence King Solomon could say: "Train a child according to his way" (Prov. 22:6; and see *Avoda Zara* 19a). Needless to say, this is not the "self-actualization" doctrine of modern psychology, which is rooted in moral relativism.[28] The only way to achieve genuine self-actualization is by becoming a servant of God, for only then can you overcome *all other forms of servitude* – be it to your own passions and prejudices or to those of others. In this way alone can you ascend to *your* highest level of freedom and perfection. For a person at that level, *the laws of morality are equivalent to the laws of nature*, except that, unlike mindless nature, he *freely* obeys that which he knows to be the crystallized thought of God. Freedom then becomes necessity, and the will becomes thoroughly rational.

As for freedom of speech, even after the Great Sanhedrin has rendered a verdict, a "rebellious elder", when he returns to his hometown, is permitted to continue teaching his dissenting views. But of course he may not act or instruct others to act against the Court's ruling, for this would violate the law, something not tolerated in a democratic society either.

Summing up, Jewish freedom differs from the freedom of contemporary democracy insofar as the latter severs freedom from reason and morality. Properly understood, freedom ultimately depends on its opposite, the restraints of authority. The purpose of authority, when exercised over the young, is to enable them, as they mature, to exercise self-restraint, hence to dispense with the need for externally imposed authority. Authority, metamorphosed as self-restraint, is therefore a precondition of freedom. This is the way of the Torah.

Equality

As was the case of freedom, the only solid and rational justification for the principle of equality is to be found in the Genesis account of man's creation in the image of God. This equality underlies a famous statement of the Jerusalem Talmud: "If gentiles [surrounding Israel] demand, 'Surrender one of yourselves to us and we will kill him; otherwise we shall kill all of you,' they must all suffer death rather than surrender a single Israelite to them" (*Terumot* 8, 9). This means that no individual may be sacrificed for the sake of his society. With respect to human life, therefore, all Jews – learned and unlearned, rich and poor – are equal. This equality, however, should not be confused with its secular counterpart. For as concerns danger to life, the conclusion that all Jews are equal is based on the premise that all souls belong to God, that the soul of an individual and his purpose in world-history is known only to his Creator.

Furthermore, unlike democratic equality, as manifested, for example, in the political principle of "one adult/one vote", equality in the Torah has nothing to do with equal rights or claims which one abstract individual may make against another. A person's "rights" depend on who or what he or she is in relation to Jewish law, the *Halakha*. For instance, in procuring their release from captivity, "A Kohane takes precedence over a Levite, a Levite over an Israelite, and an Israelite over a bastard... This applies when they are all [otherwise] equal; but if the bastard is learned in the Torah and the Kohane is ignorant of the Torah, the learned bastard takes precedence over the ignorant Kohane" (Mishna, *Horayot* 3:8). Similarly, under Jewish law "a scholar takes precedence over a king of Israel" (*Horayot* 23a).

Finally, "If a man and his father and his [Torah] teacher were in captivity [for ransom], he takes precedence over his teacher and his teacher takes precedence over his father, while his mother takes precedence over them all [if only because of her greater vulnerability]" (ibid.). Clearly, the order of precedence is determined by learning, unless a woman's life or honor is at stake. This is also true in less precarious situations. Thus, when a court has many cases on its docket, then, as the Rambam (Maimonides) points out, the case of a widow is tried before that of a scholar, a scholar's before an illiterate's, and the suit of a woman before that of a man, because the humiliation is greater in the case of a woman. Moreover, if a man has not left enough to provide for both his sons and his daughters, the first claim on the estate is that of his daughters.[29]

These examples demonstrate that equality in the Torah does not involve the leveling of distinctions characteristic of contemporary or normless democracy, where indiscriminate equality or moral equivalence prevails.

Because of its leveling tendencies, the first casualty of normless democracy is honor. Let us examine honor from the Torah perspective.

In Jewish law the honor due a person depends not only on his status but on his relationship to you. As we have seen, you are obliged to honor your teacher more than your father (unless he is also a scholar). Also, you owe more honor to your father than to your mother (unless they are divorced, in which case the honor a son owes his mother is equal to that which he owes his father, and, in the event of conflict, he may choose for himself who should take precedence). Accordingly, in Torah jurisprudence a person's honor is relational and contingent. The Torah addresses itself to reality, to the acts or accomplishments of living men, not to abstractions such as the "dignity of the individual".[30] Because man is created in the image of God, a person's merit is logically proportional to his study and observance of the Torah. A person merits honor to the extent that he reveals the infinite wisdom, power, and kindliness of his Creator in every aspect of existence – physical, moral, and intellectual. But in honoring that person, we are really honoring the Torah, the primordial source of human dignity.

It will be obvious from the preceding discussion that even though the democratic principle of equality finds no easy home in the Torah, it is only there that this important principle can be enriched and elevated. To see this more clearly, consider the precept, "You shall not give special consideration to the poor nor favor the person of the mighty..." (Lev. 19:15). This precept appears very egalitarian. Its correct application, however, requires thorough knowledge of the *Halakha*. Thus, if the parties to a dispute agree to arbitration, the judge may well favor the claims of the poor. He may also give special consideration to the poor where the adversarial party is a scholar. A famous example of this is recounted in the Talmud (*Baba Metzia* 83a):

Some porters negligently broke a barrel of wine belonging to the scholar, Raba ben Huna. In accordance with the strict letter of the law, he confiscated the porters' coats as security for its value. The porters complained to the court, and Rav, the judge, told Raba ben Huna to return the coats. "Is that really the law?" he asked. "Yes indeed," replied Rav, "so that you may walk in the way of good men" (Prov. 2:20). The porters spoke up again: "We are poor men, have worked all day, and are in need; are we to get nothing?" "Give them their wages." Again Raba ben Huna asked, "Is that the law?" And Rav replied, "Yes – and keep to the path of the righteous" (ibid.).

This judgment should not be construed simply as "acting more generously than the law requires" (*lifenim mi-shurat ha-din*). For as Rav clearly stated, he was in fact applying the law. But in this case the applicable law was the law appropriate for a scholar, not for the ordinary man.[31]

Unlike the secular world, where one finds the charming tradition that men of genius ought not be censured for moral lapses, in the Torah world the more elevated a person, the higher the level of conduct required of him. Another example makes the point even clearer.

In Jewish law, unlike other legal systems, proven ignorance of the law excuses a criminal in a court of men (*Dinei Adam*, but not in the Court of Heaven, *Dinei Shemayim*). He can only be held liable for damages. Accordingly, a person may not be punished for a criminal act unless he was warned of, and understood, its culpable nature. If, however, the malefactor is a scholar, then, capital cases aside, he may be held responsible for his crime without having been warned, since warning is only a means of deciding whether one has committed a crime willfully or not (*Sanhedrin* 8b, 41a). Here we see that equality before the law in the Torah does not result in the leveling of humanity found in egalitarian societies. The Torah provides no warrant for egalitarianism, a doctrine that subordinates all values to the principle of equality. Indeed, *noblesse oblige* is a basic Jewish principle.

Governing Principles of a Torah Community

Thus far I have examined the principle of equality without reference to governance in a Torah community. It is often said that if Israel were governed by Jewish law it would be a "theocracy". This is more a semantic than a substantive issue. If "theocracy" signifies a regime ruled by a church or by priests, Judaism is *not* theocratic. There is no church in Judaism, neither *theologically*, since there is no mediation between God and the individual Jew, nor *institutionally*, since there is no ecclesiastical hierarchy. If, however, the word "theocracy" is construed literally as the "rule of God", then Judaism is theocratic, for God is the ultimate source of law and authority. But what does this mean *operationally*?

In Judaism, no priesthood, but *only publicly tested scholarship can lay claim to any validity regarding the laws of the Torah*. This means that the Torah belongs to every Jew, whether he is a Kohane, Levite, or Israelite. Let us examine these three "classes" in relation to the principle of equality.

The first thing to be noted is that they are hereditary but not closed. The daughter of an Israelite or of a Levite may marry a Kohane and her children will be Kohanes, since "class" status is patrilineal. Hence, even though Kohanes, Levites, and Israelites have distinct duties and privileges, there is no separation of "classes". Nor is there a ruling class. Who rules is based, first and foremost, on intellectual and moral qualifications: those who are most learned in the Torah and the sciences receive the highest honors. Moreover, unlike the practice of any so-called aristocracy, in Israel education is open to, and even required of, all members of the community. Thus, thousands of years before any democracy thought of providing education for all its citizens, all the people of Israel were being highly educated as a matter of course. Far from separating or stratifying the three "classes", *Torah education is the great unifying force of the Jewish people* who, we saw, honor scholars more than kings.

Turning to governmental processes, even in a democracy, only qualified members of the court, and not the people, vote on judicial matters. Similarly, not the people but only members of the legislature vote in making the laws. Israel aside, it is true that the people elect the legislators, who in turn may appoint, or be involved in the appointment of, judges and even the executive in parliamentary systems. But this is not very different from the manner of appointing members of the Sanhedrin, which has legislative as well as judicial functions. (See Deut. 1:13, on this subject, more in Chapter 5.)

In a mature Jewish community the center of gravity lies not in any ruling class but in the body of the people. Only it must be understood that the people, as Jews, have willingly subordinated themselves to the Torah, i.e., the laws of God. (See Exod. 24:3.) It is hardly an exaggeration to say, as Rabbi Hirsch indicates, that the leaders of a Jewish community act consistently with the Torah when they make themselves superfluous.

See to it that the peasant behind the plough, the herdsman with his cattle, the weaver at his loom can be your judges and masters, the critics of your conduct and teaching; then at the same time will they be your pupils and friends, they will willingly and joyfully follow your teachings and regulations; they will understand and appreciate the spirit in which you speak and by which you are guided.[32]

This is what is meant by a "kingdom of priests, and a holy nation" (Exod. 19:6) – a people wholly animated by the teachings of the Torah.

With such a people, writes Hirsch, only

let a communal leader lay a presumptuous hand on the smallest point of the sacred Torah, let a Rabbi try to give one decision in opposition to the Torah, and the humblest Jewish apprentice will refuse obedience to the leader, and the lowliest Jewish shepherd...will rebuke the Rabbi for his error or for forgetfulness of his duty, and remind him that among Jews it is not the clerical robe and trappings nor...government decree that confer authority, that the word of the most celebrated Rabbi carries weight only so long as it accords with the...law, and is null and void if it conflicts with the law sanctioned in Israel.[33]

Because the Torah belongs to the people as a whole, no hierarchical power can impose any laws or policies or officials on a Jewish community without first obtaining its consent (on this subject, more in Chapter 7). This is not to be construed, however, in terms of secular democratic thought. There is no majoritarianism under the laws of the Torah. Under Jewish law the minority, even those who for lack of means do not contribute [to the public treasury], can compel the majority to carry out everything which is a legal obligation of the community.[34]

This should dispel the prejudice that a Torah government would be a "theocracy", a state ruled by a priestly caste.[35] In Judaism there is no "clergy" and no "laity". Indeed, the most authentic form of Jewish leadership is that of the teacher, whose power is not political but intellectual and moral. But if it is grossly misleading to equate Torah government with theocracy, it is disingenuous to identify Torah Judaism with democracy. The decency still visible in contemporary democracy has nothing to do with democracy per se; it is owed to the biblical tradition. Neither democratic freedom nor democratic equality provides any norms of conduct. What, in fact, is there about democratic freedom that would prompt a person to restrain his passions, to be kind, honest, or just? What is there about democratic equality that would prompt him to defer to wisdom or to show respect for teachers and parents? Today such qualities are conspicuous by their absence.

Conclusion

To transcend contemporary or normless democracy, it will be necessary to derive freedom and equality from the Genesis conception of man's creation in the image of God. This will provide freedom and equality with the ethical and rational constraints operative in normative democracy. Instead of assimilating Judaism to democracy, the tendency of apologists, we should assimilate democracy to Judaism. We can then incorporate the term democracy into the language of Israeli public discourse by redefining democracy as "the rule of the people under God", corresponding to the "one nation under God" theme of the American Pledge of Allegiance. This would affect the meaning of the "state". The state would cease to be a sovereign entity. Indeed, it would become the servant of the people, which is precisely what its ministers, by definition, are supposed be. This transformation of language will have a salutary influence on the behavior of politicians, and therefore on politics. Politics will tend to become "metapolitics".

How will this affect the four basic causes of Israel's disintegration? Since these causes are at least partial effects of contemporary democracy, transcending the latter is indispensable for preventing Israel's demise. Assimilating democracy to Judaism will diminish secular-religious discord and thus promote Jewish unity. Jewish unity will enable Israel to deal with its explosive demographic problem. What encourages Israel's internal and external enemies is Jewish disunity, resulting from cognitive dissonance and the government's inability to articulate a coherent, consistent, and resolute Jewish national strategy. But such a strategy is impossible given the divisiveness of Israel's political and judicial institutions. Israel's ruling elites boast of these institutions as "democratic", which to some extent they are from the parochial perspective of contemporary democracy. The more comprehensive understanding of democracy developed in this chapter can provide a foundation for reforming Israel's political and judicial institutions and thus prevent their inevitable collapse. Finally, by assimilating democracy to the Torah, it will then be possible for Israel to overcome its lack of Jewish statesmanship and direction.

CHAPTER 4
Israel's Citizenship Problem: Conceptual Therapy

The Jews have done more to civilize men than any other Nation. They are the most glorious Nation that ever inhabited the earth. The Romans and their Empire were but a bauble in comparison to the Jews. They have given religion to three-quarters of the globe and have influenced the affairs of Mankind more, and more happily than any other Nation, ancient or modern.

John Adams

Wherever the Jews have attained to influence, they have taught to analyze more subtly, to argue more acutely, to write more clearly and purely: it has always been their problem to bring people to "raison".

Friedrich Nietzsche

It was stated at the outset of this inquiry that one of the basic causes of Israel's disintegration is the disunity resulting from extreme cultural heterogeneity. Especially critical is the burgeoning Arab population. Arab voting power, by determining who shall be Israel's prime minister, can very much influence the character and even the borders of the so-called Jewish state. Israel's political elites are aware of this problem. Yitzhak Rabin's warning of May 6, 1976 bears repeating. Only now it should be noted that, in 1976, his party was not dependent on the Arab vote as it was to become a year later when Labor's twenty-nine year control of Israel's government came to an end. Thereafter it would not be politically expedient to publicly declare:

The majority of the people living in a Jewish State must be Jewish. We must prevent a situation of an *insufficient* Jewish majority and we dare not have a Jewish minority... There is room for a non-Jewish minority *on condition that it accept the destiny of the State vis-a-vis the Jewish people, culture, tradition, and belief.* The minority is entitled to equal rights as individuals with respect to their distinct religion and culture, *but not more than that.*

This last sentence, we said, unambiguously implies that the rights of Israel's Arab inhabitants do not include equal political rights. From this it would follow that Israel's Arab inhabitants can be deprived of citizenship! Of course, anyone advocating such a step would immediately be denounced as a "racist", even though one might with greater reason apply that slur to Arabs.[36] Leaving aside the fact that Jews in Arab countries do not enjoy equal rights of *any* kind, Arab intellectuals and rulers contend that Judaism is not a nationality but a religion. This might prompt some generous Arabs to conclude that the Jews of Palestine are "entitled to equal rights as individuals with respect to their distinct religion and culture, *but not more than that*"! This means that Jews are not entitled to political rights, certainly not to an independent state of their own. Thus, should Israel's Arab inhabitants become a majority, Israel would again become Palestine and its Jewish inhabitants would be disenfranchised.

In this chapter, the author will not advocate indiscriminate disenfranchisement of Israel's Arab citizens, even though sufficient evidence will be presented showing that they do not accept, in Rabin's words, "the destiny of the State vis-a-vis the Jewish people". Of course, disenfranchisement would, on theoretical grounds, be an appropriate as well as logical response to the demographic problem posed by Arab citizenship. The remedy proposed in this chapter is a bit more subtle. Since "citizenship" is but another concept that has generated cognitive dissonance among Jews, we shall clarify its meaning and then integrate the concept with ideas appropriate to a Jewish commonwealth in the Holy Land.

* * *

As everyone knows, this land, in the pre-state period, was called "Palestine", and its inhabitants, Jews as well as Arabs, were "Palestinian" citizens. Arab leaders throughout the Middle East have insisted that Israel is "Palestine", which is why the PLO, i.e., the Palestine Liberation Organization, was formed in 1964, that is, *before* Israel gained control of Judea, Samaria, and Gaza. The Arabs may be correct! By this I only mean that, from the perspective of citizenship, Israel reverted to "Palestine" when its government, on April 1, 1952, enacted the Citizenship Law. On that day another ingredient of cognitive pollution descended on the

Land of Israel and entered the minds of Jews. To dispel this pollution, we shall have to inquire into the origin of Palestine citizenship.

Palestine Citizenship

Palestine citizenship was established by the League of Nations on July 24, 1922, when the administration of Palestine, which formerly belonged to the Turkish Empire, was entrusted to Great Britain as the Mandatory Power. The Mandate, it will be recalled, affirmed the Balfour Declaration of 1917 which favored the establishment in Palestine of a national home *for the Jewish people.*

Under Article 4 of the Mandate, an appropriate Jewish agency was to be "recognized as a public body for the purpose of advising and cooperating with the Administration of Palestine in such economic, social and other matters as may effect the establishment of the Jewish national home..." The Administration of Palestine was instructed, under Article 6, to "facilitate Jewish immigration..." Article 7 required the Administration of Palestine to enact a nationality law. The law was to include "provisions framed so as to *facilitate* the acquisition of Palestinian citizenship *by Jews* who take up their permanent residence in Palestine."[37]

In pursuance of Article 7, the Palestine Citizenship Order was issued in 1925, and this order, as amended from time to time, regulated Palestine citizenship for the remaining twenty-three years of the Mandate. Subject to the right to opt for Turkish and other nationalities, all Turkish subjects – Jew and non-Jews – habitually resident in the territory of Palestine became, on August 1, 1925, Palestine citizens. Other Turkish nationals born within Palestine could also acquire Palestine citizenship even though they had not been previously resident in Palestine.[38]

Palestine citizenship could also be acquired by birth. *Any* person born to a father who was a Palestine citizen himself acquired Palestine citizenship whether or not the birth took place in Palestine. Moreover, *any* person born within Palestine who did not by his birth acquire the nationality of any other State was deemed to be a Palestine citizen. Finally, Palestine citizenship could be acquired by *any* person by means of naturalization, the main precondition being a period of residence in Palestine.[39]

These methods of obtaining Palestine citizenship differ in no essential way from the methods by which *any* person, Jewish or non-Jewish, can obtain citizenship under Israel's 1952 Citizenship Law (sections 3-5), which is also called the Nationality Law. Thus: (1) "*Any* person who, immediately before the establishment of the State, was a Palestine citizen, shall become an Israel national"; (2) "A person born whilst his father or mother is an Israel national shall be an Israel national from birth"; (3) "A person born after the establishment of the State in a place that was Israel territory on the day of his birth and who never possessed any nationality during the period between his 18th and 21st birthdays and has been an inhabitant of Israel for five consecutive years immediately preceding the day of the filing of his application"; (4) "A person of full age... may obtain Israel nationality by naturalization if... he has been in Israel for three years out of five years preceding the day of the submission of his application."[40]

The reversion of Israel to Palestine via the concept of citizenship is not affected by the Law of Return. Enacted by the Knesset in 1950, the Law of Return, by which "Every Jew has the right to immigrate to this country," has been deemed an *immigration* law, not a *nationality* law. "There is no need to argue at length," said Supreme Court Justice Moshe Landau, "in order to show that the Law of Return does not deal with nationality at all but with the right to immigrate to and settle in Israel."[41] Of course the Law of Return was decisive for the development of a Jewish majority in this country. But under section 2(c)2 of the Nationality Law, Jews exercising the right to immigrate to Israel may opt not to become Israeli citizens. On the other hand, and as we shall see later, political and legal commentators have failed to discern that the *rationale* of the Law of Return, as opposed to the language of the law itself, not only contradicts the culturally neutral principle of political equality prescribed in the Declaration of Independence, but also the Nationality Law which, in terms of the citizenship issue, is responsible for Israel's reversion to Palestine.

Without recognizing this reversion, M.D. Gouldman raises the fascinating question:

What had been the fate of Palestine citizenship immediately following the establishment of the State? Had it vanished with the Mandate, leaving former Palestine citizens (Jews and non-Jews) stateless unless they happened to be possessed of some foreign nationality? Section 11 of [Israel's] Law and Administration Ordinance, 1948 provided that the law existing in Palestine on May 14, 1948 should remain in force...subject to such modifications as might result from the establishment of the State and its authorities. Did, therefore, former Palestine citizens – or at least those that remained in Israel – automatically become citizens of the new State of Israel even though no nationality law had yet been enacted?[42]

"The latter view," according to Gouldman, "has the advantages of continuity and the prevention of statelessness." This was the position taken by Justice Zeltner in a 1951 decision of the Tel Aviv District Court, *A.B. v. M.B.*, reversing a previous decision of the same court, that a former Palestine citizen who was, in the absence of an Israel nationality law, stateless:[43]

It seems to me...that the point of view according to which there are no Israel nationals is not compatible with public international law. The prevailing view is that, in the case of transfer of a portion of territory of a State to another State, every inhabitant of the ceding State becomes automatically a national of the receiving State... So long as no law has been enacted providing otherwise, my view is that every individual who, on the date of the establishment of the State of Israel, was resident in the territory which today constitutes the State of Israel, is also a national of Israel. Any other view must lead to the absurd result of a State without nationals, a phenomenon the existence of which has not yet been observed.[44]

Obviously this decision is favorable to indiscriminate application of the principle of one adult/one vote, which principle does not take cognizance of a citizen's consent or loyalty to the State. Surely Justice Zeltner was aware of the fact that the Arabs of Palestine never consented to the establishment of the State of

Israel. Indeed, they violently opposed the Balfour Declaration and, as previously noted, never consented to the League of Nation's designation of Great Britain as the Mandatory Power.

We have here a bizarre phenomenon. Government by the consent of the governed is a basic democratic principle. So, too, is the principle of one adult/one vote. The Arabs of Israel enjoy the latter, not the former. From an abstract or formalistic viewpoint, one might argue that by voting in a national election, a person tacitly consents to the existence of the State of which he is a citizen. This view trivializes the concept of citizenship or of nationality, as well as the religious convictions and hostility of the Arabs in question.

Justice Zeltner's position – which reflects a vacuous cosmopolitanism – was rejected by Justice Kennet in *Oseri v. Oseri*, a 1953 decision of the Tel Aviv District, a decision rendered after the enactment of the Nationality Law:

Citizenship is the grant of a personal status to the citizen and it creates a *bond of loyalty* between the State and the national. The loyalty which had been created by the [Palestine Citizenship Order] was towards the Mandatory Power, which has now disappeared, and it is difficult to reach a deduction that the very law which established a bond of loyalty between the Mandatory Power and its inhabitants can create a new nationality and a new bond of loyalty between the State of Israel and its inhabitants. Such a bond cannot automatically devolve.[45]

Accordingly, Palestine citizenship did not metamorphose into Israeli nationality with the termination of the Palestine Mandate and the creation of the State of Israel. Palestine citizens were therefore held to be stateless during the period between the establishment of the State and the entry into force of the Nationality Law. But if loyalty, as Justice Kennet emphasizes, is an essential ingredient of citizenship, the Nationality Law did not, in his words, "create a new nationality and a new bond of loyalty between the State of Israel and its [Arab] inhabitants."

The Nationality Law itself acknowledges loyalty as an essential element of citizenship and nationality. Part I, section 5(c) states that prior to the grant of citizenship by naturalization, the applicant must make the following declaration: "*I declare that I will be a loyal national of the State of Israel.*" Moreover, Part II, section 11(a)3 stipulates that the citizenship of any Israel national may be revoked if he "has committed an act involving disloyalty to the State." To my knowledge this provision has never been enforced against any Arab citizen of Israel, even though many have engaged in terrorist attacks against Jews. Admittedly, unlike such attacks, the phrase "act involving disloyalty to the State" is judicially vague. But this does not refute the reversion to Palestine thesis.

By reverting in principle to Palestine citizenship under the Mandate, the authors of the Nationality Law ignored the pogroms Arabs committed against Jews during the Mandate period. Did these Jewish law-makers believe that the new State of Israel could pacify its Arab inhabitants and make them renounce their loyalty to the "Arab Nation" or Islam? Did these magnanimous but self-effacing Jews believe they could make these members of a proud Arab-Islamic civilization loyal citizens of a despised and hated Jewish state? Did these Jews believe they could buy the loyalty of Arabs by raising their standard of living in a new and prosperous Jewish country?

The twenty-year period of the Mandate mocks such wishful thinking. The progress of Jews during that period immensely improved the economic standards, health, and longevity of Palestine's Arab citizens. Not only did their per capita income greatly exceed that of any Arab country, but the rate of natural increase of Arabs in western Palestine was the highest in the Arab world. The rapid growth of Arab wages and population in Palestine was particularly striking in those areas of Jewish settlement and development. This was acknowledged by the British Peel Commission report of 1937. And yet the report noted that, "Although the Arabs have benefited from the development of the country owing to Jewish immigration, this has had no conciliatory effect. On the contrary. Improvement in the economic situation in Palestine has meant the deterioration of the political situation."[46]

Why, then, did the authors of the Nationality Law ignore this painful experience and confer citizenship, hence political equality, on Israel's prolific Arab inhabitants? No doubt they felt publicly committed to the equality provision of the Declaration of Independence. But there is more.

Israel's Supreme Court has ruled that the Declaration carries no constitutional authority and cannot serve as a foundation for any actual legal right.[47] Nevertheless, the Declaration prescribes and prompted the convening of an "Elected Constituent Assembly" to adopt a Constitution. Israel's Provisional Government arranged for the election of such an Assembly. A committee consisting of various party spokesmen was elected. A draft constitution was submitted to the committee by Dr. Leo Kohn. The draft was supported by spokesmen of Agudat Israel, Mizrachi, and Hapoel Mizrachi – the religious parties. However, the committee's majority, representing Mapai and Mapam, the secular parties, rejected the proposed constitution, which prescribed political equality for all inhabitants of the State, except that the President had to be Jewish. Secularists feared that such a provision would be deemed "racist" by the international community, even though the Declaration repeatedly refers to Israel as a *Jewish* state. This fear, I believe, very much explains why the authors of the Declaration of Independence and of the Nationality Law granted equal political rights to Israel's Arab inhabitants. Underlying this fear, however, was the secular orientation or diminished national pride and purpose on the part of the founders of the State. The reversion of Israel to Palestine should be understood in this light.

National pride, rooted in a people's sense of a venerable past, of shared triumphs and tragedies, of cherished beliefs and values, of noble and timeless aspirations – this is the core of national consciousness and of the dignity that should attach to citizenship. Israel's Nationality Law makes nonsense of nationality and citizenship, and also of Islam and Judaism, by endowing Arabs with equal political rights in a supposed-to-be Jewish state. Israel's reversion to Palestine is the price Jews are paying for this lack of national pride and purpose, indeed, of practical wisdom and courage, all of which suffer from the emasculating influence of the cultural relativism prevailing in this democratic era.

Contrast Jordan. Under the Jordanian Nationality law of February 4, 1954, a person became a Jordanian national if, "*not being Jewish*, he possessed Palestine nationality before May 14, 1948 and at the date of publication of this law was ordinarily resident in the Hashemite Kingdom of Jordan."[48] This is less a manifestation of racism than of national pride and political prudence. Making Muslims citizens of a Jewish state is even more foolish than making Jews citizens of any Muslim state, considering only the disparity in their respective birthrates. Just as only Jews are qualified to make the laws of a Jewish state – *think of the knowledge and reverence required to preserve the Jewish tradition, its religious precepts and practices, its methods of education, the memory of its great teachers and leaders* – so only Muslims are qualified to make the laws of any Muslim state.

The government of Israel has been heedless of this obvious truth. As a consequence, Israel increasingly resembles a bi-national state with the demographic likelihood of eventually becoming an Arab Palestinian state thanks to the Nationality Law and its reversion, in principle, to Palestine citizenship.

An Arab Palestinian state is now glaringly on the agenda of Israel's Arab parties. The Arab strategy, first, is to demand that Israel be transformed into a "state of its citizens". This demand actually violates the law prohibiting any party that negates the Jewish character of the State. Yet that demand is featured on the party platform of MK Azmi Bishara's National Democratic Alliance (Balad). Bishara, a Christian Arab, was a candidate for prime minister of Israel in 1999. To compound his party's illicit objective – in its own words, "to change the State of Israel into a democratic state of its citizens" – the National Democratic Alliance boldly declares that "Arab Israeli citizens are a part of the Palestinian nation and the Arab people in its national and cultural identity." Which means that Bishara's objective is *not* a "democratic state of its citizens", but an Arab Palestinian state.

His party platform continues: "The National Democratic Alliance will act to achieve...the establishment of a sovereign Palestinian state in the occupied territories since 1967 whose capital is eastern Jerusalem." Inasmuch as Bishara, a citizen of Israel, has said that "Arab Israeli citizens are a part of the Palestinian nation," it follows that he is committed to an Arab Palestinian state extending from the Jordan River to the Mediterranean.

Even while he transparently advocates dismantling Israel, Bishara sits comfortably in the Knesset and is paid rather handsomely for engaging in sedition, while the Jews in that motley assembly do little more than blink.

More blatantly disloyal and contemptuous of Jewish Knesset Members is Arab MK Abdel Wahab Darawshe (Arab Democratic Party), once a member of the Labor Party who retired from the Knesset after the 1999 elections. Darawshe's party is aligned with the Islamic Movement, an organization with a terrorist wing. (The two parties form the United Arab List which competed in the 1999 Knesset elections!) In a July 1998 interview with a Palestinian newspaper, Darawshe said: "We are part of the Palestinian people, and we reject all forms of national service on behalf of Israel. Any Arab that serves in the Israeli army is a disgusting criminal."[49] Even in the Knesset, Darawshe baldly declared: "An Arab who serves in the IDF is a mercenary and collaborator." (This statement was made shortly after Arab MK Salah Salim of the Hadash Party called for the murder of Palestinian land dealers who sell property to Jews.)[50] More to the point, however, Darawshe, speaking on Palestinian Television on December 1, 1998 in honor of the dedication of a Palestinian airport in Gaza, said that he hopes to participate in the declaration ceremony of a Palestinian state that will be established on "all of the Palestinian land".[51]

Countless other instances may be cited of what can only be termed "permissive subversion". But consider these poignant words of MK Ayoub Kara (Likud), who represents the Druze community. Referring to how he has been abused by Arab MKs during committee hearings, Kara declared on Israeli radio: "I see myself as an integral part of the Israeli people, but if they [these

Arab MKs] see themselves as Palestinians, how can they be permitted to be legislators in our Knesset, or to take part in Israel's crucial decisions on the Golan, Judea, Samaria, and Gaza, and the like?"[52]

More astonishing than the brazen disloyalty of these Arab MKs is the paralysis, to put it kindly, of Israel's political leaders. There is, however, a subterranean factor working: *One-third of the Arab vote in the 1996 Knesset elections went to Jewish parties.*[53] These parties have a vested interest in not offending Arab voters by initiating criminal charges against their Arab leaders. This, we shall see, is one of the consequences of Israel's parliamentary electoral system of proportional representation where the entire country constitutes a single district, such that many Arab votes contribute to the number of seats allocated to Jewish parties. This may very well explain the following extraordinary incident.

On December 24, 1992, at the height of the intifada, Arab MK Hashem Mahameed went to Gaza and said this to his kinsmen: "So long as the [Israeli] occupation continues, so will the struggle, and by struggle we don't mean only stones but a battle with all the means at our disposal." It requires no imagination to see that Mahameed was inciting Arabs to use firearms and other weapons against Israeli soldiers and civilians. Nevertheless, for this seditious act, a Likud-controlled Knesset, by a vote of 54 to 48, did no more than suspend for three months Mahameed's parliamentary privilege of unrestricted access to all areas of the country![54] Ponder the significance of those who voted in the negative. *Therein, one may discern the Labor Party's abject dependence on the Arab vote.* As for those who voted in the affirmative, one may discern impotence, fear of the racist slur, but also the death of outrage. The absence of Jewish statesmanship in Israel could hardly be more conspicuous, until we read the sequel.

In 1999, the same Mahameed (who supported Saddam Hussein during the Persian Gulf War and refers to Hizbullah terrorists in Lebanon as a "national liberation movement") was appointed to the Knesset's Defense and Foreign Affairs Committee, a committee which, among other responsibilities, oversees the work of Israel's secret services! We shall have to wait until the next chapter to see more clearly what there is about Israel's political institutions that conduces to such madness. But it should already be evident that normless democracy underlies this pathological state of affairs.[55]

Fear of the racist slur and self-serving motives deter all but a handful of Jewish MKs from calling for the removal of the parliamentary immunity of seditious Arab MKs, let alone the revocation of their citizenship. But human beings feel a need to justify or rationalize their behavior, and this requires some simple, basic, and non-controversial ideas or principles. The principles that dominate contemporary mentality are democratic, the most pervasive being equality. This principle obliterates all moral distinctions, to the extent of placing loyal and disloyal citizens on the same level and endowing them with equal political rights. Anyone with a scintilla of intellectual honesty will see that granting Arabs, who are hostile to the Jewish state, the same rights as Jews who fight and work for the Jewish state, is not only unjust, but suicidal.[56] What is more, this indiscriminate egalitarianism violates the rationale or logic underlying of the Law of Return.

Contrary to what was said above by Justice Landau, the Law of Return is not simply an "immigration" law. In truth the Law of Return is Israel's only *nationality* law, and it is fundamentally opposed to the Nationality Law of 1952! Let me explain.

In introducing the Law of Return in the Knesset in 1950, then Prime Minister David Ben-Gurion declared:

This Law does not provide for the State to bestow the right to settle in Israel upon the Jew living abroad; it affirms that this right is *inherent* in him from the very fact of his being a Jew; the State does not grant the right of return to the Jews of the Diaspora. This right preceded the State; this right built the State; its source is to be found in the historic and never-broken connection between the Jewish people and their homeland.[57]

Since only Jews have an *inherent* right to settle in Israel – *a right that transcends the State* – the logic of this right prohibits the Knesset from passing any law or acting on any principle (such as that of political equality) that could demographically deprive Jews of that right. Yet this is exactly what happened in 1952 when the

Knesset passed the Nationality Law. While affirming that only Jews have an inherent right to Israeli citizenship, the Nationality Law contradicts the logic of that right by making it possible for non-Jews to obtain citizenship, hence to vote, hold office, and shape the laws of the supposed-to-be Jewish state. Israel was thereby made a state for Jews and non-Jews alike, hence a "state of its citizens"! The Nationality Law thus provides the ground for denationalizing Judaism or for deJudaizing Israel.[58]

Here it should be noted that in American law, "A man's nationality is a continuing legal relationship between the sovereign State on the one hand and the citizen on the other... This legal relationship involves rights and corresponding duties upon both – on the part of the citizen no less than on the part of the State."[59] Specifically, and as Hans Kelsen writes in his *Principles of International Law*, "The most prominent amongst those duties that can be imposed only upon citizens is the duty to do military service."[60] As Gouldman points out, "In Israel, the duty of defense (both regular and reserve) is imposed not only on nationals but also on any person whose 'place of permanent residence is within the territory to which the law of the State of Israel applies.'"[61]

Nevertheless, Gouldman and almost all other commentators fail to mention, let alone criticize, the government's policy of exempting Arab citizens from the duty of national service, be it military or civilian. In contrast, the exemption of yeshiva students, especially the ultra-orthodox Haredim, never ceases to arouse acrimonious opposition across the political spectrum and even the displeasure of the Supreme Court. This double-standard admittedly contradicts democracy's indiscriminate egalitarianism. This egalitarianism, however, is only a means of achieving comfortable self-preservation, which is the ultimate aim of contemporary democracy. Viewed in this light, it is safer to draft Orthodox Jews – which is now happening – than to draft Arabs. One reason is pathetically obvious: the Arabs, generally speaking, are not loyal citizens. But given their disloyalty, which their party leaders brandish even in the Knesset, reason and justice call for the selective revocation of their citizenship.

This brings us back to Part II, section 11(a)3 of the Citizenship Law, which thus far vainly requires the revocation of any Israel national who "has committed an act of disloyalty to the State." Although far more basic remedies will be necessary, this clause, which is judicially vague to be readily implemented, should be amended to read as follows:

The citizenship of any inhabitant of Israel shall be revoked if he or she (1) engages in acts intended to impair Israel's security or welfare, such as serving in a terrorist organization whose aim is to destroy human life or property in Israel; (2) aids or abets any terrorist who has committed, or plans to commit, any act of violence against Israel, its Jewish and non-Jewish inhabitants; (3) advocates, or supports any individual, group, or nation that advocates violence against Israel; (4) publishes or distributes anti-Israel or anti-Jewish propaganda; or (5) is a member of any political party or organization that rejects Israel's existence as a Jewish state, or advocates Israel's transformation either into a bi-national state or into a state of its citizens.

These amendments to the Nationality Law are all the more necessary in view of the following proposal.

Like non-Jewish residents of the State of Israel who choose not to be citizens, but who nonetheless serve in the Israel Defense Forces (IDF), Israel's Arab citizens should also be required to perform military service. Israel's Government should therefore renounce the policy of exempting virtually all Arab citizens from fulfilling this obligation. Recognizing, however, that the induction of Arabs into the IDF poses certain dangers, the Ministry of Defense should adjust the nature of their training and assignments with due caution, but with a view to cultivating patriotic citizens.

The law governing military service should specify reasonable exemptions, but without any invidious distinction between Jews and Arabs. Aside from such exemptions, any person who refuses military service should be deprived of the right to vote in any national or local election and to hold any elective office in the State of Israel. No doubt many Arabs will refuse to perform military service despite the loss of such privileges. (Perhaps they will fear the stigma of "collaborating" with the enemy, a stigma that has resulted in the murder of Arabs by their kinsmen.) Such Arabs should be encouraged but not forced to emigrate from Israel, and they should be reasonably compensated for property left behind. As for Arabs who serve in the IDF, it goes without saying that any who commit, or conspire to commit, acts of violence against the State of Israel will be subject to the penalties of the law, including deportation. Magnanimity on the one hand, and firm justice on the other, should be the guiding principle. This will gain the respect of many Arabs and diminish the number of those who are incorrigible. Nor is this all.

Upon being inducted into the IDF, all persons, regardless of religion, should be required, just as civil servants are required, to take an oath of loyalty to the State of Israel. The oath should be framed in terms comparable to these:
(1) I do solemnly declare that I will faithfully abide by the laws of the State of Israel.
(2) I do further declare that I will neither aid nor abet any political or religious party, or any individual, group, nation, or foreign entity that advocates violence toward the State of Israel or its residents, Jewish or non-Jewish.
(3) I do further declare that I reject any political or religious precept that advocates violence toward the State of Israel or residents, Jewish or non-Jewish.*

The second and third provisions of this loyalty oath are perfectly consistent with the Universal Declaration of Human Rights which prescribes "tolerance and friendship among all nations, racial, or religious groups". Nevertheless, it will be said that such an oath, taken by a Muslim, would be tantamount to renouncing *jihad*, a

---

* Consistent with the preceding, and excluding exemptions specified by law, one of the qualifications for *de novo* membership in the Knesset should be prior national service.

basic tenet of Islam (discussed in Chapter 9). Impossible as this may seem, it places the issue, for the first time, in broad daylight. Obscuring this issue has produced no good – certainly not to Jews.

It goes without saying that a loyalty oath does not make a person loyal: witness the loyalty oath taken by Arab Knesset members. Nevertheless, a loyalty oath presupposes, in the person taking it, a moral or religious relationship to the community, his respect for its beliefs and values, a willingness to promote its good even when personally inconvenient. Such an attitude is not to be expected of all but a few Arab citizens. Indeed, it would demean them to expect such loyalty to the State of Israel. After all, the Jews not only conquered them in the War of Independence, but do not share their most cherished beliefs and values. This being the case, surely the proposed loyalty oath will appear not only futile but an insult to Arab pride. However, the purpose of the loyalty oath is not to create a bond between Arabs and Jews in the State of Israel, but to expose the absurdity and injustice of endowing Jews and Arabs with equal political rights, as if they comprised a single people. It is the height of impudence, of conceit, indeed of stupidity, to grant equal political rights to Arabs in the expectation that they will renounce their religion and 1,300 year-old civilization for a ballot box. But this smugness or obtuseness has become a syndrome in Israel. The mentality of Israel's political and intellectual elites has been rigidified by non-Jewish concepts or dogmas which prevent them from making ideological distinctions, even when life and death hang in the balance.

A Survey of Israel's Jewish Population

We have seen that a *Goy*, in contradistinction to an *Am*, is a corporate entity whose members are not united by a distinctive way of life. Israel's secular elites simply want to be like the *Goyim* – for example, multicultural America. Virtually anyone can be a citizen of that great democracy, where freedom existentially means "living as you like". Far from being an *Am*, America is a *normless* democracy where citizenship has little moral or intellectual significance. Indeed, the paucity of moral-intellectual standards in the naturalization process has stripped citizenship in America of any dignity.

From the Torah's perspective, a people is not a random or amorphous aggregation of individuals. The essence of peoplehood is *particularism*, not *universalism* – which is not to say that particularism precludes universal ideas and ideals such as ethical monotheism. A living people must have a revered past and profound sense of collective purpose, embodied in national laws and literature and vivified by national holidays and customs. Such a people will experience similar joys and harbor familiar thoughts conducive to friendship. They will feel responsible for each other, and they will respond, in righteous indignation, to assaults on their national honor. Therein is the heart and soul of a people and the reason why their government will not bestow citizenship on foreign elements whose goals or way of life clashes with their own.

Let us now examine the practices and beliefs of Israel's Jewish population. According to a comprehensive 1993 survey conducted by the Guttman Institute:[62] (1) 56% always light Shabbat candles, 22% sometimes; (2) 23% always attend synagogue Saturday morning, 22% sometimes; (3) 42% never work (in public) on Sabbath, 19% sometimes; (4) 78% always participate in Passover *Seder*, 20% sometimes; (5) 70% always fast on Yom Kippur, 11% sometimes; (6) 69% always observe *Kashrut* at home, 18% sometimes; (7) Circumcision 92%; Bar Mitzvah 83%; (8) Wedding 87%; (9) Burial/*Shiva*/*Kaddish* 88-91%; (10) *Mezuza* on front door 98%.

These Jews are typically classified as follows: Ultra-Orthodox 8%; Modern Orthodox (or Religious Zionists) 17%; Traditional 55%; Secular 20%. (Because of their high birthrate, the Ultra-Orthodox Jews today probably number 10%.) As for traditional Jews (by far the largest group), most are Sephardim from the Mediterranean or Islamic world. They are people who cherish traditional Jewish life, but modify *halakhically* required practices in those cases they believe to be personally necessary or convenient.

Most remarkable, however, are the "secularists". For the practices, as opposed to the beliefs, of a significant percentage of these Jews are quite similar to those of many traditionalists, except that they claim they maintain those practices for family and national reasons rather than for religious ones. The Guttman survey shows that 75% of the "secular" 20% follow the most common traditional religious practices. Also astonishing in this connection is a 1992 study by Tel Aviv University Professor Yochanan Peres, indicating that 23% of those who identify as "secular" believe in the Torah's divine origin![63] To this data add what was indicated in Chapter 1, namely, that between 1991 and 1997, some 330,000 Israelis, previously self-identified as "secular", became either orthodox or traditional. What makes this data all the more extraordinary is that left-wing secularists have always dominated the country's media and economy, as well as its educational and cultural institutions!

The above findings clearly demonstrate that the people of Israel are very Jewish, i.e., "religious". Thus, despite their ethnic heterogeneity, the Jews of Israel are indeed a people, thanks, of course, to the Torah.

This is not the place to explode the myth of the Palestinian people.[64] What is obvious, however, is that the Jews and Arabs living in Israel most emphatically do not constitute a people. How infinitely trivial, by comparison, are the cultural differences between French- and English-speaking Canadians. Yet the former fervently seek to separate from the latter. Contrast, too, the 15-year civil war that took place between Christians and Muslims in Lebanon, who at least speak the same language. Recall, too, the ethnic strife between Kurds and Arabs of Iraq, both of the Islamic faith, both citizens of that country. How, then, can Arabs reasonably and justly be accorded citizenship in a Jewish commonwealth? To answer this question, we need to examine the concept of citizenship from a Torah perspective.

Citizenship from a Torah Perspective

Like the concept of the sovereign state, the concept of citizenship is foreign to the Torah. Since the state is a product of human will, so too are its laws governing citizenship. Moreover, since a defined area of land is essential to a state's existence, its laws governing citizenship will apply only to that area (with exceptions of no relevance to our inquiry). But as we have seen, the people of Israel existed before they possessed a land. Indeed, it was only after receiving the Torah that they were given a land, and only for the sake of the Torah.

What also distinguishes the Torah is that any Jew who has converted to another religion will remain with all the obligations of a Jew until the end of time.[65] In contrast, citizenship is a right or privilege which can be renounced or revoked. For example, a person immigrating to the United States from Switzerland may renounce his Swiss citizenship and become an American citizen (and vice-versa). In fact, these two sovereign states may agree to allow a number of their respective nationals to be citizens of both countries. Moreover, the two countries may limit dual citizenship to those who do not serve in the army or hold an elective office of government. Clearly, citizenship is an artificial concept extrinsic to the Torah.

However, while the Torah says nothing about "citizenship", it does posit the concept of the *ger*, a proselyte or convert to Judaism. Because Judaism is a unique *philosophy* and system of *behavior*, any person, regardless of race or ethnicity, can become a Jew by learning the Torah and living according to its precepts. For the *ger* and the born Jew there is but one law. The concept of the *ger* thus provides a moral foundation for the social and political equality of naturalized citizens in any democracy. To be sure, it is reasonable and proper to require, say a President of the United States, to be a native-born American (as prescribed in the American Constitution). This qualification is anticipated in Jewish law: a convert to Judaism cannot be a king of Israel.

Although the concept of the *ger* provides a foundation for what is called a "naturalized citizen", conversion to Judaism is an infinitely more disciplined and exalting process, both intellectually and spiritually. The *ger* assumes all the obligations of a born Jew: to sanctify the Name of God by studying the Torah, serving His people, and setting an example to mankind by doing justice and kindness. The convert *earns* his equality with the born Jew, and only then is he entitled to participate in making the laws of his community. This equality of status does not extend to non-Jewish residents of Israel.

The *halakhic* category of a non-Jewish resident is a *ger toshav*. To qualify as a *ger toshav*, the non-Jew must abide by the Seven Noahide Laws of Universal Morality. Let us pause a moment and consider these laws.

Six prohibit idolatry, blasphemy, murder, robbery, adultery, and eating flesh from a living animal, while the seventh requires the establishment of courts of justice. Such courts are obviously essential to any society based on the primacy of reason and persuasion rather than passion and intimidation. The Noahide laws may thus be deemed a "genial orthodoxy". The laws of this genial orthodoxy can of course be elaborated in various ways, which means that this concise code of laws, while applicable to all mankind, is compatible with great ethnic and political diversity. Properly understood, therefore, Judaism denies any *necessary* contradiction between ethnic particularism and universalism or cosmopolitanism. Indeed, Judaism itself constitutes a synthesis of ethnic particularism and cosmopolitanism. The Noahide laws merely impose ethical and conceptual constraints on what otherwise would be an impossible dichotomy, one that would lead to interminable human conflict.

Another aspect of the Noahide laws is that they transcend the social and economic distinctions among men by holding all men equal before the law. By so doing, this genial orthodoxy places restraints on governors and governed alike and thereby habituates diverse individuals and groups to the rule of law.

Viewed in this light, the seven Noahide laws are a necessary precondition of any civilized society. Hence it is not in the least exceptional to require a *ger toshav* to abide by those laws if he is to live in the Land of Israel, that is, in a Jewish commonwealth. At the same time, however, a *ger toshav* must also acknowledge the Torah as the supreme law of the land.

Now, let us call a *ger toshav* a "citizen", i.e., a citizen of Israel. Thus understood, citizens of Israel are entitled to personal and religious freedom. They also merit the civil rights of Jews, and may have their own law courts and even their own educational institutions. In fact, the Torah requires the government to provide for their poor, their sick, and their aged whenever necessary (Deut. 15:4). However offensive this may seem to indiscriminate egalitarians, a *ger toshav* or "citizen" may not be a member of the legislative, executive, and judicial branches of government. Let us try to understand this from a Torah point of view.

What is a Jew?

For the observant Jew, the Torah is the divine source of truth and the paradigm of how man should live.[66] Hence non-Jews may not participate in making laws affecting the character of Jewish life. "A hybrid community [such as the bi-national state advocated by some post-Zionists] proclaims by its very existence that it does not consider truth to be of supreme importance."[67] It cannot be said too often that the Jews became a nation through and for the sake of the Torah, and that Israel's existence has no justification apart from the Torah. Intellectual honesty and a sense of obligation to the forefathers, Prophets, and Sages of the Jewish people – nay, to the countless number of Jews who suffered and died to sanctify God's Name and preserve the Torah – demand that only Jews make the laws of the Jewish commonwealth. Is it not the height of absurdity that Arab Knesset Members cast the deciding votes on legislation pertaining to the "Who is a Jew" issue?

Philosophically speaking, the question of "*What* is a Jew?" is far more complicated and significant than the question of "*Who* is a Jew?" (to be discussed in a moment). Here let us examine three of the many unique characteristics of the Jew.

The first is simply this: *The Jew relates every question concerning life to the Torah, i.e., the Halakha.* It needs to be understood, however, Halakhic Judaism is not fundamentalism. Rather, it is the application of the eternal words of the Written Law to the time-related needs of the Jewish people by means of the Oral Law. Here the text, which is set, confronts life, which is ever in motion. While the text prevents moral relativism and social disintegration, *Halakha* prevents social stagnation by applying general legal and ethical principles to new particulars so as to develop new branches of law appropriate to the changing needs and circumstances of the Jewish people. Such is its comprehensiveness and creativity that *Halakha* enables each Jew to make his own life a work of art while contributing to his people's perfection.

Accordingly, when Jews have a problem or controversy, they seek its resolution by consulting various legal works or some *halakhic* expert or perhaps a *Beit Din*, i.e., a court of law. Which ever the case, they are actually employing legal reasoning to relate eternal truths to the living present, such that law yields goodness and justice, as well as peace and friendship. This is why Judaism has been called the religion of law as well as the religion of reason. Now we can better appreciate why Harvard graduate John Adams, second President of the United States, could say, "The Jews have done more to civilize men than any other nation."[68] And Friedrich Nietzsche: "Wherever the Jews have attained to influence, they have taught to analyze more subtly, to argue more acutely, to write more clearly and purely: it has always been their problem to bring people to *raison*."[69]

A second unique characteristic of the Jew is that he ultimately attributes his and his people's sufferings to lapses from the Torah. This attitude of personal and national responsibility stands in striking contrast to the Christian doctrine of original sin, the Islamic and Greek concept of fate, and the psychological, sociological, and historical determinism propagated by the social sciences. (All the more ironic is the fact that the Jew has been the scapegoat of mankind!) But the Jew's profound sense of personal and national responsibility must be understood in terms of the mission of the Chosen People.

This third characteristic of the Jew is his role as the spiritual educator of mankind, a role implicit in his very name. For the word "Jew" is derived from Leah's fourth son, "Judah" (*Yehudah*), which means "to praise God". In his very name we are given to see the Jew's and Israel's world-historical function. "This People have I created for Me that they may relate My praise" (Isaiah 43:21). To relate God's praise is to reveal His infinite wisdom, power, and kindliness in every domain of existence, which ultimately requires Israel to be a holy nation – one may almost say a "nation of philosophers", the words used by Theophrastus, Aristotle's successor, to describe Israel.[70] Hence the aim of the Torah Jew is to understand the totality of existence and to live in accordance with the laws thereof.

Who is a Jew?

Turning to the issue of "Who is a Jew?" – this issue, in Israel, involves the Law of Return. As previously indicated, the Law of Return bestows automatic "citizenship" on Jews immigrating to Israel. When the law was passed in 1950, it was understood that a Jew is one born of a Jewish mother – a perfectly rational requirement if only because the certainty of a new-born child's paternity is less than 100 percent (DNA notwithstanding). But what about a convert to Judaism? Conversion according to *Halakha* was not made explicit in the Law of Return. This is the Law's basic flaw, which has resulted in the influx of hundreds of thousands of gentiles especially from Russia. What in truth was a nationality law has thus metamorphosed into an immigration law, as justice Landau *wrongly* concluded!

Moreover, until recent Supreme Court decisions, the Chief Rabbinate was unambiguously empowered by law to decide conversion matters (as it did under the British Mandate). Needless to say, the Rabbinate recognizes only conversions according to *Halakha*, and only conversions performed by qualified orthodox Rabbis are deemed legal and authentic.

Conversion is of course a most serious matter, both for the prospective convert and for the Jewish People. The gentile must first be discouraged from conversion. He must be told that he will be acceptable to God by abiding by the Seven Noahide Laws of Universal Morality. (Unlike Christianity and Islam, Judaism has no monopoly on heaven.) But if the would-be convert insists on becoming a Jew and demonstrates, to the satisfaction of a *Beit Din*, adequate knowledge of the Torah, and if the *Beit Din* has reason to believe he will abide by the precepts required of observant Jews, such as the Sabbath, the dietary laws, and the laws of family purity, then only does he merit the honor and privilege of becoming part of the Jewish People. Only then does he have an unequivocal right to participate in shaping the laws of the Jewish state.

Adequacy of knowledge and reasonable assurance of Torah observance before Jews qualified to judge of such matters – these are the basic conditions of authentic conversion to Judaism. There is nothing arbitrary or unreasonable about this.

We expect teachers and lawyers and doctors to meet the intellectual and ethical standards of their respective professions, as determined by recognized authorities. In fact, and as previously implied, higher intellectual and moral standards are expected of teachers, lawyers, and doctors than of ordinary citizens because those pursuing these learned and venerable callings can do more harm as well as more good. Therefore, the importance of preserving the highest standards of the learned professions cannot be exaggerated.

And so it is with the Jewish profession. To preserve the intellectual-moral integrity and magnificent heritage of the Jewish profession, conversion according to the standards of *Halakha* is absolutely essential. This is an awesome responsibility which the Rabbinate owes to the Jewish People as well as to any prospective convert. Only a truly Orthodox Rabbi has, or can be trusted to have, the requisite intellectual qualifications and sense of historical responsibility to perform authentic *halakhic* conversions.

I am again alluding to Israel's world-historical mission, the fulfillment of which requires the ingathering of *Jews*, not of pseudo-Jews, to the Land of Israel. Reform rabbis – and this applies to most Conservative rabbis – who deny the Divine origin of the Written and Oral Law cannot believe in the concept of the Chosen People, hence cannot but impair Israel's *raison d'être* as a light unto the nations. Because such rabbis alter Judaism to suit their own transient predilections or those of their congregations, they are not qualified to perform conversions.

Gentiles converted by such rabbis are being deluded, and with consequent embarrassment and anguish, for there are those who really want to be Jewish. There are many cases of gentiles who, having been converted by non-Orthodox rabbis, later learned of the subterfuge and underwent Orthodox conversion. In fact, some of these innocent people, who married after their original "conversion", had to remarry – and gladly did remarry – their spouse.

To justify non-orthodox conversion, Reform rabbis will adopt a plastic or pluralistic view of Judaism or Jewish law. This makes the Torah a fabrication dependent on human whim and will. The non-orthodox rabbi would have Jews believe the Oral Law is merely a rabbinical product. He thereby impugns the integrity of men of the caliber of Rabbi Akiba and Rabbi Hillel, who transmitted the Oral Law even in the face of death by cruel torture at the hands of Rome. Indeed, it would have been foolish and even criminal of the these men to resolve to suffer martyrdom if the Oral Law, whose study was prohibited by Rome, was merely the creation, rather than the logical elucidation, of human minds. One cannot but wonder whether Reform rabbis are aware of the significance of their skepticism: they are actually insinuating that the Sages were fools or frauds, and, if the latter, that they knowingly deceived the Jewish People about their heritage.

In any event, for such rabbis, the answer to the question of "Who is a Jew?" is purely subjective. How one Jewish community answers this question is not decisive for any other Jewish community. Yet these rabbis denounce Orthodoxy in the name of "Jewish unity"! Whatever the shortcomings of Orthodox rabbis, they do not succumb to the logical absurdity of calling for "unity" in one breath and "pluralism" in another. Pity they seldom show how, in the two pillars of the Talmud, *Aggada* (Jewish lore) and *Halakha* (Jewish law), Judaism allows for great intellectual latitude without succumbing to a meaningless pluralism, a pluralism devoid of rational and even ethical constraints. The rationality and creativity of the Jewish People, as Nietzsche and other gentile thinkers have remarked, is unequaled. But it is Jewish law, elucidated by its great Sages, that has preserved the People of Israel through millennia of dispersion, persecution, and genocide. Pluralism is merely a contemporary mantra.

The great Jewish philosopher, Rabbi Saadiah Gaon, declared that "Israel is a nation only through the Torah," the immutable Book of Truth. Pluralism is a denial of immutable or trans-historical truths. This is why *pluralistic rabbis lack the incentive and ability to reconcile permanence and change – a precondition of any society that knows what it stands for.* Without the stabilizing and unifying influence of truth, society can be nothing more than a transient hodgepodge of individuals and groups, each pursing its own interests. Pluralistic rabbis seem oblivious of the fact spoken of earlier: *a merely pluralistic society proclaims by its very existence that its educators do not consider truth to be of supreme importance.* Had such rabbis been the leaders of the Jewish People after the destruction of the Second Temple, the Jews would now be as extinct as the Mesopotamians.

The reader will now see why I first raised the question of "What is a Jew?" The Reform rabbi cannot really answer this question. For he or she looks upon the Jew as a *protean* being, a creature subject, like all other people, to the flux of history. In fact, one may deduce from the pluralism of these rabbis that Jews do not even constitute a people or a nation. Hence it would hardly be an exaggeration to say that Reform rabbis have more in common with liberal Protestantism than with Judaism!

Since such rabbis cannot univocally answer the question of "*What* is a Jew?" they are not qualified to convert any gentile to Judaism. Obviously this conclusion runs contrary to the shibboleths of rootless, normless, and aimless democracy.

Conclusion

The question will arise: "If a citizen of Israel, in contradistinction to a Jew, cannot be a member of the legislative, executive, and judicial branches of government, then, granting that he will enjoy all other rights pertaining to a *ger toshav*, will not this inferior status arouse his resentment?" Resentment, however, is not self-justifying. We have seen that gentiles who make Israel their permanent residence, but who choose not to be citizens, thereby disqualify themselves from voting and holding office, but still have an obligation to serve in the Israel Defense Forces. In any event, to better secure the rights of all inhabitants of Israel, as well as to improve the legislative, executive, and judicial functions of government, I shall propose a bicameral parliament in which the lower house will consist of Jews and non-Jews whose primary function will be to exercise administrative oversight. It will later be shown that this lower house will actually be more powerful and more conducive to good government than Israel's present Knesset.

That this proposal will be denounced as "racist" by indiscriminate egalitarians will remind thoughtful readers of the Mapai and Mapam members of the Constituent Assembly who, fearful of that slur, opposed a constitutional provision that the President of the State of Israel be Jewish. These egalitarians will use that slur to discredit those who wish to prevent Israel's collapse by resolving the demographic issue in terms consistent with Judaism. Like blind-deaf-mutes, they close their eyes and ears and say nothing about the seditious, not to say racist, statements and behavior of Arab Knesset Members. They cloak their fear of anti-Semitism in the guise of egalitarianism, today's easy path to moral superiority. This is a path to nothingness.

The first stage of a comprehensive solution to the Arab demographic problem is conceptual therapy. The second stage is legislative therapy. But legislative therapy will require fundamental reform of Israel's parliamentary system, the concern of the next chapter.

CHAPTER 5
Israel's Flawed Parliamentary System: A Jewish Remedy

The proper office of a representative assembly is to watch and control the government; to throw the light of publicity on its acts; to compel a full exposition and justification of all of them which anyone considers questionable; to censure them if found condemnable, and, if the men who compose the government abuse their trust, or fulfil it in a manner which conflicts with the deliberate sense of the nation, to expel them from office, and either expressly or virtually appoint their successors.

John Stuart Mill
Representative Government

We have seen that the issue of citizenship is decisive for a nation's character. This is why nations have laws limiting immigration and setting standards for naturalization. Age qualifications aside, whoever is eligible to be a citizen will usually be eligible to vote and hold office, hence exercise the legislative, executive, or judicial powers of government. Directly related to laws governing citizenship are a nation's electoral laws, which more decisively influence *Who* shall rule and for what *Ends* or purposes. In other words, the intellectual-moral character of public officials as well as the goals and policies they pursue depend very much on the method by which they are elected. The method of election will affect the relationship between rulers and ruled and therefore the extent to which a country approximates a representative democracy. As will be seen in a moment, an ostensibly democratic electoral system can enable a nation's rulers to ignore the concerns of most voters *between* elections and thereby make a mockery of democracy.

Such is the case in Israel. Accordingly, the initial purpose of this chapter is to subject to critical analysis the flaws of Israel's parliamentary electoral system. We need to bear in mind, however, that the electoral rules governing Israel's Knesset profoundly affect the policies and conduct of the executive and judicial branches of government. The analysis will itself indicate how the flaws in question may be remedied. This is not to suggest that electoral rules alone are responsible for the country's divisive political and judicial institutions. But inasmuch as Israel's parliamentary electoral rules affect not only the number of political parties but the quality of party leaders, these rules constitute the most obvious cause of the country's disintegration.

Social Structure and Electoral Rules

The number of parties in a country may be said to be an interactive function of its electoral rules and its social structure. Heterogeneous societies are likely to have more political parties than homogeneous societies, but the number will be affected by the electoral rules. Political scientist Harvey Cox asks rhetorically: "Does anyone believe that the United States would remain a two-party system, even if it adopted the Israeli electoral system [where any party receiving a mere 1.5% of the votes cast in Knesset elections can obtain two seats in the legislature]?"[71]

Despite its great ethnic, racial, religious, and economic diversity, America has a two-party system primarily because of its single-member districts with plurality rule. This two-party system is a consequence of "strategic voting". Strategic voting means voting for a candidate one believes will win, rather than for a candidate one believes will lose, even though you identify with the latter. This is why simple plurality elections on the national, as opposed to the local level, tends to eliminate third parties. An exception is Canada, which has simple plurality elections yet a long-standing multiparty system. In this case social cleavages prove to be more significant than electoral rules.

If one looks at the national level, then, of 77 countries reported as having democratic elections, 25 use electoral systems with single-member districts and plurality rule. This is not to suggest that single-member districts with plurality rule is appropriate for Israel, although I dare say it would be preferable to the existing electoral system. The typical objection to the system of single-member districts with plurality rule is that it "disenfranchises" minorities and eliminates small parties. The objection exaggerates. No successful politician will ignore minorities in a highly contested district. As for the disadvantage to small parties, we shall show that small parties can do more harm than good, even to themselves.

As for Israel, this country has less socio-economic diversity than the United States. Recall, however, that twenty-two new parties registered for the May 1999 Knesset elections, and some thirty competed for seats in that 120-member assembly! What encourages this profusion of parties is that *the entire country constitutes a single electoral district*, which necessitates proportional representation. Compounding the problem is the 1.5% electoral threshold.[72] Excluding the Netherlands (a homogeneous country), this is by far the lowest electoral threshold among some fifty states using proportional representation. Given this low threshold, almost any interest group, including casino operators, without the slightest pretension of having legislative skills or any national vision, may aspire to enter the Knesset. The Knesset has thus become a haven for single-issue parties and job-seekers. Nor is this all.

Since no party has ever won a majority of the seats in Israel's parliament, every Israeli government or cabinet has consisted of a multiplicity of parties, each with its own agenda. For example, the government formed by Prime Minister Ehud Barak after the May 1999 elections consisted of no less than eight parties, five secular and three religious.[73] This is hardly conducive to the formulation and execution of coherent and resolute national policies. But this means that Israel's parliamentary electoral rules is a basic cause of the country's disintegration.

Such is their importance that *different electoral systems can produce different party systems, even when used in the same society at the same time*! A case in point is Australia, whose House of Representatives is based on single member districts, but whose Senate is based on multimember districts. The House had three parties in 1990, while the Senate had five.

Chile and Weimar Germany more powerfully illustrate the importance of electoral rules:

In 1970 Chile had three major candidates running for president. Socialist Salvador Allende narrowly surpassed a centrist and a rightist candidate and became president, although he received only 36.3 percent of the total vote. Allende's electoral platform committed him to carry out extensive social changes. However, his support base was too narrow, and his attempt to forge ahead with radical changes despite this drawback backfired badly. The centrists became alienated to the point where they acquiesced in a military coup. The outcome was a bloody dictatorship.

History would have been quite different if Chile had different electoral rules. Chilean tradition demanded that the legislature confirm as president the candidate with the largest number of votes, although Allende was the least desirable of the three candidates for more than half the voters. In some other countries an absolute majority (that is, more than 50 percent of votes cast) is required for election. A majority can be achieved by having a second round of elections in which only the two candidates with the most votes participate. The outcome might be that the centrist candidate is eliminated, and the voters offered the choice between a rightist and a leftist. If most of the former supporters of the centrist candidate were to switch to the rightist, the latter could win, much to the dismay of many leftist voters. Instead of a second round, one can also have one round of elections but ask voters for their second preferences. In this case, the centrist candidate would presumably be the second choice of both leftists and rights, and the country would get a president at least semiacceptable to everybody.

The point here is not to argue that one of the possible methods or outcomes described above is better than the others. The point is that electoral rules matter: with the *same* distribution of votes, the presidency could go to the leftist, the centrist, or the rightist candidate, depending on the rules.[74]

Another case in point: The Weimar Republic's parliamentary system was based on proportional representation with a low electoral threshold. It has been argued that Hitler's ascendancy was helped by this electoral system, which, as one writer has put it, "preserved a maddening profusion of parties and led to a widespread yearning for a strong leader." Even if the connection between electoral rules and Hitler's political success is debatable, "the very suggestion indicates that electoral rules might have serious consequences...even for an entire nation, its neighbors – and even the whole world."[75]

What renders Israel's parliamentary electoral rules most pernicious is this: Israelis do not vote for individual candidates, but for a fixed, party-ranked list of candidates. Since parties in Israel are symbolized by a few letters on a ballot slip, most candidates on the party lists are unknown to the average voter. Various consequences follow. First, candidates for the Knesset do not compete with each other as individuals in a particular district, as in almost every other country having democratic elections. Hence the legislative performance and previous campaign promises of an incumbent are not publicly exposed by a rival for his office.

Second, since an MK is not accountable to the voters in a constituency election, he can the more readily ignore their opinions and interests. Third, having no individual representative accountable to him in a relatively small district, the voter can hardly obtain a redress of grievances by conventional political means. No wonder studies indicate that an increasing majority of Israelis feel powerless despite the ease with which parties multiply in this country![76] Powerlessness, however, can lead, and has indeed led, to violence. Alternatively, many aggrieved voters will seek redress via the courts, and this, we shall see, has so augmented the power of the Supreme Court that the latter has become the primary engine of social change in Israel, indeed, of moral disintegration.

What makes this state of affairs all the more intolerable is Israel's perilous situation in the Middle East. Israeli politicians may be no worse than others, but *Israel's political institutions magnify their vices.* The consequence is lack of public confidence in Israel's ruling elites, something a besieged country can ill-afford.

There are other pernicious consequences of fixed party lists, but these affect the Knesset Member himself. Although some parties have primaries, the party leaders can very much influence, and in many instances determine, the order of candidates on the party lists. The result is anything but democratic. Assume that the leader of party **A** is Israel's Prime Minister, and that, together with high-ranking members of his own party, the leaders of parties, **B**,

C, **D**, and **E** compose his cabinet ministers. Because a majority of the Knesset's members owe their position and perks to these parties and not to the votes of constituents, they cannot function as judges of their Government's policies as do legislators in all democratic countries. Now suppose the Government's policy regarding Jewish control of Judea and Samaria and the Golan Heights has been unduly influenced by foreign pressure. If an MK were to vote against his Government he would be committing political suicide. This will deter him from resisting a policy he deems unwise and destructive. He will then be less able to resist the same foreign pressure prompting his Government to pursue that questionable policy. Meanwhile, because the voters have no individual Knesset Member accountable to them, whom they could then expect to uphold their views and interests – which may well be opposed to the Government's foreign policy – they themselves, the voters, will become overly sensitive and more subservient to "world opinion".

Therein is a hitherto unnoticed reason why Israeli governments, no longer in the youth of Zionism, have yielded to the American State Department's post-Six-Day War policy of "territory for peace", contrary to the deepest convictions of a large majority of Israel's Jewish population. If this majority's convictions on the territorial issue have since been eroded, a basic cause is this: they lack Knesset representatives of their own choosing.

Finally, of all the pernicious consequences of fixed party lists, none is more demoralizing than the phenomenon of "party-hopping". To be reelected to the Knesset, an incumbent will of course want to have a "safe" place on his party's electoral list. Obviously this is not possible for all incumbents. Thus, to retain his position in the Knesset, a vulnerable MK may resign from his party and join another party willing to accord him "electoral", not to say, job security. And so it was that, prior to the May 1999 elections, no fewer than 29 MKs in Israel's 120-member (outgoing) Knesset switched allegiance to rival parties! Of the 32 MKs who ran on the joint Likud-Tsomet-Gesher list in 1996, 14 flew the coop, having failed to receive safe places on their party's electoral list. The motive of most was naked opportunism. But all this is a manifestation of Israel's disintegration.

It goes without saying that politicians who switch their allegiance to rival parties betray their voters. Such a phenomenon is almost unheard of in other countries, if only because 74 out of 77 countries having democratic elections rely exclusively on district elections for the lower (or only) branch of their legislature.[77] The absence of district or constituency elections, coupled to the system of fixed party lists, makes Israeli democracy a travesty. Indeed, democracy in Israel is a veneer, but thick enough to mislead the people and hinder reform. Which indicates that a state having the trappings of democracy – universal suffrage and periodic multi-party elections – can nonetheless be an alternating oligarchy, but one whose elites speak and even think in the language of contemporary democracy: normless, rootless, and aimless.

This oligarchy, rendered such by Israel's parliamentary electoral system, lowers the quality of politicians, fosters political corruption and public cynicism, undermines the people's confidence in the future, and therefore renders Israel less capable of surviving in a hostile international environment.

Thresholds[78]

The mushrooming of parties in 1999 prompted politicians and intellectuals to urge a higher parliamentary electoral threshold. Let us consider how different thresholds would have affected the outcome of the May elections of that year.

First, let us enumerate the parties that entered the Fifteenth Knesset and their number of seats: One Israel (26); Likud (19); Shas (17); Meretz (10); Center (6); Shinui (6); Israel B'Aliya (6); National Religious Party (NRP) (5); United Torah Judaism (UTJ) (5); United Arab List (UAL) (5); National Union (4); Israel Beiteinu (4); Hadash (3); Balad (2); Am Ehad (2).

Now, ignoring "surplus votes" agreements between various parties, which may slightly affect the allocation of seats, a 3% threshold would have eliminated three of the 15 parties that won less than four seats: Hadash, Balad, and Am Ehad. A 4%

threshold would have eliminated two additional parties: National Union and Israel Beiteinu. Finally, a 5% threshold would have excluded three more parties, NRP, UTJ, and the UAL. The Knesset would then have consisted of seven instead of 15 parties.

It should be obvious, however, that certain parties, endangered by a higher threshold, would form joint lists to avoid being relegated to the political wilderness. This would be a salutary development, since campaigning on a common platform would tend to enlarge their political mentality, moderate perhaps extreme tendencies, and thus elevate Israeli politics. In fact, a 5% threshold, recommended by the present writer, would streamline the Knesset and the Government far more than first appears.

Even parties with eight or nine seats would form joint lists rather than risk losing their representation in the Knesset in a "bad" election year. (A case in point: the National Religious Party dropped from nine to five seats in the 1999 elections.) After one or two elections, Israel's parliament would consist of no more than five, and perhaps only four, parties or party coalitions: a left-of-center coalition, a right-of-center coalition, a coalition of religious parties, and a coalition of Arab parties. As a consequence, the cabinet would usually have no more than two parties. This would enable the Government to pursue more coherent and more resolute national policies.

Here it may be helpful to contrast the electoral thresholds of some other countries. In Argentina, only parties whose votes exceed 3% of the number of the *registered* electorate are eligible to receive seats. In Sweden a party must either exceed 4% of the national vote or its list in the constituency must exceed 12% of the constituency vote. Germany's 5% threshold is exceeded by Liechtenstein, which, despite a population of only 32,000, has an 8% threshold. Finally, in some countries, such as the Czech Republic and Slovakia, joint lists face higher threshold requirements than single-party lists.

An alternative method of streamlining the Government – and this could supplement something less than a 5% electoral threshold – is what I shall call a "cabinet" threshold. There is precedence for this sort of thing. The Knesset used to require a party to have six seats to be represented on the Foreign Affairs and Defense Committee. The ulterior reason for this threshold was to prevent Arab MKs from being eligible to sit on that highly sensitive committee. *Hence the Knesset could require a party to have six or even eight seats to be represented in the Cabinet*!

This "cabinet" threshold would not only reduce the shabbiness that characterizes the formation of coalition cabinet governments; it would also conduce to more coherent and resolute national policies. In fact, a six-seat "cabinet" threshold would encourage small parties to form joint *electoral* lists so as to qualify for cabinet posts! A six-seat "cabinet" threshold would be equivalent to a 5% electoral threshold. And by inducing small parties to form and *campaign* on joint lists, a "cabinet" threshold would also enlarge their views and thereby conduce to greater national unity.

As for the proposed 5% parliamentary threshold, critics will object that it will eliminate small parties, hurt minorities, and thus be undemocratic. Let us consider this issue in larger terms: To what extent are small parties conducive to Israel's national interests?

Small Parties

Although the definition of a small party will be somewhat arbitrary, let us say that in a 120-member Knesset, a party having five seats – roughly 4% – is "small". A somewhat larger figure might also be reasonable, in view of the fact that many countries, including little Liechtenstein, have higher electoral thresholds. (Incidentally, David Ben-Gurion once advocated a 10% threshold.)

Now, what are the alleged advantages of a low threshold? As already indicated, its advocates first contend that a low threshold is more democratic, since it enables small minority groups to be represented in the legislature. This argument may be reduced to an absurdity, since its logic requires not only a further reduction of the threshold, but enlarging the membership of the legislature to accommodate a larger number of minute parties and interest groups. It should be obvious, however, that making an electoral system more democratic can undermine democracy. For as we have seen, Israel's permissive electoral system fragments not only the legislature, but the Government and renders the latter incapable of pursuing coherent and resolute national policies. The entire nation, including groups represented by small parties, suffers as a consequence. Democracy, therefore, is not an adequate justification for small parties.

On the other hand, if Israel had district elections, although this would eliminate small parties on a national level, some small parties may thrive on a local level. All this depends on the geographic distribution of voters. If a small party's voters are concentrated in a particular region of the country, it may be able to compete successfully as one of the two main parties locally, and this, by the way, could influence national politics. Also, and as we shall see in the case of Australia, an electoral system can be designed to preserve the influence of small parties without their having representation in parliament!

A second argument for small parties is that they can prevent the tyranny of a large party. There is no solid evidence that small parties have such power, or that tyranny is the likely consequence of eliminating small parties. The 25 democracies that have single-member plurality districts refute this contention. But to clinch the point, the low electoral threshold in the Weimar Republic made it easier for Hitler's National Socialist Party to gain power and establish a monstrous tyranny.

A third argument for small parties is that they raise controversial issues which large parties avoid in order to attract the largest number of voters. In other words, to maximize their voting appeal, large parties incline toward the center and thus tend to ignore important issues. There is some merit in this argument, but it has little if any practical significance. Consider Israel's small right-wing parties which have opposed withdrawal from Judea, Samaria, and Gaza. They have had no discernible effect on the territorial policies of Israel's Government.

True, such parties have a Knesset forum to educate public opinion regarding the deadly results of the Israel-PLO agreements. But there are members of the Likud who have denounced those agreements, which they should be able to do with greater effect on public opinion than a "fringe" party. The negative consequences of small right-wing parties in Israel far outweigh whatever good may be attributed to them, and for this reason. These small right-wing parties are usually labeled "extremist", if not "racist". Such labels, which take the place of reasoned argument, are then used to discredit and defame those who share the views of these small parties, but do so within a larger framework of ideas and political considerations. Which means that the alleged advantage of small parties, namely, that they raise controversial issues avoided by large parties, may actually prove counterproductive. An intrinsically sound or just policy may be sullied and undermined precisely because it has been endorsed by a small party! A small party may thus be more effective working within the orbit of a large party.

Voting for Candidates and/or Party Lists

We have seen that the voters of different countries, and even of the same country, have different ways to vote. In a single-ballot system the voters vote just once. In multiballot systems, two or more rounds of voting may be entailed. In many countries, including Israel, a run-off election is required when no candidate receives a majority of votes cast in the initial ballot.

Although citizens usually vote for candidates only, sometimes they vote for party lists only, and sometimes they have the option to do either or both. The number of *candidate* votes (i.e., votes cast for individual candidates) each voter possesses can range from one to the total number of candidates competing.

An exclusive *candidate* vote is one that benefits only the candidate for whom it is cast, and never transfers to any other vote total that is used for seat allocation. Single exclusive votes are cast in Anglo-American single-member districts as well as in Antigua and India. A *nonexclusive* candidate vote, in addition to appearing in the vote total for the candidate for whom it is cast, also affects other vote totals used in the allocation of legislative seats.

There are three main types of nonexclusive vote in current use: (1) the transferable vote, which transfers to the vote total of another candidate; (2) the pooling vote, which transfers to the vote total of the party list to which the candidate originally voted for belongs; and (3) the fused vote, which simultaneously affects the vote totals of candidates running for two or more different offices.

(1) The transferable vote system, also called the "Preferential Vote", is used in Australia, Ireland, Malta, Cambridge, Massachusetts, and elsewhere. Here is how it works for Australia's House of Representatives. As in single-member plurality elections used in the United States and Great Britain, elections are held in single-member districts, but the voter is required to rank *all* candidates seeking election, from first to last.

> The returning officer first sorts the ballot papers according to which candidate is ranked first. If at this stage any one candidate has a majority of the votes, he or she is declared elected. Otherwise, the candidate with the fewest first-place preferences is declared defeated. The returning officer then transfers the votes of the defeated candidate's supporters to whichever of the remaining candidates they have marked as their next preference, again checking to see if any candidate has achieved a majority of all the votes. This process continues until some candidate does attain a majority, whereupon he or she is declared elected.[79]

Of relevance to Israel, the Preferential Vote system "allows small parties to document their contribution to a large party's success. It is thus possible, even for parties that virtually never win seats on their own, to play a significant role."[80] In fact, by issuing "how to vote cards", urging its supporters to adopt a particular ranking of candidates below first, a minor party can be instrumental in deciding which major party shall head the government!

(2) The pooling vote system, used in Finland and Poland, may also be relevant to Israel. Here is how it works in Finland. Voters cast their votes for individual candidates. Once cast, however, these votes are "pooled", since candidates join together in party lists. Parliamentary seats are allocated to *lists* before they are allocated

to candidates, on the basis of *list* vote totals arrived at by summing the votes of all candidates within the list. Notice, however, that in Finland, unlike in Israel, party lists are not fixed, since the voters vote for individual candidates. But whether a particular candidate will be elected depends on the vote totals of his party's list as well as on the vote totals of other candidates on that list.

(3) By a *fused* vote, used in Uruguay, Bolivia, and Honduras, voters cast a single vote for a slate that includes candidates for the presidency as well as candidates for the Senate and the lower house. Split-ticket voting – supporting one party's presidential candidate while voting for another party's congressional candidates (as in the US) – is thus not possible.

Split-ticket voting was made possible in Israel in 1996 when, for the first time, the prime minister was directly elected by the people. Voters could then choose one party's candidate for prime minister while voting for another party list for the Knesset. This is precisely why the religious parties won 23 seats in that election, seven more than in 1992; and as we have seen, the religious parties won 27 seats in 1999. The reason is this. Prior to 1996, many voters, who identified with Shas or the National Religious Party, cast their votes for the Likud because they did not want Labor to win, either because of its secular orientation or land-for-peace policy.

To digress for a moment: What is astonishing, and what reflects on the quality of higher education in Israel, is that Labor MK Yossi Beilin, a political scientist, advocated popular election of the prime minister in the belief that it would diminish the power of the religious parties! Under the previous system, the President of the State was empowered to invite the leader of the party most likely to secure a Knesset majority to form a Government. Seeking once more to diminish the power of the religious parties, the borne-again advocates of the old system of choosing the prime minister pretend that it will restore institutional "checks and balances".[81] Admittedly, 61 votes (an absolute majority of the Knesset) are now required to topple the Government by a vote of no confidence, whereas under the previous system, *any* simple majority could overturn the Government. But the truth is that no Labor- or Likud-led Government has ever been overturned by a no-confidence vote.[82]

To revert to the old system would be the height of absurdity. Prior to the 1996 elections, it was difficult enough to form a Government when the Labor Party, for example, had more than 40 Knesset seats. As we have seen, however, Labor managed to win only 23 seats in the 1999 elections. And even though Prime Minister Barak received almost 56% of the popular vote (which included, however, 95% of the Arab vote) he found it exceeding difficult to form a solid Knesset majority. Indeed, he had to enlarge his cabinet from 18 to 22 ministers to placate his motley coalition. And so, neither the old system nor the present one is viable. Both flounder in the confusion and corruption resulting from Israel's parliamentary system: its lack of district or constituency elections, its low electoral threshold, and its allocation of seats to politicians, so many of whom – thanks to fixed party lists – are little more than job-seekers. Indeed, fixed party lists have made the Knesset a sinecure. Thus, even though Shimon Peres has never won an election, this septuagenarian is still in the Knesset! Surely he would have been returned to private life long ago if Israel had district elections. The same may be said of the late and lamented Yitzhak Rabin. Therein is the consequence and tragedy of a rigid and basically undemocratic political system. Fixed party lists entails self-perpetuating oligarchy. It is a major cause of Israel's malaise.

A Remedy Consistent With Jewish Law

Of all the various elements of political life, the easiest to change are election rules. This is not to say that election rules are easy to change, for the rules existing in any country favor entrenched interests. Nevertheless, election rules can be designed in such a way as to increase the *probability* of (1) advancing higher quality men to public office, (2) elevating debate in the Legislature, (3) improving decision-making in the Executive, (4) minimizing corruption in the bureaucracy, and, at the very least, (5) preventing majority as well as minority tyranny.

There are two extreme types of parliamentary election rules. One maximizes the power of the party leaders, the other the power or freedom of choice of the voters. Israel, more than any other country, represents the first extreme where the voter, we have seen, must cast his ballot for a fixed, party-ranked list of candidates in a single countrywide district election.[83] The other extreme, used in Switzerland, employs multidistrict elections and the voter is given the option of voting either for a party list or for a designated number of candidates running in his district without regard for their party affiliation. In fact, the voter can mix his preferred candidates from one party in with those from other parties. In this way, each voter has a say in the district's whole legislative contingent![84]

Between these two extremes are many electoral systems which more or less balance the power of the parties and the freedom of choice of the voters. Essential for any reasonable balance, however, are constituency or multidistrict elections. Some countries use what is called "Personalized Proportional Representation (PR)". For example, in Germany the voter is given two votes, one for an individual candidate and one for a party list. The candidate vote is for a single-member district contest that is won by a plurality. The second vote, however, is for a party list, and is used to provide compensatory seats to those parties which did not receive in the single-member districts the seat share proportional to their nationwide vote share. (Actually, much the same result can be achieved with a single vote, as in Denmark and Sweden.)

Alternatively, many political scientists recommend the "Preferential Vote" system described above, where voters rank the candidates on the party lists. (The present writer inclines toward this system.) As used to elect the Australian Senate, this system can be designed in such a way as to preclude gerrymandering. In the case of Israel, however, the "Personalized PR" system may be more expedient in that it would arouse less opposition by Israel's entrenched parties.[85]

The problem here is to break the power of the parties, and this can only be done by multidistrict or constituency elections as opposed to the single countrywide election that differentiates

Israel, to its detriment, from 74 other reputed democracies.[86] Indeed, at the risk of being accused of oversimplification, I dare say that district elections are a precondition of Israel's salvation. There are, however, other basic reasons why such elections are right and necessary for Israel.

First, district elections are a prerequisite of *representative* democracy. Representation is often defined as having one's views reflected in the legislative decision-making process. Representation may also be defined as having one's views reflected in actually enacted policies of government. The first raises the question: How well does the electoral system enable the national electorate to impress its opinions on the legislature? The second raises the question: How well does the actually executed policies of the government represent the opinions of the national electorate?

We have seen that Israel's single countrywide or at-large elections with fixed party lists insulates Knesset Members from the voters between elections. Hence the "representational bond" between MKs and voters is weak. Much the same may be said of cabinet ministers, since the latter, with rare exceptions, are MKs. It follows that Israel's method of electing the Knesset does not enable the electorate to impress its opinions effectively on the legislative process nor on the actually executed policies of the government. This is hardly consistent with representative democracy.

If Israel had some form of district elections, whereby the people could vote for individual candidates rather than for fixed party lists, the representational bond between MKs and constituents would be relatively strong. The electorate would thus be better capable of impressing its opinions both on the Knesset and on actually enacted government policies.[87]

Needless to say, voters can most effectively impress their opinions on candidates during election campaigns, when office-seekers solicit their support. Their views on public issues, usually conveyed by opinion polls, will obviously influence a candidate's announced position on such issues. The trouble begins after the election, when successful candidates assume office and proceed to formulate and execute public policies. For various reasons, good and bad, politicians sometimes pursue policies that contradict their campaign promises or their party's platform on certain public issues. Although this is true in United States as well as in Israel, the issues concerning the two countries are, in certain respects, fundamentally different. It is one thing for politicians to renege on promises not to raise taxes or to increase expenditures for this or that welfare program. It is quite another thing for politicians to violate campaign pledges concerning the very borders and capital of the state, and, by so doing, trample on the historic convictions and aspirations of their people. Israel's parliamentary electoral system facilitates such betrayal.[88]

Although district elections would make an MK more dependent on his constituents, it would also enable him to establish a local power base that would render him more independent of the national party. He could then resist government policies he deems unwise or pernicious without committing political suicide. What this means is that an MK, in deciding how to vote on a particular issue, will be able to make a balanced judgment between the views of his constituents, the position of his party, and what he himself deems right or expedient.

Moreover, the independence MKs gain from district elections would enable the Knesset to exercise the vital function of administrative oversight. Precisely because fixed party lists tend to transform would-be legislators into apparatchiks, MKs lack the wherewithal to scrutinize the bureaucracy headed by their party bosses, the ministers of the cabinet. This is why the annual State Comptroller Reports are replete with evidence of official corruption and of violations of the law, only to be swept under the rug by the Knesset. This is another reason why Israelis have no outlet or effective spokesman for the redress of their grievances, which means that dishonesty and injustice persist without remedy. This makes Israeli democracy a sham. Without some form of district elections, representative democracy is virtually impossible.[89]

Of course politicians can deceive voters in district as well as in a countrywide election. But when a politician, having been assured of a safe place on his party's list, does not have to campaign for reelection, he will be less concerned about public opinion. Conversely, if a politician supports a policy he opposed during his campaign for office in a district election, the voters will be reminded of the inconsistency by his political opponent. This will often deter politicians from reneging on campaign promises, at least in districts having closely contested elections. Surely this applies to politicians whose campaign promises involve such fundamental issues as the borders and capital of the state.

Second, the idea of district elections is implicit in the Torah. "Select for yourselves men who are wise, understanding, and *known to your tribes* and I will appoint them as your leaders" (Deut. 1:13).[90] The operative words in the present context are: "men...known to your tribes." Rabbi Samson Raphael Hirsch comments that each tribe (*shevet*) is to choose out of its own midst, men whose "character can only be known by their lives, which is known only to those who have associated with them." (This is the biblical source of residential requirements for Representatives and Senators in the United States.) Also, what is here called a *shevet* was called a district (*felech*) after the Second Temple.[91] Moreover, the idea of district elections conforms to the Jewish law of "agency" (*Kiddushin* 59a). This law synthesizes the "delegate" and "trustee" conceptions of representation prevalent in the non-Jewish democratic world. Whereas the delegate conception binds a representative to the instructions of his constituents, the trustee conception allows him to judge whether adherence to these instructions, when additional knowledge or new circumstances intervene, will harm his constituents' long-term interests.

Finally, it is a principle of Jewish law that "No legislation should be imposed on the public unless the majority can conform to it" (*Avoda Zara* 36a). This obviously requires legislators to consider or consult the opinions of his constituents. Hence representative democracy can be readily assimilated to Judaism simply by adding that representatives must be "men who are wise, and understanding". (This is hardly to be expected in Israel's parliament, where generals become instant legislators and even government ministers.)

It will be obvious from the preceding that Jewish law is very much based on the notion of government by consent of the governed (although it needs to be remembered that the governed here are Jews dedicated to the Torah). The extent to which government will in fact be responsive to the governed depends very much on a country's electoral rules and the overall design of its political institutions. Consider, again, the Republic of Ireland. Ireland's Constitution prescribes a system of preferential voting for its House of Representatives, a system that heightens the electoral latitude and power of the people. Consistent with respect for the people, Article 27 of the Constitution declares: "A majority of the members of the Senate and not less than one-third of the Members of the House of Representatives may, by joint petition addressed to the President...request the President to decline to sign and promulgate as a law any Bill to which this article applies on the ground that the Bill contains a proposal of such national importance that the will of the people thereto ought to be ascertained." Remarkably, on two different occasions, a referendum was held proposing to abolish the "Preferential Vote". It was defeated both times! Jewish law is no less respectful of the people. But there is still another reason for district elections.

District elections can be a partial but most important remedy to the Arab demographic problem. Recall these two questions: (1) How well does the electoral system enable the electorate to impress its opinions on the legislature? (2) How well does the actually executed policies of the government represent the opinions of the electorate?

Various polls and surveys have reported the obvious: Jewish public opinion in Israel was decidedly opposed to Arab membership in the Knesset, even before their most brazen acts of disloyalty. For reasons already indicated, only district or constituency elections can translate Jewish public opinion into decision-making in the Knesset and in the Government. Only if members of the Knesset – and several will be cabinet ministers – must campaign for reelection as individuals and in districts where they will be confronted by rivals for their offices, only then can one reasonably expect (1) the Knesset to remove the parliamentary immunity of its disloyal Arab members, and (2) the Government to enforce the law which prohibits any party that rejects the Jewish character of the State. Most Jews in Israel will not only support such measures, but they will have candidates for office who will denounce the Knesset for failing to remove seditious members, as well as the Government, for failing to indict them. All this and more may done in the name of democracy and the rule of law.

Conclusion: The Remedy

To fully remedy Israel's flawed parliamentary system, I propose a bicameral parliament consisting of a Senate and a House of Representatives. Here some will object: "Shades of the American Constitution!" To this I say the following. First, the American Constitution, which was the subject of the author's first two books, is not only excellent in itself and worthy of *selective* imitation, but its excellence is very much derived from the Torah – nay, is infinitely closer to the Torah than Israel's present form of government! Second, the parliament proposed here will be superior to the Congress prescribed in the American Constitution if only because of superior electoral rules. Third, thanks largely to the doctrine of moral relativism that dominates higher education in the United States, the American Constitution has been severed from its religious roots and transformed into a framework of almost morally neutral institutions. But as George Washington says in his "Farewell Address" (cited more fully in the next chapter), "reason and experience both forbid us to expect that National morality can prevail in the exclusion of religious principle." It is in this light that we are to understand why the United States has become a normless democracy wallowing in moral decay. In any event, the Jewish constitution proposed in this book will not, by definition, be religiously or morally neutral.

To return to the proposed bicameral parliament, its election rules will be outlined in the concluding chapter. It should be understood that only Jews, be they religious or not, will be qualified to vote for, or be members of, the Senate. However, to preserve Israel's Jewish character, Senators should possess respectable knowledge about the intellectual and moral heritage of the Jewish people, their history, customs, and aspirations. Here I am reminded of those who designed the Constitution of the Republic of Ireland. To preserve their people's cultural heritage, they established a bicameral parliament whose upper house, the Senate, consists of 60 members, 49 of whom are elected from five panels of candidates having knowledge and practical experience in the major sectors of public life, the *first* being "*National Language and Culture, Literature, Art, Education and such professional interests as may be defined by law for the purpose of this panel.*" Surely a Jewish Senate should be no less qualified.

As for the House of Representatives, as indicated earlier, it will consist of Jews and non-Jews and will exercise the function of administrative oversight (which, in John Stuart Mill's judgment, is the proper and most important function of a representative assembly). Excepting classified security matters, it will inspect the various ministries, the army, and every institution or enterprise in which a State authority participates, whether managerially or financially. Inspection shall include accountancy, legality, and appropriateness of the practices examined. The House will also conduct public hearings, investigate public complaints regarding the State administration, and suggest measures to remedy any administrative shortcomings and abuses. (The House's investigatory powers render it a formidable body, as would be appreciated by those familiar with the power wielded by any investigating committee of the American Congress.) Finally, the House of Representatives may recommend legislation to the Senate, which the Senate may amend or reject as it sees fit. But if such recommendations are enacted into law, their juridical authority will be derived from the action of the Senate.

This House of Representatives will be far more powerful than the present Knesset, and far more conducive to good government. Good government, however, will depend very much on the Executive, to which we now turn.

CHAPTER 6
Jewish Statesmanship: A Presidential Remedy

He can never be more than a second-rate statesman into whose conduct of affairs, philosophy and imagination do not in some degree enter. Without imagination, indeed, there can be no just and comprehensive philosophy; and without this there can be no true wisdom in dealing with practical affairs of a wide and complex nature.

      Henry Taylor
      The Statesman

When fortune surprises us by bestowing on us an important office, without having conducted us to it by degrees...it is impossible that we should sustain ourselves in it with propriety, and appear worthy of possessing it.

      La Rochefoucauld
      Maxims

  The concept of Jewish statesmanship is unheard of in the supposed-to-be Jewish state of Israel. Hence it is no wonder that Israel's government lacks any sense of *Jewish* national purpose, a basic reason why this country is disintegrating. A religious Jew would say that Israel's purpose is to serve God, and this Israel can best do by presenting to mankind the example of a nation in which freedom dwells with virtue, equality with excellence, wealth with beauty, the here and now with love of the Eternal. Obviously this will require Jewish statesmanship of the highest order, a statesmanship that transcends politics.

  Jewish statesmanship has three basic prerequisites: (1) statesmen possessing Jewish and secular wisdom; (2) a people whose love of freedom is embedded in a tradition that honors moral excellence, wisdom, and truth; and (3) political institutions that enable a statesman to exercise leadership yet render him accountable to his people.

The Jewish Statesman

  From the Torah's perspective, the Jewish statesman is first and foremost an educator whose power is less political than intellectual and moral. Accordingly, a Jewish statesman must be well educated in the heritage and history of the Jewish People. This is a formidable task, since the knowledge Jews have accumulated during the past four millennia is vast and unsurpassed.

Jews have excelled in virtually every discipline, especially in the domain of law. Consider Jewish law (*Halakha*), but only so far as concerns the relation between man and his fellow man (in contradistinction to the relation between man and God). That we should begin with a consideration of Jewish law in discussing Jewish statesmanship is appropriate if only because Jewish law is the one thing that has preserved the Jewish people and their national identity.

Like other legal systems, Jewish law has various branches, for example, civil and criminal law, public and administrative law. Extant Jewish legal knowledge includes 7,000 volumes or 300,000 instances of case law dealing primarily with the social and economic problems of Jewish communities dispersed throughout Europe and North Africa. Prior to the Emancipation in the eighteenth century, these communities possessed juridical autonomy and creatively applied Jewish law to the most diverse social and economic conditions. The enormous body of case law resulting therefrom is being organized at various Israeli universities, and not merely for its historical interest, but for its potential relevance to contemporary problems. (Because case law arises out of factual conditions and resolves existential controversies, it is by no means subordinate to codified law.) This repository of legal knowledge will be available to the statesman. It will teach him important principles of Jewish governance.

First, Jewish law will teach him that no one is above the law; indeed, that God Himself is bound to observe the laws of the Torah (Jerusalem Talmud, *Rosh Hashana* 1:3a). Hence our Jewish statesman will reject the Latin maxim *princeps legibus solutus est* – *the ruler is not bound by the law*. A relic of this maxim will be found in modern Israel: "No act of legislation shall diminish the rights of the State, or impose upon it any obligation, unless explicitly stated."[92]

Second, Jewish law will teach our statesman that the individual must never be sacrificed for the sake of the community.

Third, Jewish law will teach him how to secure individual equity while promoting the common good.

Fourth, since our statesman will be learned in Jewish history, he will know that Jewish law is not static but dynamic, that Judaism reconciles permanence and change. He will know that Jews survived the vicissitudes of the past because, thanks to their great Rabbis, they learned how to adapt to changing circumstances and still adhere to the Torah, mankind's first written Constitution.

Fifth, our Jewish statesman will know that only this Constitution can unite the Jewish People, and not simply because of the Torah's world-inspiring wisdom and models of human excellence. For the Torah's comprehensive and many-faceted system of law can harmonize the social and economic relations of Jews of diverse ethnic backgrounds by providing them with proven and venerable methods of resolving their differences. As Professor Menachem Elon, former Deputy President of Israel's Supreme Court, has written: "...it is precisely in all the branches of Jewish law other than marriage and divorce that it is possible...to arrive at a common language and understanding among various elements of the people who differ in their religious and social outlook."[93]

Since a vital objective of Jewish statesmanship is to promote Jewish national unity and purpose, our statesman must be sensitive to the potentially unifying influence of Jewish law. Indeed, the laws establishing Hanukah and Purim were enacted by the Sages to promote national consciousness – setting aside special days to commemorate God's deliverance of His people from the hands of their enemies. (Of course, the Sages also prescribed days of remembrance for national catastrophes, such as the destruction of the Temple.)

Sixth, Jewish law, as we have already seen, provides a rational and ethical foundation for representative democracy. However, to avoid the mischievous tendency of apologists to assimilate Judaism to democracy, the Jewish statesman will assimilate democracy to Judaism. He will understand that freedom and equality, democracy's two cardinal principles, must be rooted in the Torah's conception of man's creation in the image of God. Again, this will provide these two normless principles of democracy with ethical and rational constraints.

Finally, although our statesman will be educated in Jewish wisdom, he will have learned from such masters of Jewish law as the Rambam and the Vilna Gaon that thorough knowledge of the Torah requires veridical secular knowledge. It follows that "Jewish identity" is not a sufficient condition for Jewish statesmanship. Israel's religious parties have "Jewish identity". However, because of their long dependence on secular parties, they lack the breadth of vision and spiritedness required for Jewish statesmanship. Regrettably, the narrowness and timidity of Israeli politics have infected them. Without denying the accomplishments of the religious parties, too often they use Torah for politics rather than politics for Torah. The Jewish People require statesmen who strive for the unity of thought and action prescribed in the Torah. Conversely, Jewish statesmanship requires a Torah-oriented people.

The Jewish People

Chapter 4 referred to various studies of the beliefs and practices of Israel's Jewish population. The Guttman Institute reported that 55% believe in the divine origin of the Torah, and that some 80% are either Orthodox or Traditional. This degree of religiosity is a precondition of Jewish statesmanship. Let us see why via this passage from George Washington's Farewell Address:

Of all the dispositions and habits which lead to political prosperity, Religion and morality are indispensable supports... Whatever may be conceded to the influence of refined education on minds of peculiar structure, reason and experience both forbid us to expect that National morality can prevail in the exclusion of religious principle.

The theme of Washington's Farewell Address is *national unity*. National unity, he believed, requires national morality, a precondition of which is religion. Religion and morality counter man's natural inclination to self-indulgence and his tendency to be preoccupied with the immediate gratification of his own desires.

Religion and morality foster self-restraint and consideration of others. Far more than secular humanism, religion inspires men with reverence, with deference to wisdom, with concern for posterity. Alexis de Tocqueville points out that religion gives men a general habit of conducting themselves with a view to eternity.[94] These are Jewish traits. Such traits are indispensable to Jewish statesmanship and national purpose, more so in this secular age, where men typically yield to their daily casual desires and renounce whatever cannot be acquired without protracted effort.

The Jewish people have been celebrated for the quality of their family life, where reverence and deference begin. There is a passage in the Talmud, "It is not a great honor for the princess when her praise comes from her friend; it should come from her rival." Although it would be inaccurate to call Friedrich Nietzsche a rival, this gentile philosopher had a deep understanding and respect for Judaism, polemical statements to the contrary notwithstanding. Allow me to quote at length from *The Dawn of Day*, where he speaks of "The People of Israel":

In Europe they have gone through a school of eighteen centuries, such as no other nation can boast of, and the experience of this terrible time of probation have benefited the community much less than the individual. In consequence whereof the resourcefulness in soul and intellect of our modern Jews is extraordinary. In times of extremity they, least of all the inhabitants of Europe, try to escape any great dilemma by a recourse to drink or to suicide which less gifted people are so apt to fly to. Each Jew finds in the history of his fathers and grandfathers a voluminous record of instances of the greatest coolness and perseverance in terrible positions, of the most artful and clever fencing with misfortune and chance; their bravery under the cloak of wretched submissiveness, their heroism in the *spernere se sperni* [despising their despisers] surpass the virtues of all the saints.

One can hardly say this is true of Israel's political leaders today. But Nietzsche continues:

People wanted to make the [Jews] contemptible by treating them scornfully for twenty centuries, by refusing to them the approach to all dignities and honorable positions, and by pushing them all the deeper down into the mean trades and, indeed, they have not become genteel under this process. But contemptible? They have never ceased believing themselves qualified for the highest functions; neither have the virtues of all suffering people ever failed to adorn them. Their manner of honoring parents and children, the reasonableness of their marriages and marriage customs make them conspicuous among Europeans. Besides, they know how to derive a sense of power and lasting revenge from the very trades which were left to them (or to which they were abandoned)... Yet their vengeance never carries them too far, for they all have that liberality even of the soul in which the frequent change of place, climate, customs, neighbors, and oppressors schools man; they have by far the greatest experience in human relationships...

Now Nietzsche concludes his encomium:

Where shall this accumulated wealth of great impressions, which forms the Jewish history in every Jewish family, this wealth of passions, virtues, resolutions, resignations, struggles, victories of all sorts, where shall it find an outlet, if not in great intellectual people and work? On the day when the Jews will be able to show as their handiwork such jewels and golden vessels as the European nations of shorter and less thorough experience neither can nor could produce, when Israel will have turned its eternal vengeance into an eternal blessing of Europe: then once more that seventh day will appear, when the God of the Jews may rejoice in Himself, His creation, and His chosen people and all of us will rejoice with Him![95]

Now, what is remarkable is that a unique renaissance is taking place in Jewish philosophy, especially in Israel. Unlike the Rambam, whose *Guide of the Perplexed* assimilates the Torah to Aristotelian philosophy, or unlike Hermann Cohen, whose *Religion of Reason* assimilates Judaism to Kantian philosophy, Jewish thinkers today avoid such apologetic and dated efforts by using concepts intrinsic to the Torah to illuminate reality, revealing, *en passant*, the shortcomings of much that passes for secular knowledge.[96] Of profound significance, Jews educated in the rigorous sciences are returning to the Torah.[97] They are beginning to transform the map of knowledge. This renaissance in Jewish philosophy is a precondition of Jewish statesmanship. Jews with strong Jewish roots are now well represented in the country's academic institutions, in the Israel Defense Forces, and in the professional sectors of Israel's economy. Conditions are thus emerging for the assumption of national leadership by a Jew with this background of talent and sense of Jewish awareness. However, without well-designed political institutions, Jewish statesmanship is more ardently to be wished for than expected.

Political Institutions

Jewish statesmanship, we said, requires political institutions that enable a statesman to exercise leadership and still render him accountable to his people. Political institutions are not morally neutral mechanisms. They can influence the character and conduct of those who make the laws and policies of a state as well as their relationship to the governed. As Montesquieu has written: "At the birth of societies, the rulers of republics establish institutions; and afterwards the institutions mould the rulers."[98] Although even the best-designed political institutions cannot ensure wise and virtuous leadership, still, how institutions are designed can either restrain or liberate human egoism, the bane of good government.

Egoism is as old as Adam. In Israel, however, egoism wears not even a fig leaf. Egoism has been institutionalized in this country in two basic ways. First, the multiplicity of parties spawned by Israel's low parliamentary electoral threshold fosters "egocentric pluralism". This egocentric pluralism enters the Prime Minister's cabinet which, as previously noted, consists almost exclusively of members of the Knesset. The parties that form the cabinet do so, said David Ben-Gurion "not on the basis of a common program but merely to divide up the positions of influence and the national budget."[99] Because cabinet ministers appoint the directors of dozens of public corporations, each ministry is a veritable fiefdom. This egocentric pluralism undermines national unity and national purpose. It enfeebles Jewish national consciousness and leaves no vista for Jewish statesmanship.

Hence the present writer urges the adoption of a presidential system of government. It may seem, however, that popular election of the Prime Minister is equivalent to such a system; and indeed, its proponents were partly motivated by the idea that it would augment the power of the Prime Minister and render him less subject to political extortion by small parties, the religious in particular. But as we have seen, the reformers miscalculated: the power of the religious parties increased as a consequence of split voting, and their weight in the Government has become even more pronounced. Prime Minister Netanyahu's Government collapsed, ostensibly because of the Wye River Memorandum of October 1998, but more fundamentally because he was burdened by a cabinet consisting of seven of the Knesset's discordant parties. A presidential system will remedy this anarchy, for the cabinet will no longer be drawn from the Knesset. Instead, Israel for the first time will have a *unitary* Executive.

The multiplicity of parties in the cabinet renders it a plural Executive, which is utterly incompatible with *any* form of statesmanship, let alone Jewish statesmanship and national unity. Let us try to understand this.

National unity is the first concern of any statesman. This should be the constant concern of politicians in a country like Israel, surrounded as it is by malevolent Arab regimes and divided within by a largely disloyal Arab population. A unitary Executive, but therefore a presidential system of government, is best calculated to remedy the divisive and hostile forces now endangering Israel's survival.

Happily, a presidential system is perfectly consistent with Jewish law. The Torah discourages collective leadership. When Moses instructed Joshua to consult with the elders and follow their advice, God countermanded him, saying that Joshua alone should lead the people into the Land of Israel. "There can be but one leader for a [people] and not two." (See Deut. 31:7 and *Sanhedrin* 8a.)

Israel lacks even collective leadership. How can it be otherwise when the Prime Minister's cabinet consists of diverse party leaders animated by their own personal ambitions and partisan interests? In fact, various cabinet members in the past have been known to consort with Israel's enemies.[100] Also, cabinet ministers sometimes conspire with each other to topple the Government.[101] The truth is that Israel's system of coalition cabinet government magnifies the vices of men. Needed is a unitary Executive, meaning a President whose cabinet constitutes a team committed to a coherent body of ideas and programs.

A most lucid and compelling defense of a unitary Executive was made by Alexander Hamilton in *The Federalist Papers*, one of the greatest works on statesmanship and the most authoritative commentary on the American Constitution. His argument is more valid for Israel today than it was for America in 1788.

In *Federalist 70*, Hamilton writes: "Energy in the Executive is a leading character in the definition of good government." By energy Hamilton does not mean power, but mental energy, which springs from wisdom and self-confidence.[102] (As Henry Taylor said in *The Statesman*, "The energy of the statesman should be as purely as possible intellectual; it should be of that rare species which can be combined with equanimity."[103]) But Hamilton also has in view the *institutional* prerequisites for the exercise of energy, the first of which is *unity*: "That unity is conducive to energy will not be disputed. Decision, activity, secrecy, and dispatch will generally characterize the proceedings of one man [far more so] than the proceedings of any greater number; and in proportion as the number is increased, these qualities will be diminished." He goes on to say, "This unity, can be destroyed in two ways: either by vesting the power in two or more ministers of equal dignity and authority; or by vesting it ostensibly in one man, subject, in whole or in part, to the control and cooperation of others, in the capacity of counselors..." Clearly Hamilton would have deplored coalition cabinet government.

Admired by no less than Talleyrand as the greatest statesman of the age, Hamilton probes the defects of a plural Executive. Because a plural Executive inevitably gives rise to difference of opinion, there inevitably follows the danger of "personal animosity" among those composing the government. Such dissensions

lessen the respectability, weaken the authority, and distract the plans and operations of those whom they divide... [T]hey impede or frustrate the most important measures of the government, in the most critical emergencies of the state. And what is still worse, they might split the community into the most violent and irreconcilable factions, adhering to the different individuals who composed the magistracy.

Hamilton then turns to the psychological consequences of a plural Executive, or rather, how such an Executive can arouse the frailties of human nature:

> Men often oppose a thing, merely because they have had no agency in planning it, or because it may have been proposed by those whom they dislike. [A common experience in Israel's cacophonous cabinet.] But if they have been consulted, and have happened to disapprove, opposition then becomes, in their estimation, an indispensable duty of self-love. They seem to think themselves bound in honor, and by all the motives of personal infallibility, to defeat the success of what has been resolved upon contrary to their sentiments. Men of upright, benevolent tempers have too many opportunities of remarking, with horror, to what desperate lengths this disposition is sometimes carried, and how often the great interests of society are sacrificed to the vanity, to the conceit, and to the obstinacy of individuals, who have credit enough to make their passions and caprices interesting to mankind.[104]

How well these perceptive remarks describe the behavior of Israeli cabinets, whose ministers, as party leaders, feel obliged to exert their egos or independence lest they lose credit among their party followers. Hamilton continues:

> But one of the weightiest objections to a plurality in the Executive...is that it tends to conceal faults and destroy responsibility... It often becomes impossible, amidst mutual accusations, to determine on whom the blame or the punishment of a pernicious measure, or series of pernicious measures, ought really to fall. It is shifted from one to another with so much dexterity, and under such plausible appearances, that the public...is left in suspense about the real author. The circumstances which may have led to any national miscarriage or misfortune are sometimes so complicated where there are a number of actors who may have had different degrees and kinds of agency, though we may clearly see upon the whole that there has been mismanagement, yet it may be impracticable to pronounce to whose account the evil which may have been incurred is truly chargeable.

One can hardly better describe the confusion surrounding the Yom Kippur War and the question of who in the Golda Meir cabinet was most responsible for that disaster. To this day the most confidential aspects of the Agranat Commission investigating Egypt's "surprise" attack on Israel in 1973, specifically, the failure of the Israel Defense Forces to launch a preemptive strike, have not been released to the public. Something of this nature may also be said of the Oslo or Israel-PLO Declaration of Principles. Was it concocted by Foreign Minister Shimon Peres and imposed on Prime Minister Yitzhak Rabin and his cabinet as a *fait accompli*? And if that agreement was illegal, as learned attorneys maintain,[105] the fact that it was approved by Israel's cabinet makes it all the more difficult to assign responsibility (which, Hamilton says, is of two kinds, "censure" and "punishment").

After citing ancient and modern experience, revealing the defects and dangers of a plural Executive, our philosophic statesman concludes:

It is evident from these considerations that the plurality of the Executive tends to deprive the people of the two greatest securities they can have for the faithful exercise of any delegated power, *first*, the restraints of public opinion, which lose their efficacy, as on account of the division of the censure attendant on bad measures among a number, as on account of the uncertainty on whom it ought to fall; and, *secondly*, the opportunity of discovering with facility and clearness the misconduct of the persons they trust, in order either to their removal from office, or to their actual punishment in cases which admit of it.

The Jonathan Pollard espionage affair should be viewed in this light. To what extent was then Prime Minister Shimon Peres – but surely Defense Minister Yitzhak Rabin – responsible for that debacle? If a Secretary of Defense or other cabinet secretary in the United States was under suspicion for having committed a grievous error, the President would ask him to resign, and public resentment would be assuaged. In Israel, however, the blunder of a minister affects the standing of the entire cabinet including the Prime Minister. Although collective responsibility should oblige the Government to resign, as may rightly be expected in a parliamentary system, this never happens in Israel. In fact, prior to 1981, the Prime Minister could not even fire a cabinet minister. Nor is this to be expected now if the minister is a member of a party other than the Prime Minister's. For example, between 1986 and 1988, when Shimon Peres served as Foreign Minister under a government of national unity led by Likud chairman Yitzhak Shamir, Peres went to foreign capitals to promote, on his own initiative and without cabinet approval, a Middle East international peace conference. Yet, even though Mr. Shamir denounced Peres's escapade as "madness" and "suicidal", he did not dismiss him from the cabinet – surely because Peres was chairman of the Labor Party.[106]

Clearly, and as anticipated above, to secure unity in the Executive, the President's cabinet must share his ideas and ideals as well as the programs advocated during his election campaign. This is why no member of the President's cabinet should head any political party or hold any other public office. *It is through the President and through him alone that the combined forces of the people are concentrated to a distinctively Jewish national purpose.*

Since a primary purpose of the President is to promote national unity, the mode of his election, his tenure and re-eligibility, and of course the powers of his office will be of major importance. Interestingly, and of profound significance for Israel, the mode of electing the President of the United States was the most difficult problem that occupied the framers of the American Constitution. America's Electoral College system of choosing a President was designed only after the most protracted debates. Many other methods were considered. Although we have little more than the sketchy notes of James Madison, a reconstruction of the debates regarding each proposed method reveals the following. The framers were seeking a method of election that would accomplish four basic objectives. *First*, it should be politically as well as physically convenient (remember, travel in those days was slow and hazardous). *Second*, the method should increase the probability of obtaining a President widely known for wisdom and virtue. *Third*, it should safeguard the President's independence and integrity. *Fourth*, the method of election should attract the widest possible public support. The system of Electoral Colleges convening in each state and chosen in a manner determined by the state legislatures fulfilled these four objectives, as I have elsewhere shown in great detail.[107]

Paradoxically, although the Electoral College system of choosing the President of the United States was a failure almost from the outset, it nonetheless represents not a "bundle of compromises", but one of the pinnacles of American statesmanship which Israel would do well to reflect upon. Let me set forth the most salient points and their relevance to Israel.

The early Electoral Colleges consisted of the most prominent citizens. Anticipating this, Hamilton could say in *Federalist 68*, "the immediate election [of the President will] be made by [a small number of] men capable of analyzing the qualities adapted to the station, and acting under circumstances favorable to deliberation [i.e., in camera]...and most likely to possess the information and discernment requisite to such complicated investigations."

Consistent with the first and second objectives mentioned above, the President of Israel should be nominated by the Senate, i.e., the Upper House of Parliament (which is another reason why members of the Senate should possess a sound knowledge of their people's heritage and history). For purpose of illustration, let us suppose that the Senate consists of seventy members, and that twenty are required to nominate a President, such that no more than three candidates will be nominated. The nominations will obviously be made by the parties or party coalitions in the Senate (which should satisfy the fourth objective). The candidates will then compete in a popular election. A majority of the popular vote will be required for the election of a President, so that a run-off election may be necessary. So much is simple enough and not uncommon in the democratic world.

Complications begin with an incumbent's *re-election*, and here is where James Madison had a stroke of genius. He discerned, late in the debates, that to preserve the President's independence and integrity (the third objective), his re-election must not depend on any fixed or permanent body of men, such as the Congress (which he himself had originally proposed). This is the primary reason for ad hoc Electoral Colleges. In the case of Israel, however, the Senate is not an ad hoc body. If it nominates the President and he seeks a second term, he will be dependent on the Senate for his renomination. If he should then be re-elected, he will very likely enter office encumbered by "political debts", which cannot but impair his independence and integrity vis-a-vis the Senate.

There is a solution to this dilemma, though it may astonish many readers. The solution is to make an incumbent President *automatically re-eligible for re-election*! He will then not be simply dependent on the Senate for a second term. Meanwhile, the members of the Senate will be free to nominate, if they wish, three other presidential candidates who, together with the incumbent, will vie for the popular vote. Needless to say, if no candidate receives a majority, the two receiving the highest number of votes will compete in a run-off election.

Remarkably, Brazil offers a parallel solution to the renomination problem. Brazilian law requires parties to renominate their incumbent federal representatives should the latter so wish![108] Obviously this makes representatives utterly independent of their parties. Our proposed solution to the renominating problem is less drastic, for the Senators who initially nominated the President could deny him support for a second term simply by nominating another candidate. Although this is not a likely scenario, an incumbent President will be deterred from treating his initial senatorial supporters with disdain, as may happen in Brazil.

Regarding the President's tenure, the present writer recommends a fixed four-year term. This will preclude votes of no confidence which, in Israel we have seen, have never overturned a Labor- or Likud-led Government. Also, the proposed President will not possess the power to dissolve parliament. (I shall address myself to inevitable objections later.)

More complicated is the number of terms to which a President will be eligible. A four-term limit would be far more appropriate for Israel than the two-term limit now imposed on the office of the Prime Minister. Again it must be emphasized that the primary justification of a presidential system of government in Israel is that, if properly designed, it will be most conducive to Jewish statesmanship, hence to the attainment of Jewish national unity and purpose. This is precisely what is most lacking in Israel, and which this country must soon remedy lest it collapse.

If a talented man, say fifty years of age, were to become President and prove worthy, it would be absurd to preclude him from the presidency when he reaches the age of fifty-eight, and it would not even be democratic. Every teacher knows that talent is exceedingly rare. Rarer still is the combination of talent and virtue required of statesmanship. Witness only the paucity of great statesmen in almost every century. How many Churchills can the twentieth century boast of? A two-term limit is more a confession of political mediocrity than a guard against tyranny, the shibboleth of timid and prosaic men.

Again let us recur to Hamilton, this time in *Federalist 72*, where he defends the *indefinite* re-eligibility of the President prescribed in the original US Constitution. Re-eligibility, he says, is necessary to give a President "the inclination and the resolution to act his part well, and to the community time and leisure to observe the tendency of his measures, and thence to form an experimental estimate of their merits." Stated another way, a President's eligibility for re-election "is necessary to enable the people, when they see reason to approve of his conduct, to continue him in his station, in order to prolong the utility of his talents and virtue, and to secure to the government the advantage of permanency in a wise system of administration..."

Conversely, a constitutional limitation on the President's re-eligibility would deprive the community
of the advantage of the experience gained by the chief magistrate in the exercise of his office. That experience is the parent of wisdom, is an adage the truth of which is recognized by the wisest as well as the simplest of mankind. What more desirable or more essential than this quality in the governors of nations? Where more desirable or more essential than in the first magistrate of a nation? Can it be wise to put this

desirable and essential quality under the ban of the Constitution, and to declare that the moment it is attained, its possessor shall be compelled to abandon the station in which it was acquired, and to which it is adapted?

These are compelling arguments, and they are relevant to Israel. This country needs statesmen with vision, statesmen capable of pursuing long-term and comprehensive policies of national significance. Such policies require time and patience as well as fortitude to effect. If the Presidency is limited to two terms, the office will attract not men of vision but mediocrities and short-term pragmatists. It will also result in frequent changes in the laws and also in the administration, which "insiders" will know how to exploit at the expense of the public. Limiting the Presidency to two terms would preclude Jewish statesmanship, hence Jewish national unity and purpose.

Refuting Arguments Against Presidentialism

Let us now anticipate and refute various arguments made against presidential vis-a-vis parliamentary government. Some political scientists contend that, given the president's fixed term of office, the political process becomes broken into discontinuous, rigidly determined periods without the possibility of continuous readjustments as political, social, and economic events may require. No scientific array of evidence, however, is offered to substantiate this academic and largely impressionistic contention. One may argue that most governments under parliamentary systems run their allotted tenure of four years and are equally discontinuous.

Alternatively, it could be argued that presidentialism reduces the uncertainties and unpredictability inherent in parliamentary governments. Parliamentary systems usually involve a large number of parties whose leaders and rank-and-file legislators often undergo changing loyalties and realignments. As a consequence, these parties can, at any time between elections, make basic policy changes and even change the head of the Executive, i.e., the Prime Minister. A country like Israel, surrounded by hostile dictatorships, requires strong and predictable executive power, hence presidential government.

Presidentialism also provides accountability and identifiability. The voter knows who he or she is voting for and who will govern should this candidate win. This may also be true in parliamentary regimes consisting of only a few parties with highly visible leaders. But it is certainly not true in a multiparty system (like Israel's) where no party can expect to gain an absolute majority, in which case the voter does not even know which parties will form a governing coalition.

Critics of presidentialism also refer to the phenomenon of "grid-lock", when the legislature is dominated by a party other than that of the President. Studies indicate, however, that, "grid-lock" in the United States is very much a myth. Politicians of both major parties know that the public's business must be done if they are to remain in office, so that compromise between President and Congress is the rule. On the other hand, Israel's current system of coalition cabinet government, which so often leads to paralysis, can hardly be deemed preferable to America's presidential system, which has nurtured the wealthiest country in the world. Besides, one may well argue that "grid-lock" is less to be feared than the stagnation, if not tyranny, that may occur in a parliamentary system which gives a single party control of both the Executive and Legislative branches of government. The American system of checks and balances has its disadvantages, as does any human contrivance, but that system has been most conducive to liberty and creativity.

There is, however, one significant advantage of parliamentary systems: they often have a well-known shadow government, whereas a president-elect starts naming a cabinet only after his election. Unfortunately, this advantage of parliamentary systems does not apply to Israel, whose fragmented parliament yields a cabinet consisting of dissonant parties. Alternatively, suppose presidential candidates were required to designate, during their election campaign, say five cabinet ministers – for example, foreign affairs, defense, finance, education, and religion. Consider the probable consequences. Those designated would most likely be men of experience, usually well known to the public. Although they would not constitute a shadow government, they could form the nucleus of a very solid cabinet. What is more, the public would know in advance the leading cabinet ministers. This would induce presidential candidates to choose the most worthy members of the community as cabinet colleagues. The cabinet would then consist of five ministers virtually elected by the people, while the remaining cabinet ministers – say ten – would be nominated by the President with the advice and consent of the Senate.

Finally, critics of presidential government point to the poor record of such systems in South America. But the political culture of South American countries is no more promising to parliamentary systems. John Quincy Adams predicted early in the nineteenth century that it might require two hundred years for republican government to take root in South America! But this, only in passing.

We have been referring, of course, to a presidential system where the President exercises executive power (to be outlined later in our proposed constitution). Opponents will raise the bogey-man of dictatorship. This is sheer nonsense. Besides, in addition to what was said above about the potential tyranny lurking in parliamentary systems, we have proposed a parliament far more powerful than the existing Knesset, which is little more than a cipher vis-a-vis the Government.

It should not be forgotten that the Labor Party was in power for the first twenty-nine years of the state; that it dominated virtually every aspect of public life. Not even the debacle of the Yom Kippur War produced a change of the guard. Israel needs a presidential system of government. This will become even more evident when we discuss foreign policy and diplomacy. But first we must examine Israel's judicial system, in particular, its Supreme Court.

CHAPTER 7
Israel's Flawed Judicial System: A Democratic Remedy

If you see a generation which is constantly on the decline, go and investigate the Judges of Israel.

Babylonian Talmud
(*Shabbat* 139a)

Democracy consists as often as not in the free use of the people's name **against** *the vast majority of the people.*

Walter Bagehot

Israel's Supreme Court renders thousands of decisions a year affecting the political, social, economic, ethnic, and religious character of the State. It does so in the name of democracy but with only occasional references to the laws and moral principles that ennoble the heritage of the Jewish people. No other court in the world ignores the legal heritage of its own people. We ask: Can Israel endure as a Jewish state when its judicial system, which subtly influences every aspect of daily life, is deliberately and primarily based on non-Jewish law? Implicated in this question is the halakhic status of Israel's secular courts. Are they halakhically Jewish or non-Jewish?

The present writer, a political philosopher, has no pretensions of being qualified to discourse on Jewish law per se. However, one does not have to be a Talmudist to determine the logical consistency of arguments concerning the halakhic status of Israel's judicial system. Also, one does not have to be expert in Jewish law to project the political and psychological consequences of a Supreme Court whose judges employ gentile laws and principles in making decisions affecting the beliefs and values, the memories and aspirations, hence the very national consciousness of their fellow citizens.

This chapter will examine divergent opinions regarding the halakhic status of Israel's secular courts from a logical, philosophical, and political perspective. Since Israel's Supreme Court can and does resort to gentile legal systems, the present author will present prima facie evidence indicating that Jewish law is more rational, more humane, and more ethical than these other systems. He will argue, moreover, that the adoption of Jewish civil law will facilitate Jewish national unity and thus render Israel more capable of confronting the relentless animosity of its Arab-Islamic neighbors. Finally, he will propose practical measures by which to facilitate and hasten the incorporation of Jewish civil law into Israel's legal system such that it will be at least *primus inter pares* (first among equals) vis-a-vis English, Continental, and American law.

A Question of Logic

Certain rabbinical scholars contend that Israel's secular courts are halakhically non-Jewish because their judges decide the vast majority of cases by non-Jewish laws and concepts. Professor Yaakov Bazak disagrees. He asserts at the outset: "it is imperative to emphasize that the problem of the State and Jewish law is not essentially a religious-halakhic one, but rather a national-cultural one."[109] He thus attributes to Judaism – perhaps unwittingly – a dichotomy between religion and nationality which, though foreign to the Torah, is quite compatible with Israel's secular judicial system. This is not all. By holding that the problem of the State and Jewish law is essentially a "national-cultural" one, Bazak can the more readily base his conclusion that Israel's secular courts are Jewish on the premise that they have been "established by law, with the concurrence of the public" (p. 208). Even then, however, he needs to relate this premise to some sort of "religious-halakhic" argument.

This he seemingly does by emphasizing the flexibility of Jewish civil and criminal law or of its great medieval expositors. He first quotes the Rosh: "In financial matters, the court has the power to enact [legislative] enactments [*takkanot*] according to the times and the need, even if they overrule Torah law..." He then cites the Ribash: "...the court may punish not in accordance with the law, even without proper testimony, according to the need of the hour" (pp. 207-208).

We have here a non sequitur. Although the quoted remarks illustrate the flexibility of the halakhic authorities, they provide no logical support for Bazak's thesis that Israel's court system is halakhically Jewish. The Rosh and the Ribash were referring to courts learned in Jewish law, something lacking in Israel's secular judicial system. The courts of which these two halakhic authorities speak can rightly enact *takkanot*, i.e., legislation, according to the needs of the time. But one can hardly make a norm of necessity. Israel's secular judges do not make occasional exceptions to Jewish law when dealing with the needs of the hour. Their judicial norm or modus operandi ignores Jewish law if only because they were not educated in that rigorous discipline, one that requires far more than three years of study at a university.

Nevertheless, Professor Bazak finds support for his thesis in the *Shulkhan Arukh* (*Hoshen Mishpat*, Ch. 8.1): "Any community may accept the authority of a court not qualified by Torah law" (p. 208). Actually, this ruling is a commentary of the Rema, which was incorporated in the chapter of the *Shulkhan Arukh* just cited. Contrary to the Rema, however, Professor Bazak fails to mention that a community may accept the authority of a lay court *only in the absence of halakhic scholars*, a situation that does not obtain in Israel. Yet, without going further, Bazak believes he has proven his case, saying: "...anyone who labels the Israeli courts (established by law, with the concurrence of the public) 'non-Jewish'...does not know what he is talking about" (ibid.). But he does go further.

He turns to the Rambam, who writes: "Anyone who litigates before non-Jewish laws or in their courts...is an evildoer and is considered as though he has blasphemed and raised his hand against the Torah." Bazak maintains that the law against recourse to non-Jewish courts, as it appears in the Rambam and in the Talmud, "is explicitly directed against appearing before the judicial bodies of a foreign government, rather than utilizing the courts of the Jewish community" (p. 209).

Bazak's quote from the Rambam is tendentious. He fails to mention the sequel, where the Rambam refers to the Talmud's explanation of Exodus 21:1 in tractate *Gittin* 88b: "And these are the ordinances which you shall place before them – before them and not before non-Jews; before them and not before *laymen*."[110] Here laymen include Jews not learned in Jewish law, which applies, of course, to Israel's secular courts. Instead of quoting this halakha, Bazak selects a related one from *Gittin* 88b: "Wherever you find congregations of non-Jews, even though their laws are the same as Jewish law, you may not have recourse to them" (p. 209). This halakha has no relevance to Bazak's thesis, which concerns only Israeli courts, not gentile courts.

Professor Bazak's position is doubly paradoxical. For while he contends that Israeli courts are halakhically Jewish, he admits that their judging disputes according to non-Jewish law is a serious defect! He has the highest respect for Jewish law, and he not only prefers it to gentile law, but also urges its eventual incorporation into Israel's legal system.

Perhaps a well-informed public would share Professor Bazak's preference. Even now much of the public might turn to rabbinical courts if the latter's jurisdiction were comparable to that of the secular courts, as was proposed in 1947 by Israel's first Chief Rabbi, Isaac Herzog. This suggests that Israel's court system is not the result of public acceptance but of resignation to a *fait accompli* occurring at the establishment of the State.

Indeed, it can be shown that Supreme Court decisions frequently violate the abiding beliefs and practices of a very large majority of Israel's Jewish population, 55% of which, recall, believe in the divine origin of the Torah, and 80% are either orthodox or traditional. To mention only a few examples of its ultra-secular orientation, the Supreme Court, *without legislative authority or judicial precedent*, has (1) ruled that the Chief Rabbinate does not have final jurisdiction over conversions; (2) ordered the Minister of Interior to register Reform conversions; (3) ruled that rabbinical courts must adopt the same criteria as civil courts when deciding property settlements in divorce cases; (4) directed the Minister of

Religious Affairs to sign appointments of Reform and Conservative members to religious councils; (5) ruled that kibbutz shopping centers may remain open to the public on the Sabbath; (6) declared "illegal" the Defense Ministry's policy of exempting yeshiva students from military service (yet blanket exemptions from any form of national service has remained "legal" for Arab citizens); (7) ruled that forbidding the import of non-kosher meat infringed Basic Law: Freedom of Occupation;[111] (8) ordered the return of a girl to a secular school after her father withdrew her; (9) awarded four Jewish children to their Muslim father instead of their mother (who had returned to Judaism); and (10) overruled the Education Minister's decision to delay the screening of a program on homosexual youth.

Although the Supreme Court will not deny that Israel is, or is supposed to be, a Jewish as well as democratic state, it exalts *democratic* rights in almost total disregard of *Jewish* rights, ignoring, therefore, the convictions and customs of a large majority of Israel's Jewish population. And while the rule of the majority is not the last word of democracy, or even of Judaism, it is nonetheless a basic principle of both. In fact, the Court's president, Justice Aaron Barak, baldly states that his duty is to be "faithful to the views of the enlightened population," meaning Israel's intellectual and cultural elites – ultra-secularists alienated from the Jewish heritage.[112]

These facts shake the foundation of Professor Bazak's thesis. He has said that "Israel's secular courts are halakhically Jewish," and he bases this thesis on the supposition that Israeli courts were "established by law, with the concurrence of the public". This supposition ignores the great ideological disparity between the Supreme Court and the public (even though much of the public may not be aware of this chasm).

Bazak also ignores a fundamental Jewish and philosophical principle. A Jewish community's acceptance of a law or legal system does not necessarily make it Jewish or lawful. *Sanhedrin* 26a states that the majority in a community may consist of wicked men, and that the "agreement of transgressors is not a lawful decision." (As Abraham Lincoln once said, the majority has no right to do what is wrong).

Finally, Bazak's contention that Israel's court system is Jewish because it has been "established by law, with the concurrence of the public" may be reduced to a logical absurdity. Suppose Supreme Court decisions repeatedly entail a desecration of the Sabbath. Suppose, further, that the Court, by adhering to foreign laws and concepts, repeatedly violates Jewish marriage laws. To be more specific, suppose the Court, in imitation of American jurisprudence, legalizes sodomy and same-sex marriage.[113] Suppose the Court also fosters adultery, by affirming a Knesset statute that gives a share of a decedent's estate, equivalent to the share of the decedent's lawful spouse, to one who was not legally married to, but cohabited with, the decedent, and was the decedent's commonly reputed spouse. Suppose, moreover, that the Supreme Court goes so far as to declare, in the process of interpreting said statute, that an agreement between a couple to live together as man and wife, even if either or both are married to others, "is not in any way prohibited, immoral, or contrary to the public interest."[114]

Can such a court, even if it were *originally* "established by law, with the concurrence of the public", rightly be called "Jewish"? If not, it might then follow, according to the Rambam and other halakhic authorities, that any Jew who litigates, *ab initio*, before such a court or does so without having first received permission from a rabbinical court or Beit Din, is "an evildoer and is considered as though he has blasphemed and raised his hand against the Torah." This, at first glance, would seem to be the position of Rav Yaakov Ariel, to whom we now turn.

A Question of Justice

Rav Ariel contends that "The general spirit of the [Israeli legal] system, as well as most of the judges, is alien to Jewish tradition. Most religious Jews, under the impression that 'the law of the land is law' (*dina d'malchuta dina*) applies to [Israel], are unaware of the seriousness of the prohibition on litigating before secular Israeli courts."[115] Let us pause a moment to discuss this principle.

The principle of *dina d'malchuta dina*, the law of the "land" (literally the "kingdom") is the law, applies to Jews living in the Diaspora. It means that the laws of a gentile government are binding on Jews even when they differ from the laws of the Torah. However, this principle applies primarily to the collection of taxes; and the Talmud, wherein this principle is laid down, states that the "*law* of the government is binding", but not "the *robbery* of the government."[116] Hence the principle of *dina d'malchuta dina* is of rather narrow scope. It does not apply to marriage and family law. Nor is it binding if inconsistent with Jewish law in the area of *forbidden acts*. Moreover, "the law of the land" is not law if it violates the rights of the people. Finally, according to the Rashbetz, the principle of *dina d'malchuta dina* is no authority for governmental appointment of a judge over the Jewish community where such an appointment involves an infringement of the basic principles of justice embodied in Jewish law.[117] Needless to say, the Rashbetz ruling has appalling implications for the State of Israel and its secular courts, and perhaps even for the rabbinical courts whose jurisdiction shrinks continually because of encroachments by the Supreme Court.

Returning to Rav Ariel, he writes: "Since the State of Israel is the state of the Jewish people, it should be governed by authentic, traditional Jewish law. In the same way that it is inconceivable to have a Jewish state without a Jewish language as the official language, the Jewish calendar as the official calendar, and an explicit relationship with the Jewish people (the Law of Return), so too a Jewish state without Jewish law is inconceivable" (p. 213).

Most religious Jews, he avers, do not understand that secular law or justice, like secular education, shapes the social and economic relations among men and therefore the daily life and ultimate character of the community. "Perhaps the political struggle to ensure religious education resulted in the neglect of the problem of religious justice" (p. 214).

Rav Ariel blames religious jurists for the general indifference of the religious public to this problem. The burden of his essay is to refute those "who, in contradiction to the unanimous opinion of Torah scholars in recent generations, developed the theory that the prohibition on non-Torah judiciaries does not apply to the Israeli court system" (ibid.).

He begins his halakhic argument with Exodus 21:1: "And these are the ordinances which you shall place before them." As noted above, *Gittin* 88b explains the words "before *them*" as meaning "not before non-Jews" as well as "not before laymen." This dual prohibition clearly prohibits recourse to *any* court that does not adjudicate on the basis of Torah law. This obviously applies to Israel's secular courts, or so Rav Ariel concludes.

He defends this conclusion by a complex but logically rigorous elucidation of such authorities as Rashi, the Rambam, the Ran, the *Shulkhan Arukh* and other basic halakhic sources.[118] When all is said and done, however, the premise or reasoning of these authorities is rooted in *Gittin* 88b. Exceptional circumstances aside (inevitable in the Diaspora), all agree that it is impermissible to adjudicate before a non-Torah court, hence before laymen or gentiles.

Shifting to ideological grounds, Rav Ariel points out that, under the Torah, "The human judge derives his moral values, his legal reasoning, and his judicial authority [not from the public or some transient political assembly but] from the Supreme Judge, Creator of the world, Who created man in His image so that he might lead a life of truth and justice" (p. 217).

"Justice," he continues, "is not a product of mere human intelligence, designed only to facilitate social utility and efficiency. Jewish social existence possesses a divine purpose and reflects a divine order" (ibid.). "He who renders true judgment becomes a partner of God in the creation of the world" (*Shabbat* 10a). These exalted ideas obviously transcend the intellectual horizons of secular judges entrenched in Israel's Supreme Court, otherwise known as the High Court of Justice.

For Rav Ariel, "it is inconceivable that the entire system of justice [in Israel] be entrusted in principle to human agreement. This would make justice dependent on the vagaries of current modes of thought" (p. 218). Such a system would succumb to the moral relativism that now permeates the secular democratic world. There would be no absolute standards by which to distinguish right from wrong. Judicial decisions would vary according to the personal predilections of judges or the whims of Israel's opinion-makers, its assimilated intellectual and political elites.

(To deliberately abandon Jewish law and adjudicate according to non-Jewish or gentile laws and principles is to pursue a policy of assimilation: the assimilation of Judaism from which will inevitably follow the assimilation of Jews – their loss of Jewish national consciousness.)

Rav Ariel admits that a system of "relative or temporal justice" is sometimes necessary, but such a system, he adds, should not deviate excessively from the absolute standards of the Torah. This is especially pertinent in the domain of civil law, which profoundly affects the social and economic life of the community. To abandon this source of divine wisdom as irrelevant to contemporary Israel, and to litigate before its secular court system on the grounds that "the law of the land is law," is to uproot the Torah. To paraphrase the Rashba: "Who would need the holy books of the Mishna and the Talmud? One might as well teach children Israeli or gentile law in their classrooms. Heaven forfend that this should occur in Israel" (ibid.).

Concerned about the long-range consequences of a Jewish state without Jewish law, Rav Ariel argues that it is forbidden to appoint laymen instead of Torah scholars as *permanent* judges. Of course, to choose laymen "incidentally" to arbitrate a particular dispute is permissible. So, too, is the permanent appointment of a non-Torah judiciary in a locality where no scholars are available. Whether a secular court system constitutes a denial of the Torah therefore depends on the availability of a rabbinical alternative.

To prevent the abandonment of Jewish justice in Israel, Torah jurisprudence, says Rav Ariel, must be at least equal to that of foreign law. This may be accomplished legislatively by making rabbinical courts equal in authority and power to the secular courts (pp. 218-219). Until this happens, however, we are compelled to ask, What are religious Jews to do when involved, say, in civil law disputes? Also, must not long and arduous work be done to render the enormous body of Jewish civil law applicable to contemporary social and economic needs and problems? Finally, must not rabbis who undertake this task be knowledgeable about secular or gentile law, as were the leading halakhic authorities of the Middle Ages?

Rav Ariel does not address these questions in his admittedly brief essay. Nor does he solve, in that essay, the halakhic dilemma of Jews compelled to litigate before Israel's secular courts. We are left with the vexing problem: Is it halakhically permissible to litigate before such courts *ab initio*?

Jewish Law is a "Member of the Family"

Enter Professor Menachem Elon, a man learned in both Jewish and secular law. Elon discusses the halakhic status of Israel's judicial system in his monumental work, *Jewish Law: History, Sources, Principles*.

He, too, refers to *Gittin* 88b, but he dismisses, "for both halakhic and historical reasons", the argument prohibiting recourse to Israeli courts consisting of Jews unlearned in Jewish law. Referring to the same section of the *Shulkhan Arukh* cited by Professor Bazak (*Hoshen Mishpat*, Ch. 8.1), Elon states that "litigation may be brought before laymen with the consent of the parties" (IV, p. 1916, n. 47). As already indicated, however, this ruling is from the Rema's commentary incorporated into the code of the great Joseph Karo, who is more stringent than the Rema. In fact, the Rema's emendation begins with the halakha that permission to litigate before laymen depends on the non-availability of a rabbinical alternative, a ruling held by all halakhic authorities. Moreover, litigation before laymen also depends on the nature of the case. Thus, while lay courts may hear cases involving *both* loss of money and of frequent occurrence, such as loans, sales, and purchases, cases involving penalties, as in theft, assault, and rape require ordained judges. (See *Sanhedrin* 3a, *Baba Kamma* 84b.)

Furthermore, and as a matter of historical fact, Jewish litigants before and after the codification of Jewish law in the *Shulkhan Arukh* (1564) usually preferred courts having a Rabbi, if only because such courts proceeded more quickly and deliberately and entailed much lower costs. (This sometimes prompted gentiles to take their disputes to Jewish courts!)[119] The eminent historian Salo W. Baron, a rabbi with doctorates in jurisprudence and political science (often cited by Elon), says this of Jewish communities that enjoyed juridical autonomy prior to the eighteenth-century Emancipation:

All family matters, including inheritance, were administered in accordance with religious law by coreligionists...

Questions pertaining to the synagogue, cemetery, ritual bath, ritual food, and so forth, at least insofar as they did not affect the dominant creed or royal treasury, were almost invariably adjudicated by the Jewish authorities. In the legal domain, moreover, the opinion of the ritualistic expert carried great weight even where there existed no permanent rabbinate and the judiciary had a predominantly lay character. In this vast field, it may be asserted, the general validity of Talmudic law was uncontested.[120]

Because these Jewish communities enjoyed juridical autonomy, rabbinical insistence on the exclusivity of Jewish law was the rule in theory and in practice. Medieval gentile courts, in addition to being notoriously corrupt – bribery was common – required oath taking and other judicial features that were Christian oriented. Recourse to Jewish lay courts was the lesser of two evils.[121]

Elon himself admits that "The goal of preventing resort to non-Jewish courts and of protecting Jewish juridical autonomy motivated the halakhic authorities in the post-Talmudic period to permit the appointment of three laymen to function as a court, even if none was *gamir* [learned in Jewish law], in a locality where even the minimal requirement that the court include one *gamir* could not be met" (I, 23; see also II, 794).

This was so even when such lay courts resorted to gentile laws or customs. After all, unlike now, Jews did not have a state of their own and were therefore subject to most unfavorable circumstances.

Nevertheless, to bolster his opinion on the halakhic status of Israel's secular courts, despite their primary reliance on non-Jewish laws and principles, Professor Elon resorts to eloquence. He reminds us that, "Today, even the most strictly observant Jews throughout the Diaspora turn to the courts of the countries in which they reside," and adds: "It is thus particularly ironic that the prohibition against "resorting to non-Jewish courts" is invoked precisely with regard to the Jewish courts of a Jewish state in which Jewish law is a "member of the family" – or at least a frequent guest" (IV, p. 1917).

With all due respect, one cannot but wonder why Elon singles out those who claim that the prohibition against resorting to non-Jewish courts applies to Jewish courts in Israel, when he elsewhere admits that *Gittin* 88b also prohibits recourse to courts consisting of Jews unlearned in Jewish law.

Professor Elon's eloquent statement requires further scrutiny. First, that religious Jews in the Diaspora litigate before non-Jewish courts is logically irrelevant to the halakhic issue in Israel where Jews litigate before courts of Jewish laymen. Besides, and as another commentator observes,

Even today, among the Orthodox everywhere from New York to Bombay, it is considered a disgrace for a Jew to summon a fellow-Jew before the courts of the land. A decent respect for Jewish observances still requires that the aggrieved party should first apply to a rabbinical court to have the matter adjudged there. Only after the defendant ignores the rabbinical summons, is it proper to sue in the courts of the land.[122]

Second, in referring to "a Jewish state in which Jewish law is a 'member of the family' – or at least a frequent guest," Elon has in mind the Foundations of Law Act of 1980, which authorizes the Supreme Court, when there is a gap or ambiguity in the law, to apply "the principles of freedom, justice, equity, and peace of the Jewish heritage." But as he well knows and deplores, the Court pays only lip service to the Foundations of Law Act.

Third, whatever he means by saying Jewish law is a "frequent guest" in Israel's secular courts, Elon knows, and profoundly regrets, that only a minute fraction of Jewish law has been incorporated into Israel's legal system. Moreover, this partial and condescending recognition of Jewish law is misleading, since its salutary effect, as Rav Ariel points out, "is apparent only at the outset... [For] as the law becomes part and parcel of the body of secular law, explicated and modified by secular jurists who use the mental framework and conceptual world derived for the most part from non-Jewish sources, it gradually loses its Jewish character" (p. 222). In fact, Israel's Supreme Court has adopted the permissiveness and moral equivalence underlying American jurisprudence, in consequence of which the Court is pursuing the anti-Torah agenda evident in its decisions regarding adultery and sodomy, as well as the Sabbath and conversion.

(This must be regarded by any candid observer as a deliberate assault on the beliefs and feelings of a very large majority of Israel's Jewish population.)

Now let us juxtapose our three authors. All would agree that when religious Jews in the Diaspora litigate before gentile courts, they do so under the halakhic category "the law of the land is law" (which, remember, does not apply to matters of personal status and forbidden acts). Rav Ariel denies the propriety of using this exilic category to justify litigating before Israel's secular courts. Bazak and Elon deny the applicability of *dina d'malchuta dina* to Israel since they both regard its secular courts as halakhically Jewish. Bazak, however, is a case apart. For the error, or supposed error, of applying *dina d'malchuta dina* to justify litigation before Israel's secular courts may be logically derived from the avowed premise of Bazak's essay! Recall his (astonishing) assertion that "the problem of the State and Jewish law is not essentially a religious-halakhic one, but rather a national-cultural one." Bazak does not venture to define these terms, nor can he readily do so since Judaism (unlike Christianity) does not separate religion from nationality. Professor Elon rightly states that the connection between religious law, ethics, and nationality in Judaism "is so integral and organic that while boundaries may possibly be marked between them, the connection cannot be completely severed" (IV, 1904). This fact undermines the halakhic status of Israel's secular judicial system and renders more plausible the application of *dina d'malchuta dina* in the Jewish state. Elon, I believe, unsuccessfully avoids this discomforting conclusion. Whatever the case, we must turn elsewhere to fully appreciate the subversive consequences of Israel's judicial system.

The Consequences of Litigating in Secular Courts

In *Litigation in Secular Courts*, Rabbi Simcha Krauss (who refers to Professor Elon's argument in *Jewish Law* as "eloquent") commences as follows:

The Shmona Esrai, which a Jew says three times a day, contains our innermost and most profound prayers. In it we express and articulate our most basic needs – we pray for national liberation, the rebuilding of Jerusalem and the redemption brought by the Moshiach. And in practically in the same breath, we pray "restore our judges as of yore."[123]

Needless to say, that Jews in Israel pray for the restoration of their judges of old, places in question the character and perhaps the halakhic status of their country's secular judges.

Rabbi Krauss begins, however, not with Israel's secular courts but by explaining the severity of the prohibition against resorting to gentile courts. This he does by citing the strictures of various halakhic authorities. Rashi warns that whoever resorts to gentile courts "desecrates God's name". (Recourse to gentile laws conveys the impression of their being superior to the laws of the Torah.) The Rambam adds: "Whoever submits a suit for adjudication to gentile judges in their courts, even if the judgment rendered by them is in accord with Jewish law, is a wicked man." The *Shulkhan Arukh* quotes this Rambam and cautions us that the prohibition in question exists even if "both [parties] have agreed [to settle their dispute] before the gentile courts" (pp. 38-39).

This prohibition is not a denial of *dina d'malchuta dina*. Since Jewish communities in the Diaspora exercised judicial autonomy, they had either a rabbinical alternative to gentile courts, or, in localities where that alternative was lacking, they had halakhic authority to adjudicate before Jews not conversant in Jewish law.

With the establishment of the State of Israel, however, a dilemma confronts serious Jews. The Knesset, a secular institution, enacts all but a handful of laws without reference to the Torah, while Israeli courts interpret Knesset laws and adjudicate disputes according to gentile law and principles. Now, to quote Krauss, "It is one thing for exilic Jews in the pre-Emancipation era to have resorted to lay courts when no rabbinical alternative was available. But today, for Jewish legislators in a Jewish state to make laws in disregard of the Torah, and for Jewish judges to interpret and adjudicate these laws is a quite different matter" (p. 50).

To litigate before Israeli courts that ignore Torah law and adjudge according to foreign legal systems violates, *prima facie*, the halakhic prohibition of resorting to gentile law. By so doing, Jewish judges genuflect to, or affirm the value of, gentile law over the Torah. This is the desecration of God's name that Rashi and others authorities refer to in their strictures against resorting to non-Jewish courts.

Rabbi Krauss concludes: "The essence of...the prohibition of resorting to a secular judicial system is the deinstitutionalization of Torah law and its subsequent nullification by atrophy and neglect, through the conscious choice of criteria other than Torah law. That this 'other law' is made by Jews in the Knesset and interpreted by Jews in the Israeli judicial system does not alter the fact that a conscious choice was made to forgo Torah law for other law" (p. 51). Thus, *should Jewish law cease to operate in social and economic life, it will become little more that an intellectual exercise, as if the Halakha were still in exile, relegated to the private domain of the family, the synagogue, the congregation, and the Jewish school.* Jewish law will then cease to be creative, indeed, will wither and decay. The consequence is *headless* Judaism.

Apply the previous paragraph to Israel and it follows that *the halakhic prohibition of resorting to a judicial system that ignores Jewish law ultimately involves Israel's survival as a Jewish state.*

Surely reliance on *dina d'malchuta dina* to justify litigation before secular courts, whether halakhically correct or not, is nothing more than a fig leaf. It may suffice for Jews in America, hardly for Jews in Israel. A judicial system that promotes headless Judaism in Israel is a grave matter, more so in a country surrounded by hostile Islamic regimes. The serious reader will see, therefore, that merely to discuss the status of Israel's secular courts on halakhic grounds does not go far enough. If discussion of this subject is to have a politically significant impact on Jews in general, and on non-religious Jews in particular, it will have to be shown that Jewish law is inherently preferable to gentile law, and that its incorporation into Israel's legal system is essential for the country's survival. This leads me to Rabbi K. Kahana's book, *The Case for Jewish Civil Law in the Jewish State.*[124]

A Matter of National Consciousness

Writing in 1960, Rabbi Kahana, who taught at Jews' College, London, declares at the very outset of his book: "That a civilized people should administer its own laws in its own country is a proposition which, indeed, should not call for discussion" (p. 1). Such discussion, however, is urgently necessary in Israel, for its legal system is undermining the people's sense of national consciousness. Severed from its own laws and constitutional history, a country's political, economic, and social history will be largely unintelligible. Its legal heritage will cease to have practical relevance. Fewer and fewer people will understand their past, the way their forefathers related to each other in daily life, the conditions under which they lived, their way of thinking. *Without such knowledge Israel will forget its world-historical mission.*

Ignorant of their legal heritage, Israel's opinion-makers and policy-makers can have no clear sense of national purpose. Their public statements, their political and judicial decisions, especially when influenced by a pluralistic mode of thought, will lack coherence and direction, indeed, will be all the more prone to foreign influence and pressures. At stake is a people's emotional security, their solidarity and confidence in the future, their very ability to withstand adversity.

"By turning to our own system of law," says Rabbi Kahana, "instead of borrowing from other systems, the State of Israel would give expression to the inner feelings of its citizens" (p. 12). "The more we delve into Jewish law and into its history the more we find there the reflection of the creation of our own national ideas" (p. 14). These are the noble ideas of Torah Judaism which sustained the Jewish people through centuries of humiliation, torture, and decimation. *These ideas enabled the Jewish people to despise their despisers.*

Rabbi Kahana's "plea for the acceptance of Jewish law is not based only on the idea of tradition; it is an appeal for the recognition of the Jewish people's instinctive feeling that their law is founded on ethics and justice" (ibid.). This sense of ethics and justice may be seen in the following laws incorporated into Israel's legal system: the Wage Delay Prohibition Law (1955), the Prohibition of Defamation Law (1962), the Severance Pay Law (1963), and the Right to Privacy Law (1981) – all based on the Torah.[125]

However, to borrow piecemeal from diverse legal systems to meet various needs and fleeting circumstances without reference to well-established unifying principles can only result in complications and bewilderment as well as resentment and social tensions. Conversely, when the legal order accords with a people's abiding sense of justice and national consciousness, the laws will not be felt as arbitrary or coercive. Respect for law will then follow, as will mutual confidence and social harmony.

Jewish Civil Law and Its Gentile Competitors

To facilitate the acceptance of Jewish law by secular laymen, Rabbi Kahana focuses on Jewish civil law (*Mishpatim*), in contradistinction to religious law (*Hukim*). *Hukim* are laws which would be disparaged as unreasonable by man's sensual nature and by the non-Jewish world, such as the prohibition of pork or the scapegoat used for the Day of Atonement. The reasons for these laws are unknown and not intended to be known. They relate to "commandments" and concern the relationship between man and God. In contrast, *Mishpatim* are those laws which, were they not contained in the Torah, would have been prescribed by human intelligence, such as the prohibition of theft and murder. In other words, *Mishpatim* are laws that can be explained in a rational manner, for they concern the affairs of man and his neighbor. In fact, one meaning of the term "*Mishpat*" is "an act of judgment".[126] This is why the expression "judgment" and not "commandment" is used in Jewish civil law.

It should be emphasized that Jewish civil law covers the largest domain of the *Halakha*, and in no other area is the human intellect allowed so much freedom to decide according to the insights of the judge and the circumstances of the case. "A judge has nothing to guide him but that which he sees with his own eyes" (*Sanhedrin* 6b). His aim, however, is to unite truth and goodness by reasoned inquiry.

Jewish civil law, says Rabbi Kahana, is so rational that the term "imposition" will not be found where *Mishpat* is introduced in the Torah. The Talmud requires the teacher to explain *Mishpat* solely on the basis of reason. Jewish civil law not only requires public officials to understand the laws they have to administer; it also "exhorts the people to realize that it is for them also to learn its rules and principles, so that they know what are the rights and duties of individuals in relation to their neighbors and the community at large" (p. 29).

Because Jewish civil law is rooted in reason, it provides, like any science, a basis for future development. Rabbi Kahana draws a comparison between Jewish and Roman law:

It is universally admitted that Roman law is a consistent logical system, which, though it is old, has survived and it is still being used in many parts of the world. No lawyer or judge, in the countries where it is used, complains that it does not lend itself to being adapted to modern conditions. How much more does this apply in the case of Jewish law which, in addition to its consistency, has its own theoretical basis and can be more easily understood, applied and extended to every age!...

Whatever praise is given ... to Roman law, as far as justice and its ethical underlying ideas are concerned it does not attain the high standard of Jewish law (pp. 30-31).

While Roman law has the "logical formal rationality" required of a sound legal system, it lacks the "substantive rationality" of case law, which endows legal principles with concrete meaning on the one hand, while promoting justice and neighborly relations on the other. The logical rigidity of Roman law may be seen in this example. "By the Roman law every man had a right to dig in his own land for the purpose of improving it, even though he should thereby intercept the water which supplied his neighbor's fountain" (p. 60, n. 1). Here jurisprudence is confined to legal principles divorced from ethics. In Jewish law, more than in other legal systems, a man who merely anticipates that his own property may suffer from what his neighbor does or is about to do can obtain a court injunction (p. 60).

Turning to English law, on which Israel's Supreme Court still heavily relies, its development has been haphazard. Although English law is based on case law, a precondition of "substantive rationality", examination of actual cases reveals that inconsistency permeates English jurisprudence. In certain cases, judges have upheld violated laws over considerations of morality; in others they have upheld morality over the law. The subject is discussed by the late Professor Moshe Silberg, a former Deputy President of Israel's Supreme Court (one of its few members educated in Jewish law). Silberg begins by citing two cases that occurred in the nineteenth century.[127]

[The first] involved two Frenchmen who had immigrated to London, and one of them, a priest by profession, had been stricken with syphilis. His colleague cured him through the use of various drugs, and he sued him for twenty pounds as the fee for curing him. The defendant did not deny the facts. He admitted that he had been fully cured, thanks to the attention of the claimant who was an expert. He argued, however, that his colleague was not legally permitted to attend to him because...no one was allowed to practice medicine in London...unless he were licensed by the medical association. He therefore claimed that his cure of syphilis was a violation of the law, and that one could not claim to be paid for doing something which transgressed the law, that one had to do it without a fee! The Court did not recognize this argument, and ordered the defendant to pay the full amount of the claim.

In the second instance, which was tried the same day and by the same judge, the claim was for payment of the cost of a certain fabricated article – bricks. The defendant claimed that the bricks did not conform to the size prescribed by law, and that it was, therefore, forbidden for the seller to sell them, and that he could not, therefore, claim their price. The Court accepted the argument and dismissed the claim.

Silberg comments that, to this day, no one is clear as to the difference between the two decisions, "except for the relative emotional difference between…the ingratitude of the person who was cured and a merchant's refusal to pay." After examining more recent cases of English law, Silberg states that, "Two mutually contradictory tendencies played on the loyalties of the judges: the desire to defend the validity of the legal proscription on the one hand, and the desire to grant redress to the aggrieved claimant on the other."

However, had the judges followed Jewish law in such matters, then the recipient of illegally dispensed goods or services would be compelled to render payment to the aggrieved claimant, but who would then be fined to that (or a greater) amount for violating the law. Jewish law will therefore oblige a man to pay a prostitute her agreed fee although the liaison is illegal. As one commentator put it: "Why should a dishonest fornicator indulge himself for free at the expense of another? The court will oblige him to pay the sum agreed upon, in order that he should not have the sin of dishonesty added to that of immorality."

Returning to Silberg, he points out that, in English law, the contradiction between law and morality "is not accidental, partial, or hidden." It permeates modern English jurisprudence and indeed all other systems of modern law. In contrast, "there is no legal system in the world, ancient or modern, in which the principles of morality and law are so intertwined as in Jewish law." Here a digression is necessary.

We have been using the terms "morality" and "ethics" uncritically, as if their meaning is obvious and as if they are Torah concepts. For the purpose of this inquiry, let us ignore the differences which writers may ascribe to these terms. Both ethics and morality involve standards or rules of good behavior; both may be associated with such qualities as modesty and generosity, mercy and justice. However, there is no distinct term for ethics in the Torah or in the Talmud because in Judaism the goal of ethics and law coalesce. The Prophets and Sages of Israel looked upon law, in the larger sense, as ethical jurisprudence. As a recent scholar puts it: "...ethical criteria are so structured into halakha that they are themselves halakhot... The general duties of showing good manners, sympathy, understanding, love and selflessness toward others, are left largely undefined...[because] they are the product of the personality reared upon and shaped by Torah."[128] Thus, just as Judah Halevi, in his *Kuzari*, could say, "God forbid there should be anything in the Torah that contradicts reason," so the Sages of the Talmud could say: God forbid there should be anything in the application of the law that contradicts ethics or morality.

While morality is a basic aim of Jewish law, Jewish law is solicitous of human freedom. Since moral conduct hinges on free will, Jewish law does not impose morality (which actually begins in the family). Rather, it promotes morality by means of rational, just, and equitable rules of social and economic intercourse. The intended result is considerate and kindly behavior or the perfection of refined and friendly and therefore cheerful human beings.

Now let us assimilate the term morality to the Torah by defining it as "*the imitation of God's ways*" (*Imitatio Dei*). Thus, "You shall be holy, for I, the Lord your God, am holy" (Lev. 19:2). Just as God is gracious, so too we must be gracious. Just as He does justice, so too we must do justice. Thus understood, morality may then be rooted in the Torah's conception of man's creation in the image of God. Created in God's image, man is endowed with reason and free will. Reason and free will are preconditions of moral conduct. But conduct cannot be moral unless consistent with the ways or laws of God. Judaism therefore avoids the dichotomy of law and morality that has long divided and perplexed Western civilization.

One other point needs to be emphasized. It is precisely from the Torah's conception of man's creation in the image of God that we may derive the most exalted ideas of human dignity. This is why human dignity, indeed, the sanctity of human life, is a cornerstone of Jewish law.

A distorted view of human dignity will be found in a September 1999 ruling of Israel's Supreme Court. In the very midst of an upsurge in Arab terrorism, the Court, in an opinion delivered by Justice Aaron Barak, held that the use of "moderate physical pressure" in the interrogation of terrorists violates Basic Law: Human Dignity and Freedom. To this it may be replied that terrorists are themselves inhuman, or that their barbarous acts constitute a denial of human dignity. It may also be said that Barak's opinion denies the human dignity of the Jews who have been the victims of Arab terrorism. Finally, it may be said that the same judge has turned down petitions against the release of Arab terrorists who, it is well known, go on to commit further acts of savagery against Jewish men, women, and children. Israel's Supreme Court, which condones pornography and sodomy, has made a mockery of human dignity. But this highlights the question of whether Israel can survive its judicial system.

We may now return to Rabbi Kahana who shows that regard for human dignity has not played a central role in the development of English (or in Roman) law. As late as the eighteenth century, it was a crime punishable by death to hunt or steal a deer or a rabbit or a fish from any place where such creatures were usually kept, or to cut down or otherwise destroy a tree planted in an avenue or garden. The number of persons, including minors, executed in England for trivial offenses is shocking. At the outcome of a single court session, thirteen persons were hanged for associating with gypsies! Sir Robert Peel, in his speech to Parliament in 1830, said, "Capital punishments are more frequent, and the criminal law [is] more severe, on the whole, in this country than in any other country in the world."[129] By the early years of the nineteenth century the number of crimes visited by capital punishment had risen to over two hundred!

In Jewish law, theft and robbery, although considered heinous wrongs, were never subject to capital punishment. So restrictive are the rules of evidence in Jewish law – circumstantial evidence and confession are not admissible – that, prior to the destruction of the Second Temple and the demise of the Sanhedrin, the death sentence issued by a Jewish court must have been very rare indeed. We read in the Mishna: "A Sanhedrin that puts one man to death in seven years is called "destructive". R. Eliezer b. Azariah says: Or one in seventy years. R. Tarfon and R. Akiba say: Had we been in the Sanhedrin none would ever have been put to death" (*Makkot*, I, 10).

Until the last century, and quite contrary to the long history of Jewish law, imprisonment for debt was common in English and Continental law. Also, as concerns the creditor's power over the debtor, Jewish law is far more humane than Roman and English law. In Jewish law the security for a loan was always limited to the property rather than the person of the debtor. Because its aim is to promote kindly as well as just relations among men, especially in economic affairs – which can engender callous and even felonious behavior – Jewish law is very protective of the needy, the economic rights of workers, and what may be termed the social rights of former criminals. In Jewish law, and apart from cases involving manslaughter, all criminals who have paid the penalty for their misdeeds and have done *teshuva* are not only qualified to resume their former occupations, honors, and offices, but are eligible to be appointed or elected to new ones for which they are qualified.[130] Also, by prohibiting disclosure of a person's past misdeeds, Jewish law facilitates his rehabilitation, repentance, and self-respect. Manifested here is Jewish law's concern for human dignity, indeed, its affirmation of man's creation in the image of God.

"For the Jewish people," writes Rabbi Kahana, "the law was based neither on command nor on sanction. The validity of the law was based on the fact that it was good and just" (p. 101). This is why *lifenim mi-shurat ha-din*, i.e., to act more generously than the law requires, is a basic principle of Jewish law.[131] Recall the incident of Raba ben Huna, the scholar who was required to pay the wages of some porters, who had negligently broken a barrel of his wine. Jewish law, we have seen, demands higher standards of conduct from the leaders of the community. The reason is simple enough. The leaders of the community, especially its educators, politicians, and jurists, possess the power to do great harm as well as great good, for they shape the standards of the living and posterity.

The Jewish principle of requiring higher standards of conduct from people in high places is aristocratic (*noblesse oblige*) and conforms to a lofty conception of human dignity. That principle was emulated by American law until 1967, when it was nullified by the US Supreme Court on the grounds that it violates the equal protection clause of the Fourteenth Amendment of the American Constitution.[132] American jurisprudence, like American higher education, is tainted by moral equivalence or indiscriminate egalitarianism. Here are recent cases in Israel.

The Supreme Court has ruled that homosexual couples are entitled to the same benefits as *other married couples*, in consequence of which employers must grant full benefits to the partners of their gay employees. (This has encouraged Reform rabbis to perform same-sex marriages.) The Court has also ruled that Israel's air force cannot exclude female pilots unless they are pregnant! (A pretty piece of biological obscurantism.) More pregnant of mischief is the Court's ruling in an "affirmative action" case. Imitating American law, Israel's Corporation Law mandates "approximate representation" of women on the boards of directors of public corporations. Consistent therewith, the Supreme Court vetoed the appointments of three men because of gender.[133]

How ironic that the American "quota system", which discriminated and still discriminates against some of the most gifted members of that country, should become part of the law and jurisprudence of Israel. Israel's Supreme Court seems to have forgotten that Israel is supposed to be a nation of "priests" (a dreadful rendering of *Kohanim*), meaning men of preeminent intellectual and moral character – noblemen. Israel can hardly become a light unto the nations when its laws and jurisprudence ape the leveling egalitarianism or stupidity of the world's greatest democracy.[134]

Jewish law does not sacrifice reason on the altar of emotional or indiscriminate equality. Unlike other legal systems, Jewish law unites "formal" and "substantive" rationality. This it can do because Jewish law consists of the Written Law of the Bible and the Oral Law of the Talmud. To paraphrase Rabbi Kahana: "While the Bible embodies the formal rationality of the law, its juridical rules and principles, the Oral Law is concerned with their case by case application in the daily life of the community. Also, whereas the Written Law presents to us the legal institutions and the nature of our rights and duties, the Oral law teaches us the practical application of those institutions and the working out of those rights and duties in social conduct."

...vital as it is to extract the principles of law, something further is necessary – their application to human experience. The rules of law in the Torah have not been fixed in advance. There is in the Torah an organic body of rules and principles with an inherent power to grow. The machinery for its development is the Oral Law... Principles acquire full meaning only when applied to cases...

It is indicated over and over again in Jewish juristic literature that the legal material of the Bible must not be interpreted according to the mere letter; it is the concept behind the word which is of crucial importance (pp. 34-35).

Rabbi Kahana emphasizes that the Oral Law was needed not because the Torah was incomplete, but because the Written Law, by its very nature, demanded the Oral Law. Any written statement, standing by itself, may be open to more than one interpretation and indeed misinterpretation. But conclusions reached after adequate discussion, such as took place among the Sages in the great Jewish academies, can dispel ambiguities. While the Written Law gives only headings and principles, which may give rise to disputes over their exact meaning, the Oral Law clarifies those headings and principles by their application to concrete cases. "It was not accidental that the Bible leaves development to the Oral Law; it is because the Bible recognizes that life is a process of continuous growth and therefore the law must possess vitality to allow growth" (pp. 39-40).

How Early Secular Zionists Viewed Jewish Law

Strange as it may now seem, secular Zionists in the pre-state period recognized that Israel's national renaissance and the rebirth of its national consciousness required the restoration of Jewish civil law. As early as 1909, the Israel office of the Zionist Organization in Jaffa established a Jewish Court of Arbitration which declared:

Our law is one of the most valuable assets of our national culture, and a unifying force [among Jews] throughout the world. The Jewish people have developed and maintained a remarkable system of law, whose foundations were laid at the dawn of our national existence; hundreds of generations have toiled over it, perfected it, and adorned it, and even today it retains the powers to renew its youth and to develop in a manner appropriate to the outlook of our time. During the thousands of years of the existence of our nation, this law was influenced by many material and spiritual factors. It absorbed religious and ethical concepts; it reflected cultural, economic, and social values; and it can still faithfully reflect the life of the people throughout the future.[135]

True, the Jewish Court of Arbitration was committed to the renewal of Jewish law "without any admixture of religion". Its goal was to restore Jewish law only insofar as it governs the relation between man and his fellow. The court respected the Jewish religion, but viewed Jewish law as something apart – something of value to everyone, religious or not.

Unfortunately, the Jewish Court of Arbitration failed to take root in the *yishuv* (the Jewish community), and not primarily because of religious opposition. It was a lay court that simply applied general principles of equity, justice, and social welfare without the guidance of any systematic legal system, Jewish or otherwise. Most of its judges, though intelligent, were not only ignorant of Jewish law but often had no legal training.[136] Still, it should be remembered that here were secular Zionists who recognized that the laws governing the Jewish community in Israel should be based on Jewish law.

The same attitude was expressed by the Jewish Law Society, established in Jerusalem in 1918 soon after the Balfour Declaration. The Society's purpose was to create an institute for research into Jewish law and to make Jewish law an active force in the Land of Israel. It recognized that if Jews were eventually to establish an independent state, the state would require a system of law in harmony with its people. Such a legal system, it was obvious, could not be simply imported from abroad. "Even those foreign legal principles that merit being treated as models or incorporated into Jewish law must first be adapted to fit our own historical legal characteristics and must pass through the channels of our nation's creative processes to take on a national form consistent with the needs and temperament of the people."[137]

The Jewish Law Society sought to unite jurists throughout the Land of Israel and to make contact with scholars and jurists in the Diaspora. The aim was not only to conduct research into development of Jewish law from its beginnings to the present time, but to make it compatible with the legal systems of the West and the East, and to formulate proposals for legislation prescribing the future governance of the Land of Israel. Remarkably, these secular Zionists discerned that it would be necessary to recreate *Jewish national consciousness* before creating the Jewish state!

While acknowledging the creative development of Jewish law down through the centuries, the Society had to confront the fact that, given the religious culture of the Jewish people, the Jewish legal system was closely tied to religious law. Hence, according to Professor Elon, it would be difficult to discern the boundary between law and religion in many cases. However, some halakhic authorities maintain that, as a general rule, a principle derived from religious law cannot be applied to civil law. This does not mean that it would be a simple task to incorporate Jewish civil law into Israel's legal system, especially now after the establishment of the State and the consequent operation of non-Jewish law. Elon nonetheless believes it can be done. On the other hand, he questions whether the creative development of Jewish law during the past two millennia can "continue if its national and religious aspects are uncoupled."[138] Without minimizing this problem, it bears repeating that non-religious Zionists recognized that the restoration of Jewish national consciousness requires a Jewish state whose legal system is based primarily on what Rabbi Kahana calls Jewish Civil Law.

The Barak Court and Its Consequences

This is not the attitude of Israel's Supreme Court, as may be clearly discerned by examining Justice Aaron's Barak's position regarding the Foundations of Law Act mentioned earlier. The Act severed the Israeli legal system from the binding force of English law and created an official link with Jewish law, making Jewish law a complementary part of Israeli positive law. Thus: "Where a court finds that a legal issue requiring decision cannot be resolved by reference to legislation or judicial precedent, or by means of analogy, it *shall reach its decision* in the light of the principles of freedom, justice, equity, and peace of the Jewish heritage (*morasha*)" (italics added).[139]

Despite the imperative "shall reach its decision", Justice Barak contends that Jewish law should not be given a preferred status even as a merely persuasive source when there is doubt as to the meaning of a particular statutory provision. He writes: "It should never be said that a particular [legal] system has the primary claim to interpretive inspiration." (Imagine a US Supreme Court justice teaching his fellow-countrymen, "*It should never be said that the American legal system has the primary claim to interpretive inspiration!*")

Returning to Barak, he goes on to say, in utter opposition to the secular Jewish Law Society: "In my view, not only is there no advantage in giving priority to Jewish law, but such priority runs counter to the essential nature of the interpretive process."[140] This "in my view" gives judges complete license to ignore Jewish law, indeed, to impose their personal preferences on the judicial process and on their countrymen (especially via the boundless power of Israel's undefined Basic Law: Human Dignity and Freedom).

Israel has thus come a long way from the non-religious Zionists of yesteryear to the irreligious post-Zionists of today. Many are the causes contributing to this decline, not the least of which is the abandonment of Jewish law. The adverse psychological impact on Jews escapes superficial observers. By forsaking the legal heritage of their country, legislators and jurists assault the emotions and expectations of the older population while rendering young people rootless and aimless, placing all at the mercy of whim, chance, and accident.

Judges who habitually apply foreign jurisprudence and concepts to problems in Israel, despite Israel's unique people and precarious situation, know not what they do. They not only undermine Israel's foundations and world-historical purpose – "From Zion shall go forth the law" – but they unwittingly undermine the rule of law, which ultimately depends on a people's respect for that which is firm and abiding. The consequence is the arbitrary rule of men. Is this not evident in the so-called "activism" of the Supreme Court, which goes so far as to dignify a law suit against circumcision, a 4,000 year-old Jewish observance? Is not the arbitrary rule of men evident in the anarchy of Israel's Government, wherein a multiplicity of parties compete for power while Israel's enemies arm and plan for this country's destruction?

There can be no rule of law in a country whose judges have forsaken their people's legal heritage. Contempt for law in Israel is obvious, corresponding to contempt for the past. For this we may thank Israel's intellectual, political, and judicial elites, untutored as they are in Jewish wisdom. They are even indifferent to the wisdom of gentiles, whose greatest philosophers and statesmen understood that the rule of law requires reverence for the law, but that one can hardly revere that which is ephemeral.[141] Yet Justice Barak has declared that Israel's Basic Laws should be easily amendable![142] Having abandoned the past, people of Barak's mentality live only in the fleeting present. Of them Goethe has written, "He who cannot draw on three thousand years is living from hand to mouth."

As previously indicated, Jewish law reconciles permanence and change and thereby endows the present with background and purpose. This is why Jewish law is at once unifying and conducive to freedom and creativity. It was the wisdom of the Torah and its Sages that united and preserved Jewish communities throughout the Dispersion. It was because of that wisdom that the Jews, without a state and land of their own, never lost self-government. Throughout the Middle Ages, Jewish communities, whether *de jure* or *de facto*, were autonomous entities – virtually a "state within a state". These communities had a highly developed system of jurisprudence, their own officials, and were usually governed by democratic institutions. They enacted secondary legislation (*takkanot*) to deal with new and diverse conditions and still preserved their loyalty to the primary law of the Torah. Moreover, and thanks to their Rabbis, the Jews were the first to develop a comprehensive system of public education without parallel in the history of civilization until the modern public school era. Theirs indeed is a religion of reason through law.

Not that these Jewish communities were without human failings, or never succumbed to the defects which all institutionalized religions are susceptible, such as rigidity and individual submissiveness. But these defects, says Salo Baron, "were minimized in the medieval Jewish communities, though not entirely eliminated, by the absence of permanent, hereditary leaders and of sacramental distinctions between rabbis and laymen, by the perfect equality before God, by the dynamism of the messianic aspiration and by the progressive nature of Jewish law which had long before developed an almost perfect system of checks and balances, apparently able to combine basic continuity with surface change."[143]

This ability to reconcile continuity and change is one of the hallmarks of Jewish law. Because of the timeless principles of the Written Law and the Oral Law's application of those principles to novel social and economic conditions, a Jew could find himself at home even when suddenly expelled from the place of his birth and upbringing to a distant country. Jewish law can therefore unite Jews having diverse ethnic backgrounds, as witness the intermarriage of Ashkenazi and Sephardi Jews in Israel. I will go further: Jewish law is absolutely essential to the preservation of the family, the cornerstone of Judaism. Hence, any assault on Jewish law, whatever the motives, is more serious than outbursts of anti-Semitism.

Summary and Conclusion

I must now offer a remedy to the subversive jurisprudence of the Barak Court. But first, a brief summary of the dilemma confronting Jews in Israel.

We have seen that Israel's secular courts adjudicate primarily according to non-Jewish or gentile legal systems and concepts. With all due respect to Professor Menachem Elon and his magnificent work, a powerful case was made by Rabbis Ariel and Krauss that the *halakha* prohibits recourse to Israeli courts *ab initio* since they do not adjudicate according to Jewish law. The halakhic prohibition aside, Rabbi Kahana presents solid reasons why Jewish law is intrinsically preferable to English law. It so happens, however, that the case he made for the adoption of Jewish civil law was made some forty years ago, with no discernible impact on Israel's judicial system. So what are religious Jews in Israel to do?

Inasmuch as the authority of Israel's rabbinical courts extends only to personal status and not to the vast domain of civil law, it appears, at first blush, that Jewish law leaves Jews in limbo. To avoid this dilemma, recourse has been made to the principle of *dina d'malchuta dina* – "the law of the land is law" – a principle appropriate to Jews in the Diaspora. This principle can hardly be comforting to Jews living in the supposed-to-be Jewish state of Israel.

Profoundly concerned about this paradoxical and vexatious situation, Rav Ariel proposed that legislation be enacted that would endow the rabbinical courts with the same power and authority of the secular courts. That was in 1980. There is little prospect that the Knesset will enact such legislation in the foreseeable future. Recall, however, that in 1980 the Knesset did pass the Foundations of Law Act. According to Professor Elon, this Act should have made Jewish law "first among equals" vis-a-vis the gentile legal systems to which the Supreme Court resorts in its decisions. But as indicated above, the Court has unofficially ignored that basic piece of legislation.[144]

Nevertheless, since the Knesset is the creator of the country's entire system of governance, including the judiciary, it is not bound by any Supreme Court decision. If the Knesset disagrees with the Court's interpretation of any law, it may change the law, as it has done on various occasions.[145] We have already seen, however, that according to the Babylonian Talmud, "No legislation should be imposed on the public unless the majority can conform to it" (*Avoda Zara* 36a). This principle is expressed differently in the Jerusalem Talmud: "...any legislation enacted by a court but not accepted by the majority of the public is no law" (*Avoda Zara* 2:8). It follows from this principle of Jewish law – and here I quote Professor Elon: "(1) Before legislating the legislator must examine and investigate whether a majority of the public will be able to conform to the proposed enactment, and (2) if, after the legislation is enacted, it appears that a majority of the public do not accept it, the legislation is legally ineffective."[146] This applies to decisions of the Supreme Court.

Now, in view of the fact that the power and authority of Israel's Supreme Court is derived from Basic Law: The Judiciary, enacted by the Knesset, it seems to the present author that it would be far easier for the Knesset to amend the Foundations of Law Act to require the Court to regard Jewish law as *primus inter pares*. Whether this would overcome the halakhic prohibition of resorting to secular courts I leave others to determine. However, two salutary consequences would follow. First, putting teeth into the Foundations of Law Act would induce the Supreme Court to consult halakhic authorities whenever gaps or ambiguities in the law require resort to Jewish principles. Second, a rightly amended

Foundations of Law Act would prompt members or would-be members of the legal profession to study Jewish law, especially if the term "heritage" (*morasha*), appearing in the act, had an explanatory note indicating that the term included *Jewish law*.

To hasten the process, the Knesset should alter the method of appointing Supreme Court justices, today the most undemocratic method in the free world. Only Israel allows almost no role for elected officials in the selection process. Three members of the nine-member selection committee are sitting members of the High Court, including the Court's president, two are representatives of the Israel Bar Association, and four are members of the two leading parties, including the justice minister and a member of the Knesset Law Committee. The committee's majority, therefore, is unelected. Moreover, the two members of the Bar are subject to various forms of pressure by the president of the Court before whom they may frequently appear. For similar reasons, the justice minister can also be manipulated by the Court's president. And since the Court's president handpicks the judges for every case, he can very much determine the selection of his own successor as well as the Court's character as a whole. In short, Israel's High Court of Justice is a self-perpetuating oligarchy.

Unlike the American Supreme Court, which includes "liberals" and "conservatives", what distinguishes Israel's Supreme Court – which preaches pluralism – is ideological uniformity. Of its current fourteen members, all graduated from the same law school, only one wears a *kippa*, and only one is Sephardi. In contrast, the Knesset has no less than 33 Orthodox Jews – 27.5% of that 120-member body. As for the Sephardim, they number 50% of the Jewish population. Hence Israel's Supreme Court is extremely unrepresentative of Israeli society.

Even though the Court, unlike the Knesset and cabinet ministries, lacks the complex factual knowledge required to resolve problems in various areas of public concern, it nonetheless arrogates to itself jurisdiction over matters concerning security, counter-terrorism, and even traffic regulations.[147]

To remedy this unheard of as well as undemocratic state of affairs, justices of the Supreme Court should be nominated by the Prime Minister and their appointment should require the approval of a majority of a Knesset plenum.

It goes without saying that solidifying the Foundations of Law Act will not immediately resolve the halakhic dilemma posed by Israel's secular court system. Nor will it soon restore Israel's judges as of yore, as Jews pray for in the Shmona Esrei. Nevertheless, it would facilitate Israel's complete restoration as a Jewish state. Otherwise, metaphysical reasons aside, it is doubtful that Israel will survive its judicial system.

Appendix: A Jurist's Critique of the Supreme Court

A remarkable interview of Israeli-born and Oxford-educated Professor Ruth Gavison was recently published in *Ha'aretz* Magazine (Nov. 12, 1999). Professor Gavison is one of Israel's senior jurists and leading experts in Israeli law. Currently Professor of Human Rights in the Faculty of Law of the Hebrew University of Jerusalem, Gavison had this to say of Israel's Supreme Court, despite her secular, left-wing reputation:

Our Supreme Court is very impressive. All told, it has excellent people, it enjoys a very strong status at home and high professional prestige abroad... At the same time, this is a court that has opened its doors to everyone and every matter and has shed almost every [judicial] limitation. As such, it is very different from the old court, which was far more modest, which showed far more respect for authority and for the autonomy of the elected political authorities; it believed that justiciability has limitations and thought its role was to be a supreme professional judicial authority, not a tribunal of social reformers and moral tutors...

I think it is proper for the court to give expression to our common values, such as the basic human rights. But I do not think it is right for the court to make use of its power to give priority to the values of one group in society at the expense of the values held by other groups. I do not think it is right for the court to decide in favor of Westernism and against traditionalism; or in favor of modernity and individualism and against communitarianism. I find that very problematic.

I also do not think that it is the court's role to be the supreme moral arbiter of society. That was not why it was appointed, and it is also unclear that it has the necessary skills for that. Judges in Israel are not selected on the basis of their integrity [sic] or their ethical code or for the social leadership they have demonstrated. They are chosen on the basis of their professional ability as jurists. There is nothing in their training that affords them the right, the authority or the ability to determine moral norms, to be the teachers of the generation.

The paradox is that precisely when the court purports to be a supreme moral authority, it undercuts its legitimacy as a supreme judicial authority. So it is the court itself, with its attempts at role expansion, that endangers the legitimacy of the legal system. Because as a supreme moral authority it is far from clear that the court is better than [Shas spiritual leader Rabbi] Ovadia Yosef. And it is equally unclear that the supra-legal values of the [so-called] enlightened [secular] public in whose name the court acts [N.B.] are worthier than the supra-legal values of the religious public... In Germany, Italy and South Africa there are constitutional courts that have far-reaching powers. But those courts are subject to a clear constitution and were established especially to fulfill that function; accordingly, their members are chosen by the political branches and are appointed for a limited period. In the United States there is a Supreme Court that has taken on itself the power to overturn laws, but it does this in a lengthy process and on the basis of a crystallized constitution, and its justices are appointed in a political process.

In Israel, by contrast, there is no crystallized constitution, there is no lengthy process and there are no justices who represent the entire society or who serve for a limited period. The result is a situation in which one court, which effectively appoints itself, creates the constitution by means of its interpretation of the Basic Laws. And this occurs without any of the control mechanisms that exist in the United States. So from this point of view our situation is quite distinctive. The combination of judicial criticism of Knesset legislation, in a state where there is as yet no crystallized constitution, by a court whose justices are not elected but are appointed for life by the judicial system itself, creates a very problematic situation...[f]rom the point of view of democracy and the democratic decision-making process...

What is equally serious is that this process is not accompanied by public discussion worthy of the name. In the United States, where there are activist courts, there is an ongoing, lively debate. Opinions are voiced on both sides of a question. Whereas in Israel, some sort of rhetoric is generated that creates the feeling that anyone who is critical of the court is the enemy of the rule of law. I do not accept that. I think the very opposite is true. I think that within the judicial community there are deep disputes today over all the questions on the public agenda: over a constitution, the Basic Laws, the status of the court... All these questions are in dispute, but generate no public reverberation because of the attempt to close ranks and create a front of homogeneity toward the [public] outside.

It is true that there are attacks on and threats to our judicial system, and it is true that the political system does not always protect judicial independence strongly enough. But the need to protect the court and its independence cannot justify the systematic, protracted and sweeping avoidance of any public discussion of the court's place in our life. I do not like ideological collectivity in general and judicial ideological collectivity in particular. Certainly not in a judicial system...

[Consider] the appointment of judges. Nowhere else in the world is there a situation in which judges have control over the process of appointing judges. It is very good that judges have input in the process, but it is very bad when they have control over it. It gives those who head the system too much power, and it turns the system into a kind of closed sect, which is too uniform and which effectively perpetuates itself...

[T]he court cannot solve all our problems. What we get is a kind of quick fix, which may work for a moment but does not resolve the basic problems, the problems that the political system has to resolve, the problems that our elected representatives have to cope with. The attempt to bypass our tribulations and bypass a genuine public debate over what is needed by rushing to the High Court of Justice, and the attempt to curb our unhomogeneous and non-Western and not necessarily secular elected political system by subordinating it to a homogeneous judicial system that is Western and secular, is an attempt that is doomed to failure. It is liable to foment a very grave crisis.

CHAPTER 8
The Nature of the Muslim-Jewish Conflict:
The Philosophical Foundations of the "Peace Process"

Therefore, hear the word of Hashem, O scoffing men, O rulers of this people who are in Jerusalem. For you say, "We have made a sealed covenant with Death and made a compact with the Grave; when the scourge passes through it will not affect us, for we have made Deceit our shelter and taken refuge in Falsehood."

Isaiah 28:14

The propagandists of secularism, who leave out of account the religious factor in the Palestine problem, ignore the fact that this is the only bone of contention in the world which has persisted for thirty centuries and is still based on religious and spiritual foundations.

Abdallah al-Tall

Nowhere in this country is disintegration more evident than in Israel's piecemeal retreat toward its indefensible 1949 armistice lines. The problem before us is to understand the reasons for this retreat, more precisely, to understand the mentality of those who have championed Israel's policy of "land for peace". This will require, among other things, a philosophical analysis of the nature of the Arab-Jewish conflict and how it has been perceived and addressed by Israel's political elites. Any philosophical conclusions, however, must be confirmed by empirical evidence, an abundance of which will be set forth in this chapter.

The question confronting scholars as well as policy-makers is whether genuine and abiding peace is possible between ideologically antagonistic regimes such as Israel and its Arab-Islamic neighbors. Rightly or wrongly, political scientists classify Israel as a democracy and her Arab-Islamic neighbors as autocracies.[148] None deny that intensifying this political antagonism are profound religious and cultural differences. Yet, Western pundits and policy-makers suggest that this clash of civilizations is not an insuperable barrier to genuine and abiding peace in the Middle East. Many convey the idea that economic prosperity and cooperation can dissolve the Muslim-Jewish conflict.[149]

This very much describes the attitude adopted by Shimon Peres, who applied for Israel's membership in the Arab League when he was Yitzhak Rabin's foreign minister![150] The Arab League secretary, having yet to define man as *homo economicus*, informed Peres that the Jews of Israel should first become Muslims.

Peres' non-ideological attitude is widespread in the West. The policy of "land for peace" is not based simply on the assumption that "returning" the territory Israel gained in the Six-Day War would alone pacify her Arab neighbors. More fundamental is an assumption about human nature, an assumption that transcends political and religious ideologies, namely, the primacy of economics in human affairs. This assumption led to the Oslo negotiations which culminated in the Israel-PLO Declaration of Principles of September 13, 1993.

A socialist Labor government in Israel negotiated that agreement in Norway, a socialist country, and the agreement was sponsored by the United States, a capitalist country par excellence. The Western participants obviously believed in the primacy of economics versus politics and religion in the Arab-Jewish conflict. This idea of the primacy of economics is related to the idea of "conflict resolution" prevalent among political scientists throughout the democratic world. I shall examine these related ideas on theoretical grounds via Karl Marx and Thomas Hobbes and then test their validity by means of empirical evidence. Since the Muslim-Jewish conflict has a religious aspect, it is not irrelevant to point out that whereas Marx was an unabashed atheist, Hobbes, writing in seventeenth-century England, was a disguised one.[151]

Marx and Hobbes at Oslo

Marxism was implicit in the Oslo negotiations insofar as they were based on the primacy of economics. It would be more accurate to say, however, that the Oslo negotiations were influenced by "paraMarxism", for Oslo was also an exercise in "conflict resolution", in contrast to Marx's doctrine of revolution.

The notion of "conflict resolution" may be derived from the basic presupposition of Hobbes's political science, that *violent death is the greatest evil*. The fear of violent death, together with the desire for comfortable self-preservation or commodious living, impels men to seek peace. Hobbes not only denied perdition, providence, and paradise. He was the first systematic political philosopher to substitute bourgeois or utilitarian morality for aristocratic pride or honor. That is why the aim of the state, for Hobbes, is *peace at any price*.[152]

Hobbes may also be deemed a progenitor of capitalism insofar as capitalism fosters the unlimited acquisition of wealth or avarice. Hobbes not only avowed that money is the blood of the commonwealth, but he attacked the traditional doctrine that covetousness is a vice.[153] With Marx, the father of socialism, and Hobbes, a precursor of capitalism, we are prepared to examine the mentality underlying the Oslo negotiations.

* * *

As is now well known, while public negotiations between Israel and Arab Palestinians were going on in Washington, secret negotiations were taking place in Oslo between representatives of Israel's socialist Labor Party and high-ranking members of the PLO.[154] Oslo was chosen for these talks because the socialist parties of Israel and Norway had developed close relations over the years, and the Norwegians, who had long welcomed the PLO in their capital, had won PLO chief Yasser Arafat's confidence.

Leading a team of mediators was the late Norwegian foreign minister Johan Jorgan Holst, a socialist who had a long standing connection with the European Economic Community – the EC. Paradoxically, the EC was to become the model for making peace between Jews and Muslims – paradoxically if only because Europe is predominantly Christian and democratic. It seems, however, that the EC model for Middle East peace-making originated among American economists at Harvard University. In November 1991, the month following the Madrid Middle East Conference, the Americans brought together Israelis, Arab Palestinians, Jordanians, Lebanese, Syrians, and Egyptians for a unique symposium at

Harvard on the economic consequences of the Middle East peace process. The Americans believed that only economic prosperity and cooperation could overcome the Israel-Arab conflict in general, and the Israel-Palestinian conflict in particular.

Accordingly, throughout the latter part of 1992, left-wing Israeli politicians, economists, and academics met clandestinely with PLO representatives in Cairo and London. These meetings led to the Oslo negotiations with the on-going cooperation of the Harvard economists. Cooperation between socialists and free marketeers highlights the primacy of economics in the mentality of the democratic world. Let us probe this mentality.

Although the terms "social democrats", instead of socialists, and "liberal democrats", instead of free marketeers, might be more accurate, they obscure the centrality of economics. It goes without saying that Israel's socialist Labor Party has been influenced by a Marxist mode of thought. This may also be said of countless value-free social scientists, be they socialists or not. *According to Marx, the ultimate cause of human conflict is not inherent in human nature – in egoism or self-preference – but in the penury of external nature, more precisely, in economic scarcity.* Nature simply does not provide enough for human needs. Economic scarcity can be overcome, however, by the conquest of nature through scientific technology. Hence there is an economic or technological solution to human conflict.

Marx nonetheless insisted that the economic solution to human conflict must be preceded by a political revolution of violent proportions. Communists must seize state power and abolish private property. In less advanced states they must industrialize the country, establish industrial armies for agriculture, and transfer agrarian populations to urban centers. Eventually, this corporate state will wither away and be replaced by genuine democracy, where men and women are animated by fraternal disinterestedness: "*From each according to his ability, to each according to his needs!*"[155] From Marx's *Economic and Philosophical Manuscripts*, we learn that history will reach its end in "*the complete and conscious restoration of man to himself...as a social, that is, human being."* Man will then be a fully *"conscious species-being, that is, a being related to its species as to its own essence..."*[156]

If this utopian aspect of Marxism has no application to the Middle East, what shall we say of the economic model for Middle East peace? Marx was realistic enough to know that profound political and psychological change must precede the termination of international conflict. *Such change in the Middle East would necessitate a radical transformation of the political-religious character of the Islamic world.*

Islam, however, is not about to wither away like Soviet communism. Unlike Marxism, Islam is not a political ideology but the heart of a proud, 1,300 year-old civilization. It may well be argued that Islamic regimes are capable of absorbing scientific technology without undergoing a Marxist democratic revolution or the pacifism implicit in Hobbes.[157] No country was more advanced in science and technology than Nazi Germany. But let us probe even deeper into the economic model for peace in the Middle East.

Explicit in Marxism is the assumption that the products of human consciousness – such as political and religious ideas – have no independent status. Marx referred to such ideas as "phantoms" or "ideological reflexes".

The phantoms formed in the brain, are bound to material premises. Morality, religion, metaphysics, all the rest of ideology and their corresponding forms of consciousness, thus no longer retain the semblance of independence.[158]

Evident in Marx is the doctrine of historicism or historical relativism, which still permeates higher education in the West.

Now, if "forms of consciousness" are simply the reflexes of "material premises", they must be relative to time and place. In other words, if ideas merely reflect economic modes of production which change from epoch to epoch, or which differ from country to country, it follows that the political and religious ideas of nations have no independence or inherent validity. *Change their economic conditions and you will change their ideas.* Hence the economic model for Middle East peace.

The primacy of economics versus ideology in Marx corresponds to the primacy of the passions versus thought in Hobbes. Hobbes writes: "*Thoughts are to the desires as scouts and spies to range abroad and find the way to the things desired.*"[159] Moreover: "*Whatever is the object of any man's appetite or desire, that is it which he for his part calleth good; and the object of his hate or aversion, evil... For these words of good [and] evil...are ever used with relation to the person that useth them: there being nothing simply and absolutely so; nor any common rule of good and evil, to be taken from the nature of the objects themselves; but from the person of the man, where there is no commonwealth.*"[160]

The doctrine of moral relativism could hardly be stated more lucidly and concisely. Professor Allan Bloom and others have shown that relativism dominates education in the democratic world. One should therefore expect relativism to influence, however subtly, the mentality and policies of democratic politicians.[162] Relativism, which denies the truth of any system of moral and religious values, fosters hedonism or the primacy of economics or material values.[163] The same doctrine, which renders all ideologies equal, readily lends itself to the policy of "conflict resolution" and thereby insinuates that no cause or ideological conflict is worth dying for. (Hobbes's peace at any price.)

Relativism has disturbing consequences in the Middle East. Because this doctrine undermines religious convictions, it arouses Islamic contempt and hostility toward the West, a matter emphasized in the writings of Professor Seyyed Hossein Nasr, a Harvard-educated Muslim of profound erudition.[164] Muslims regard Israel as a bastion of the West. Israel's academic and political elites – whether socialist or liberal – have been very much influenced by relativism. Their relativism, however, is obscured by a leveling internationalism or secular humanism.

Consistent with Marx, these liberal socialists deem the nation-state a mutable product of history. Their Israeli counterparts have become "post-Zionists". Gad Yaacobi, Israel's former ambassador to the UN, told a Harvard group: "There is no such thing as Jewish land. There are only Jewish people." This was not merely a casual remark. Even the adjective "Jewish", has become an encumbrance to post-Zionists. Thus, Tel Aviv University professor of philosophy, Asa Kasher, having been assigned by the Rabin Government to draft a new ethical code for the Israel Defense Forces, deleted not only "Zionism" and the phrase "love of the land" from the Soldiers Code of Ethics, but "Judaism"![165]

Viewed in this light, the economic model for peace-making is intended to expedite the "end of ideology" in the Middle East, which Harvard professor Daniel Bell, writing in 1961, associated with the West. Here a brief digression is in order.

Bell attributed the end of ideology to the success of capitalism and the welfare state. The ascendancy of affluent, consumer societies has virtually eliminated class conflict. The masses can no longer be inspired by utopian ideas; they are preoccupied with commodious living, enjoying the fruits of science and technology in a thriving market economy.[166] Capitalism and socialism have converged. The Russian religious philosopher Nikolai Berdyaev defined socialism as the more equal distribution of the bourgeois spirit. He saw both capitalism and socialism as corrosive of religion.[167] We are back in the Middle East.

Pristine capitalism, in opposition to religion, purveyed the doctrine that human misery and conflict can be overcome by the wealth of nations promised by economic laissez-faire and the liberation of acquisitiveness: *"Private vices, public benefits."* Adam Smith proclaimed that war could be replaced by economic competition. From this one may infer that war on behalf of any ideology is irrational – the position of Shimon Peres. In his own words: *"Wars are born in the womb of error."*[168] Hence, as in Hobbes, there is no such thing as a *just* war. Clearly, the idea of "conflict resolution" links socialists and capitalists. The kinship goes further.

Insofar as capitalism fosters, along with greed, multinational corporations, it tends to dilute patriotism. During an April 1995 press conference, President Clinton complained about American billionaires who had renounced their citizenship. Although they may not be as cosmopolitan as socialists, capitalists proclaim that free trade can overcome ideological and international conflict: "Trade builds bridges." Socialists agree, hence the European Union. *Europe, however, is not the Middle East.* *Homo economicus* may reign in democratic Europe, where Christianity has been secularized. But most denizens of the Middle East should be classified *homo religiosus*.

To expect the Arab-Islamic Middle East to yield to the economism or consumerism of the West is to expect more than twenty regimes to self-destruct. This is hardly a short term prospect. An economic strategy that trivializes the political-religious dimension of the Muslim-Jewish conflict is not an adequate basis for peace-making.

Besides, some Arab spokesmen – including Egyptians – contend that economic cooperation is a strategy by which Israel seeks to dominate the Middle East. Aqba Ali Saleh wrote in the leading Saudi daily *Asharq al-Aswat* that "*The merging of technologically backward economies with [a] high-tech economy necessarily entails domination by the latter...*" (meaning Israel).[169]

It should be noted that whereas the combined Gross Domestic Product (GDP) of Egypt, Syria, Lebanon, and Jordan was three times that of Israel's in the 1960s, it dropped to two-to-one in the 1970s, and by the late 1980s the figure had evened out. In 1995, five million Israelis produced a GDP of more than $70 billion compared to the $68 billion produced by seventy-seven million Egyptians, Syrians, Lebanese, and Jordanians. If this trend continues over the next decade, Israel's GDP will eventually be double that of its neighbors.[170]

Juxtapose the fact that the Arab states spent $58 billion on conventional arms alone in the thirty-six months between January 1991 and July 1993 and the idea of an economic solution to the Muslim-Jewish conflict smacks of secular mysticism.[171]

True, Israel and Egypt signed a peace treaty in March 1979. Yet, not only is trade between the two countries minuscule, but Israel's late Minister of Defense, Mordechai Gur, reported that Egypt is trying to exclude Israel from any Middle East economy.[172] Moreover, former Director General of Israel's Defense Ministry, Maj. General (res.) David Ivri, declared, "*The peace with Egypt is not peace. It is actually a cease-fire...*" Ivri warned that "*[Egyptian President Hosni] Mubarak has not created any Egyptian interest in Israel's continued existence.*"[173] The massive growth of the Egyptian army, said General (Res.) Matan Vilnai, is "Israel's most dangerous enemy".[174] In fact, shortly before the October 30, 1991 Madrid Conference (in which Israel met with Syria, Lebanon, Jordan and proxies of the PLO), Egypt, along with Syria, Lebanon, Jordan, the PLO, and fifty-seven other Arab-Islamic states, met in Teheran where they signed resolutions calling for Israel's destruction.[175] It were as if Egypt had never signed a peace treaty with Israel!

Perhaps Jordan's signing the Teheran resolutions was intended for "domestic" purposes. The late King Hussein knew very well that the existence of his regime depends largely on Israel, given Syria's territorial ambitions. In any event, Jordan's 1994 peace treaty with Israel merely formalized the *de facto* political cooperation which has long been the policy of their respective governments – and this, in the absence of economic relations. It should be borne in mind, however, that Jordan has paramount obligations to the Arab League which, judging from the Teheran Conference (and more recent evidence), remains committed to Israel's demise.[176]

* * *

Many Western pundits seem to ignore or minimize the fact that Israel, flaunted as a secular democratic state, poses a threat to the political-religious power structure of Arab-Islamic regimes. Nothing is more condescending than for Western politicians and intellectuals to expect Arab Muslims to betray their heritage or sacrifice their religious convictions for economic pottage.

The West parades as the patron of peace in the Middle East, to which it sells enormous supplies of sophisticated weaponry. Strange that the West, which abhors war, is itself steeped in violence. Witness the United States: While murder is a daily occurrence in the nation's capital and in other American cities, where people live under the same laws, America's political and intellectual elites offer an economic panacea to the Muslim-Jewish conflict!

Trade may build bridges, but man does not live by bread alone. France and Germany were the greatest trading partners before the Franco-Prussian War. So were Russia and Germany before the First and Second World Wars. Nationalistic and imperialistic ambitions transcended economic interests.

Especially relevant to the Middle East is the previously mentioned Britain's Peel Commission Report of 1937 which concluded that the Jewish contribution to Arab prosperity in Palestine only increased Arab hatred.[177] And thus it was after 1967 when Israel gained control of Judea, Samaria, and Gaza. Thanks to Israel's economic and technological assistance, not only did Arab income in these areas multiply four-fold, but the Government established new hospitals, health centers, primary and secondary schools and universities. Predictably, except to paraMarxists and naive capitalists, these schools and universities became hotbeds of insurrection.[178]

But consider the most extensive case of Arab-Israeli economic cooperation. The employment of more than 100,000 Palestinian Arab commuters inside Israel knit together the two economies and has brought individuals from the two communities into person-to-person contact. Yet this daily contact did not overcome Arab animosity toward Israel and may even have contributed to the intifada.[179]

No less revealing are Greece and Turkey, old adversaries which have been at peace for more than seventy years. "The two neighbors [both members of NATO] have economies that should be complementary, as Turkish textiles could be traded for Greek industrial goods. Yet their trade flow in 1992 was a paltry $250 million, less than 0.7 percent of either country's total trade flow."[180]

The ideological significance of such data does not penetrate the minds of secularists tainted by socialist and capitalist ideas. Such is their surreptitious contempt of Islam, that the secularists who have ever dominated the modern State of Israel should invariably minimize the all-important religious dimension of the Arab-Israel conflict. As the Arab commentator cited in the headnote put it: "*The propagandists of secularism, who leave out of account the religious factor in the Palestine problem, ignore the fact that this is the only bone of contention in the world which has persisted for thirty centuries...*"[181] This Arab spokesman, like many others who may be quoted, regards neither economics nor territory as the decisive issue in the Muslim-Jewish conflict. In fact, his statement was made before Israel gained control of Judea, Samaria, and Gaza, along with the Sinai and the Golan Heights in 1967.

Proud of their heritage, Muslims regard the secular democratic state of Israel as an outpost of Western decadence. Erasing this state from the map of the Middle East is a political and religious imperative. Although Muslims differ as to how and when this is to be done, their ultimate goal is the same. Anwar Sadat put it this way in an interview with *al-Anwar* on June 22, 1975: "*The effort of our generation is to return to the 1967 borders. Afterward the next generation will carry the responsibility.*"[182] Nor is this all.

In a *New York Times* interview dated October 19, 1980, Sadat boasted: "*Poor Menachem [Begin], he has his problems... After all, I got back...the Sinai and the Alma oil fields, and what has Menachem got? A piece of paper.*"

A year after signing the March 1979 peace treaty with Israel, Sadat ominously declared: "Despite the present differences with the Arab "rejectionist" rulers over the Egyptian peace initiative, the fact remains that these differences are only tactical not strategic, temporary not permanent."[183]

Sadat also said: "Fear is the second layer of skin of every Israeli or Jew."[184] Some may dismiss this statement as Arab arrogance. But if the "peace process" inaugurated by the Rabin-Peres Government and continued by their successors is indeed animated by the Hobbesian fear of violent death disguised by a paraMarxist promise of Middle East prosperity, that venture may hasten a catastrophic war with dire consequences for Israel.

CONCLUSION

This philosophical analysis of the mentality underlying the "peace process" served a two-fold purpose. It exposes and at the same time refutes the rationale of those who live in a state of "denial" regarding the implacable nature of the Muslim-Jewish conflict. Neither Marx nor Hobbes, nor the ideologically neutral social sciences they fathered are very helpful in dealing with this conflict – actually a protracted war punctuated by armistice agreements and peace ploys. War has many causes, of which economic motives are often trivial. As for the fear of violent death, which may incline nations to peace, the same fear also prompts nations to appeasement, as occurred before the bloodiest war in human history.

A nation's attitude toward peace and war depends on its form of government, on riches and poverty, and on what its people deem most important or sacred. Regarding democracy, a word from Alexis de Tocqueville is sufficient. Not only do most citizens of democracy possess property, but such is the paramount importance they attach to property that they are psychologically disinclined to war.[185] This cannot be said of non-democratic societies steeped in poverty. It is a grave error for democrats to mirror-image or project their love of ease and comfort upon the rulers and people of such societies. No invidious comparisons are intended. After all, there have been 1,000 wars in the Western world alone during the last 2,500 years.[186] Those who deplore the bellicose nature of Islam should bear in mind that Europe, the home of Christianity and humanism, has been drenched periodically in rivers of blood.

Even though Muslims and/or Arabs do not dwell in abiding peace with each other, Shimon Peres seems to believe they would live in peace with Jews, if only they enjoyed something comparable to a Western standard of living.[187] Arabs might deem this an insult. A group of Arabs once wrote Vladimir Jabotinsky, saying: "*You are the only one among the Zionists who has no intention of fooling us and who understands that the Arab is a patriot and not a prostitute (who can be bought).*"[188]

The idea that Arabs can be bought is certainly a bourgeois prejudice to be found among socialists and free marketeers alike. And yet, perhaps our philosophical analysis of their mentality, valid in itself, obscures a simpler explanation of the peace process. For example, one might argue that Israel's retreat to its indefensible 1949 borders is simply a consequence of foreign, especially American, pressure. The efficacy of foreign pressure, however, depends on the domestic resistance that can be mobilized against it. One must then inquire into the factors or ingredients of domestic resistance. Surely the most important is the human factor.

Some men are obviously more susceptible to pressure than others. Much depends on their moral and intellectual character, their wholehearted dedication to a cause, which depends on their conviction regarding the justice of their cause. Such dedication and conviction will be diminished if they have been tainted, wittingly or otherwise, by moral or cultural relativism (which brings us back to Hobbes and Marx). Perhaps this relativism underlies a statement Ehud Barak made in 1998, before he became Israel's Prime Minister, namely, that had he been an Arab, he too would have been a terrorist; which implies that had he been a German, he would also have been a Nazi. Being a terrorist or a Nazi would then seem to depend on sociological conditioning or the pressure exerted by one's society. If so, we should not expect much intellectual or moral independence on the part of a prime minister concerned about American pressure, especially when the object of such pressure is to induce Israel to yield land for peace – land having no metaphysical significance to this prime minister.

All other things being equal, a secular prime minister is more apt to be susceptible to foreign pressure than a Torah-oriented prime minister. A secular prime minister would thus be more inclined to pursue the policy of "land for peace". Surely a prime minister who regards the Golan Heights as "tank land", and not as "holy land", as did the late Yitzhak Rabin, will the more readily yield to pressure and agree to withdraw from this strategic area. Mr. Rabin had no doubt about the strategic importance of the Golan. Indeed, just prior to the June 1992 national elections – the elections that made him prime minister – he declared: "As for the future, it is inconceivable that even in peace time we should go down from the Golan. Whoever even thinks of leaving the Golan wantonly abandons the security of Israel."[189] Yet he agreed to withdraw. What was decisive here was not Rabin's military assessment, but his lack of any moral or ideological commitment to this ancient part of Israel, which his soldiers, in 1967, regained with their blood. In all probability, a Torah-oriented prime minister would be more steadfast, especially after twenty-five years of no war with Syria, a brutal military dictatorship whose signature on a peace treaty would not be worth the paper it was written on.

This is not to suggest that all religious Jews are "hawks" and that all secular Jews are "doves", to use the puerile language of contemporary discourse. But two facts need to be juxtaposed: (1) Israel has never had anything but secular prime ministers, and (2) most of the 220,000 Jews living beyond Israel's pre-1967 borders are either religious or traditional. Given that number of Jews, who moreover have family and friends and supporters in the rest of Israel as well as in the Diaspora, this country would surely be in a better position to withstand American pressure if it had, at the helm, a Jewish statesmen as defined in Chapter 7.

As we have seen, however, a Jewish statesman's effectiveness will depend largely on the structure of his government. A plural Executive is less capable of statesmanship, hence less able to resist foreign pressure, than a unitary Executive. And let us not forget the impotence of a parliament based on fixed party lists, with an electoral threshold more conducive to egotistical pluralism than patriotism.

Consider, too, the phenomenon of what I call "self-induced pressure". Judging from the statements and arms buildup of Israel's Arab adversaries – see the Appendix below – any candid observer would have to admit that the policy of "land for peace" is a deadly hoax. But once Israeli politicians committed themselves to this policy, they could hardly back out of it without confessing, as it were, that they had committed a blunder of the first magnitude, a blunder responsible for the murder of many Jews. Hence they became (and are still) trapped in their own rhetoric, the "rhetoric of peace", which may also be called the "politics of peace", for every politician, Left and Right, had to intone the mantra of "peace" lest he be discredited. This is especially true of left-wing parties since, as we have seen, the land-for-peace policy gains for its advocates the Arab vote. The peace charade had to go on, resulting in self-induced pressure.

And yet, mediocre men cannot remain comfortable in falsehood – and Israel has had no lack of mediocrity at the helm. Such men must somehow find a rationale for the irrational policy of land for peace. Some of its advocates will say, "We must not rule over Arabs; it is neither consistent with democracy nor with Judaism." The present writer has shown that Israel's governmental system of ruling Jews is neither consistent with democracy nor with Judaism! Besides, the choice confronting Israel is to rule over Arabs (benevolently) or to be ruled by Arabs (despotically). Also, those who say "We must not rule over Arabs" will also defend the policy of land for peace on paraMarxist grounds, again, that a prosperous New Middle East will relegate the Muslim-Jewish conflict to the dust heap of history. We have come full circle.

Let us see if we can break out of this circle in the next chapter.

Appendix

To fully appreciate the mendacity of the "peace process" and of those who foist this deadly charade on the public, two documents should be juxtaposed. First, consider the 1998 Fateh Constitution, bearing in mind that Fateh, the ruling faction of the PLO, controls and bankrolls the Palestinian Authority. There is not one iota of the Fateh Constitution that does not have the approval of PLO chief Yasser Arafat, Israel's "peace partner" so often dignified by President Bill Clinton. Below are nine of the Fateh Constitution's 27 paragraphs:

A. Principles

(1) Palestine is part of the Arab world, the Palestinians are part of the Arab nation and their struggle is part of the struggle of the Arab nation.

(2) The Palestinian struggle is an integral part of the worldwide struggle against Zionism, colonialism and international imperialism.

(3) The liberation of Palestine is a national duty demanding physical and spiritual assistance from the whole Arab nation.

(4) The Zionist movement is racist, colonialist and aggressive in its ideology, its goals, its organization and its methods.

(5) The foundation of Israel's existence in Palestine is the Zionist occupation, based on colonialism.

B. Goals

(6) The complete liberation of Palestine and the economic, political, military and cultural elimination of Zionism.

(7) Establishment of an independent, democratic state in all of Palestine with Jerusalem as its capital.

C. Method

(8) A revolutionary military struggle as the sole method of liberating Palestine.

(9) A military struggle is not a tactic but a strategy, and the military revolution of the Arab Palestinian nation is a decisive component in the struggle for the liberation and the removal of the Zionist entity; the struggle will not be complete until the Zionist state is destroyed and Palestine in its entirety will be liberated.

That these are not mere words intended for "domestic consumption", consider a second document. Thus, on December 10, 1996, the US House of Representatives "Task Force on International Terrorism and Unconventional Warfare" issued a detailed report which states, *inter alia*:

Approaching the end of 1996, the Middle East may well be on the verge of a major regional war. Numerous sources in the region report that the supreme leaders – both civilian and military – in most Arab states (including Egypt and Jordan), as well as in Iran and Pakistan, are convinced that the present vulnerability of Israel [resulting from the "peace process"] is so great that there is a unique opportunity to, at the very least, begin the process leading to the destruction of Israel. Toward this end, several Arab states, as well as Iran and Pakistan, have been engaged in a frantic military build-up and active preparation in the last few months...

[T]he PLO's preparations for an imminent war are evident. In Gaza, Arafat ordered the marked acceleration of the building of a personal bunker four stories deep. Moreover, the PLO is rapidly building, all over Gaza, a chain of command centers, ammunition and weapons-storage areas – all of them underground and well fortified to even withstand Israeli bombing and shelling. The PA's [Palestine Authority's] security forces are also accumulating large stockpiles of anti-tank and anti-aircraft weapons, including missiles, even though they are forbidden by the Oslo Accords.

Those who ignore the primacy of politics and religion in the Muslim-Jewish conflict, or, more generally, those who believe there is an economic or technological solution to the human problem, trivialize human nature. And inasmuch as they disdain human history, they call to mind Orwell's chilling phrase: "*A generation of the unteachable is hanging upon us like a necklace of corpses.*"

CHAPTER 9
Democratic Versus Martial Diplomacy: A Jewish Alternative

Magnanimity is not to befriend the enemy, but to spare them, and remain on your guard against them.

Ibn Hazm (994-1154)

Reconciliation with our enemies is only a desire of bettering our condition, a weariness of contest, and the fear of some disaster.

La Rochefoucauld

The four basic causes of Israel's disintegration are, again, (1) lack of Jewish statesmanship and purpose, (2) fragmented political institutions, (3) cultural incongruity, and (4) secular-religious discord that obstruct the development of a foreign policy appropriate to a Jewish commonwealth.

Foreign policy obviously entails diplomacy. Hindering an effective diplomacy is the cognitive dissonance associated with normless democracy.

In formulating and executing foreign policy, the Jewish statesman should have one question uppermost in mind: How to make Israel more united, more independent, more self-confident, more *Jewish*! I did not say more "secure". Israel suffers from a security syndrome rooted in the nineteenth-century Zionist movement's understandable reaction to anti-Semitism. Nor did I mention "peace". Every decent nation desires peace. But this means that peace is not a distinctive national goal. The mere fact that peace is ever on the lips of Israeli politicians is itself indicative of the lack of Jewish statesmanship and purpose.

Nor can we expect a Jewish foreign policy given a multiplicity of parties in the cabinet, i.e., a plural Executive. Israel's enemies at home and abroad will play one party against the other. The Arab issue is of material interest to the capitals of the democratic world, and it should never be forgotten that the nations of this world are more concerned about material interests than about justice.

As for the impact of secular-religious discord on Israel's foreign policy, this does indeed involve anti-Semitism, which secularists are a bit more likely to fear than religionists. The reason is this. Secular Jews, by definition, are more assimilated than religious Jews, hence are more inclined to imitate, or at least not irritate, the *Goyim*. Leftists in particular tend to be "internationalists"; they want Israel to be like the nations. This very much explains Mr. Peres's bizarre effort to make Israel a member of the Arab League.

Finally, Israel's democratic mentality yields a democratic diplomacy which, we will now see, cannot compete well with the martial diplomacy of its enemies.

Theoretical Analysis

Negotiation between democracies and dictatorships is bound to be rendered difficult by the basic differences in the political character of the two regimes.* Diplomacy is not an ideologically neutral affair. How and why states negotiate – their methods and objectives – depend mainly on their principles of government. The diplomacy of a government based on consent – on freedom of discussion, pluralism and compromise – will differ profoundly from the diplomacy of a government based on coercion, propaganda and conformity.

Sir Harold Nicholson, a theoretician and practitioner of diplomacy, makes a fundamental distinction between martial and democratic diplomacy.[190] Whereas martial diplomacy regards negotiation between adversary states as a form of warfare pursued by other means, democratic diplomacy – largely the product of commercial societies – regards negotiation between adversaries as a means of conciliation requiring mutual concessions leading to lasting agreement and peace.

The methods of martial diplomacy resemble a military campaign or a series of maneuvers the ultimate goal of which is victory over

---

* The reader should bear the following in mind. Although Israel is not an authentic democracy from the perspective of its political and judicial institutions, the *mentality* of its political leaders is indeed, democratic, and this is decisive for their conduct of negotiations.

the enemy, if not his complete destruction. The purpose of negotiation is to outflank your enemy, to weaken him by all manner of attacks. If the opponent is a democracy, attempts will be made to manipulate public opinion through the media, the object being to undermine popular support for the government's negotiating position. Efforts will also be made to divide the government itself by subtle appeals to political factions and opposition leaders. And of course there will be attempts to drive a wedge between the government and its allies. The principle is *divide and conquer.*

The tactics of martial diplomacy against democracies are also military in character. First of all there is the use of surprise – what Nicholson calls "sudden" or shock diplomacy. Its purpose is to demonstrate strength, to cause concern and confusion and thereby increase the opportunity for direct and indirect pressure. A recent example took place in Cairo in 1995 before the entire world. Appearing on television with Israeli, American, and Egyptian leaders and diplomats for the purpose of signing the second Israel-PLO agreement, Yasser Arafat suddenly refused to do so! This bold maneuver left Israel's Prime Minister Yitzhak Rabin with the choice of calling the televised spectacle off or making additional territorial concessions to the cunning terrorist. Rabin, lacking Arafat's nerves, yielded.

Another tactic of martial diplomacy is the use of indirect force to compel concessions. Syrian President Hafez al-Assad employs terrorist organizations such as Hizbullah to attack Israel's northern frontier as a "bargaining chip" on the Golan Heights negotiating table. (This also applies to the PLO and its collusion with Hamas to squeeze concessions from pliant Israeli governments.)

Then there is the extensive use of deception. Negotiating demands are couched in moralistic and democratic language such as "peace" and "self-determination". To spread the glad tidings of peace to the unwary, or to promote divisions in the ranks of the enemy, flattering interviews are granted to susceptible journalists and other opinion-makers. Statements are issued to promote goodwill and a sense of security before turning to more aggressive offensives, such as propaganda campaigns designed to alienate the enemy's allies. Some of these statements are so palpably mendacious as to create doubt as to their very mendacity or at least their malevolence.

While martial diplomacy attempts to disarm the adversary through guile and professions of peace, these attempts are punctuated by veiled or less-than-veiled threats of war. This use of cunning and intimidation by the martial school of diplomacy reflects the basic character of dictatorial regimes. Obviously, under such a system of negotiation, trust, fair-dealing and conciliation are not easy. A concession made or a treaty concluded is apt to be regarded not as a final settlement of a conflict, but evidence of weakness and retreat, an advantage which must soon be exploited in preparation of further advances and triumphs. Here martial diplomacy is aided by the fact that democracies, more than other kinds of regimes, ardently desire peace and, even in the absence of pressure, will make gratuitous concessions to the extent of taking "risks for peace". Indeed, the very principle of compromise intrinsic to democracies renders them more yielding than dictatorships. Knowing this, the leader of a military regime – and many civilian dictatorships are actually animated by military principles – will launch his diplomatic campaign from a negotiating position involving impossible demands from which he will hardly deviate. For example, Syrian dictator Assad insisted that Israel withdraw entirely from the Golan Heights *before* he would even consider signing a peace treaty!

What makes this demand even more outrageous is that not only did Israel capture the Golan Heights in a war of self-defense, but this once barren land was purchased in 1892 by Edmonde de Rothschild from nomadic Arabs for the purpose of settling the area with Jews. (The purchase has been confirmed by Turkish and French authorities and, in 1957, the deeds of purchase were deposited in the Land Office of the Government of Israel.) But if Assad's demand was outrageous, the willingness of Labor Party leaders to withdraw from the Golan Heights, and without even pressing Israel's purely legal claim to this most strategic territory, appears incomprehensible. An explanation of this extraordinary state of affairs will deepen our understanding of democratic and martial diplomacy.

Israel under left-wing governments represents the epitome or extremity of democratic diplomacy. The principal reason is this. Israel's left-wing elites have substituted democracy for Zionism and Judaism as the only legitimate and respectable basis for Israel's existence. As we have seen, they regard Israel not as "the state of the Jews" but as "the state of its *citizens*", almost 20 percent of whom are Arabs, without whose votes the Labor Party would become politically passé. This attitude is very much rooted in the anti-religious cosmopolitanism of Karl Marx. As a consequence, Israel's left-wing elites are devoid of Jewish national consciousness. Moreover, because of the increasing proportion of religious to non-religious Jews in Israel, Israeli leftists parade under the banner of a pluralistic, democratic society. This makes them or left-wing Israeli governments the easiest victims of martial diplomacy.

Calculating upon the divisions inherent in pluralistic societies, those guided by the martial school of diplomacy will seek to maneuver their opponent into negotiating with himself, a task rendered easier when the opponent lacks a strong sense of national pride and solidarity. Israel's most prominent internationalist illustrates the point. "We live in a world," said Peres in 1994, "where markets are more important than countries." Hence, in negotiating with Yasser Arafat over Israel's heartland, Judea and Samaria, Peres ignored Arafat's brazen violations of the Israel-PLO agreements, saying: "I don't believe we should judge the [peace] process by the performance of Yasser Arafat. We're not negotiating with Arafat. We're negotiating with ourselves..."(!)[191] The first remark suggests a Marxist-cum-bourgeois mode of thought. As for the second remark, the reader may draw his own conclusions.

Returning to our theoretical level of analysis, when negotiating with a democracy, the ruler of a dictatorship will try to force his opponent into piecemeal surrender or into a militarily indefensible position. The morality of martial diplomacy is quite simple: "What's mine is mine and what's yours is mine – or at least negotiable." In contrast, democratic diplomacy is based on the assumption that compromise with one's rival is generally more profitable than his total destruction. Negotiation is not merely a phase in a death-struggle, but an attempt to reach some durable and mutually satisfying agreement. The means used are not military tactics but the give and take of civilian or commercial intercourse. The problem is to find some middle point between two negotiating positions which, when discovered, will reconcile their conflicting interests. And to find that middle point, all that is required is goodwill, frank discussion and compromise.

Not only naïve journalists but even sophisticated politicians and political scientists often think that merely for adversaries to meet and talk to each other is a positive step toward peace, when, as history has shown, and as martial diplomacy intends, it may only be a lull before the storm.

Because democracies are based on discussion, the general tendency of democratic diplomacy is to overestimate the ability of reason to produce confidence and lasting agreement. This tendency of democratic diplomacy results in a number of errors when confronted by martial diplomacy.

First, there is the error of making gratuitous concessions, sometimes as gestures of goodwill. The hope is for reciprocity, hardly to be expected, however, from dictatorial regimes. As Henry Kissinger has written, anyone succeeding in the leadership struggles of such regimes "must be single minded, unemotional, dedicated, and, above all, motivated by enormous desire for power. [Nothing in the personal experience of dictators would lead them to accept gestures of goodwill at face value.] Suspiciousness is inherent in their domestic position. It is unlikely that their attitude toward the outside world is more benign than toward their own colleagues."[192] The inherent asymmetry between democratic and dictatorial regimes renders reciprocity dubious, and, in the case of Israel, virtually impossible. For a democracy to yield territory, something tangible and irreversible, for nothing more substantial than a dictator's written and revocable promise of peace, is a curious quid pro quo. Yet this defines the relation between Israel and the Palestine Authority, itself a military dictatorship. The latter, consisting of "former" terrorists (including murderers of Jews and Arabs alike), is being given control of most of Judea, Samaria, and Gaza in return for the suppression of Arab terrorism, even while this latest Arab despotism teaches Arab school children to hate Jews and to exalt suicide bombers!

The second error of democratic diplomacy is the prejudice that international conflict is caused primarily by lack of mutual understanding – the supposed root of mutual fear and suspicion. The assumption, so typical of the liberal democratic mind, is that men are by nature benevolent, and that through discussion they will discover that what they have in common is more important than their differences.

Third, guided by that liberal prejudice, the democratic school of diplomacy tends to minimize conflicting ways of life or ideologies. In his July 1996 address before a joint session of Congress, then Prime Minister Benjamin Netanyahu gratuitously denied any "clash of civilizations" between Israel and her Arab-Islamic neighbors. Such is the influence of democracy on the intellect that even political scientists tend to think that ideological conflicts can be overcome by "confidence building" measures, such as cultural exchange and economic relations. Given only mutual tolerance and material prosperity, war can be made a thing of the past. Such sentimental materialism is characteristic of bourgeois as well as socialist democracies preoccupied as they are with enjoyment of the present. Thus, when Shimon Peres said "We live in a world where markets are more important than countries," he was suggesting that national borders or wars fought over territory are things of the past. Forgotten is the high degree of commercial (and cultural) intercourse between France and Germany before the Franco-Prussian War. Also forgotten is that Russia and Germany were the greatest trading partners before the First and Second World Wars. (Incidentally, on January 1, 1900, the *New York Times*, the *London Times*, and *Le Monde* uniformly predicted that economic prosperity, made possible by scientific technology and democracy, would produce an era of universal peace.)

Unfortunately, history has little significance for democratic societies, whose politicians and diplomats are animated by election-oriented and short-term pragmatism. Hence Hasannin Heykal, former editor of Egypt's leading daily *Al-Ahram*, could say:

Israelis and Americans have always been at fault in approaching situations in what they believe to be a strictly pragmatic way. They have dealt only with what they could see, concentrating on the present to the almost total exclusion of the past. How often in talks with Rogers, Kissinger, and Sisco and others has Egypt heard Americans say, in effect, "We're not interested in raking over the past: Let's look at the situation as it is today."[193]

This NOW mentality renders democrats impatient for results, and dictators know how to exploit this impatience. They know that democratic leaders have a personal political interest in the appearance of successful negotiations. They can violate agreements confident that a democratic prime minister will be reluctant to admit any failure in his own diplomatic achievements. Indeed, instead of condemning such violations, democratic leaders may not only minimize, but sometimes defend them. (Notice how Israel's political leaders have ignored Arafat's repeated calls for a *jihad*, his complicity in Arab terrorism, his indoctrinating Arab children to hate Jews – to mention only a few of his violations of the Israel-PLO agreements.[194] Yet, while Arafat praised Arab suicide bombers as "holy martyrs", Israel's left-wing elites referred to their helpless Jewish victims as "sacrifices for peace".)

Last, and perhaps the most serious error and weakness of democratic diplomacy, is that it makes too sharp a distinction between peace and war, that is, it fails to take seriously the already noted fact that for martial diplomacy, peace is war pursued by other means. Stated another way, *to men of goodwill, unrelenting malevolence is incomprehensible.*

And yet, along with this dangerous prejudice, democratic diplomacy harbors the contrary prejudice that autocrats are temperamental types that must be handled with kid gloves. Dictators often foster this prejudice in order to discourage democratic statesmen and other opinion-makers from enlightening public opinion about the vicious nature, methods and objectives of dictatorial regimes. (Notice the silence of American and Israeli politicians regarding the atrocities committed by the Assad regime in Hama and in Lebanon.) *There is nothing dictators fear more than truth, which is why their media are government-controlled.*

The very character of dictatorships – centralized decision-making, control of public opinion, ruthlessness – gives them certain negotiating advantages which cannot be overcome unless democracies negotiate from a position of dauntless power; in which case these advantages, paradoxically, can be made to work for us rather than against us. Take the Machiavellian flexibility of totalitarian states. The most notorious example is the Hitler-Stalin Pact: one day mortal enemies, the next day brothers in blood. A more recent example was Anwar Sadat's shift from a pro-Soviet to a pro-American foreign policy, designed to terminate Washington's unofficial acceptance of Israel's control of the Sinai.

This extreme flexibility should teach us that dictators are not moral purists or doctrinaires. Whatever their ideological principles or long-range objectives – *and these should not be obscured or minimized* – they are quite capable of postponing them when unfavorable circumstances require. And precisely because they are dictators, they can do so with remarkable rapidity, depending on the force brought to bear upon them. Dictators respect force; it is the cornerstone of their regimes. But knowing how to negotiate with these professional students of power can shorten conflicts and sometimes even prevent them.

The Unspoken Price of Negotiating with Dictatorships

Political scientists fail to emphasize that *whenever a democracy and a dictatorship negotiate publicly as equals, the dictatorship gains enormously.* Such negotiation places these two types of regimes on the same moral level. This moral equivalence corrupts public opinion in the democratic world, a world already mired in the university-bred doctrine of moral relativism. Consider the case of Israel.

It may sound quixotic, but Israeli politicians – Left and Right, secular and religious – degrade Israel by seeking the recognition of Arab regimes whose media (especially Egypt's) vilify Jews and the Jewish State.[195] *To demand the cessation of this anti-Semitism as a precondition of negotiation would enhance Israel's honor, a crucial element given the overweening pride of Arab-Islamic culture.*

Instead, Israeli spokesmen are forever boasting that it is great progress to meet and shake hands with Arab negotiators, even though some are leaders and supporters of on-going Arab terrorism. Moreover, for Israelis to negotiate with their Arab adversaries is to convey the impression that Arab regimes are no less disposed to candor and peace than Israel, and that agreements reached with Arab autocrats will bind their successors despite the fact that the latter represent no one but their own cliques and have no scruples whatever about adhering to the agreements of their predecessors. On the other hand, for Israeli politicians to be candid about the bellicose and devious character of Arab regimes is to preclude negotiation. Arab rulers need not worry: *It is against the law in Israel to tell the truth about the militant nature of Islam, hence of Israel's Islamic enemies.* To do so is to impugn Israel's own Muslim citizens and expose oneself to the charge of racism – in Israel a felony. It matters not that these citizens have forever been exempt from military service for security reasons, indeed, that most *openly* supported Saddam Hussein in the Persian Gulf War despite his threat to incinerate Israel, including themselves.

Facts such as these demonstrate that the contradictions between democracy and Arab-Islamic culture are so many and so profound that negotiation between Israel and any Arab state will not enhance Israel's security, to say nothing of her dignity, *so long as such states remain dictatorships.* Israel's peace treaty with Jordan is no exception. For that piece of paper the left-wing government of Yitzhak Rabin yielded 330 sq. km. of land on which seven school children were subsequently murdered by a Jordanian. That land, moreover, can be shown to be Jewish land, even in terms of international law. Be this as it may, the Israel-Jordan treaty merely formalized the *de facto* political cooperation which has long been the policy of their respective governments vis-a-vis any threat from Syria and Iraq. Besides, not only does the treaty take no precedence over Jordan's commitment to the Arab League, but Amman remains the headquarters of Arab terrorist groups, and it remains a capital offense to sell property to Jews.

Contradictions between Israel and its Neighbors

The contradictions between Israel and its Arab-Islamic neighbors need to be examined from the perspectives of political philosophy and culture. What follows is a summary of those contradictions.

First of all, democracy, as we saw, is based on consent, pluralism and persuasion. This adorns democracy with a certain easy-goingness. Past grievances are readily swept aside and political opponents can be friends despite their differences. Differences are resolved by discussion and mutual concessions, and agreements are usually abiding. In contrast, Arab culture is based on the primacy of intimidation and even violence. Agreements between rival factions do not really terminate animosities, which is why such agreements are so short-lived.

Second, thanks to the biblical influence on the West, democracy is based on the primacy of the individual. This influence did not penetrate Arab-Islamic culture which is based on the primacy of the group – be it the village or the extended family. The individual Arab or Muslim has no identity outside the group; it is to the group that he owes his loyalty. This is one reason why internecine conflict has been endemic among Arabs throughout their history.

Third, freedom, including freedom of speech, is one of the two cardinal principles of democracy. This is not the case of Arab-Islamic culture, which is strictly authoritarian and whose media are government-controlled.

Fourth, unlike democracy, whose other cardinal principle is equality, Arab-Islamic culture is strictly hierarchical. Top-down leadership is a fundamental principle of Islamic theology.

Fifth, democracy, we saw, is generally regarded as a *process* – the "rules of the game" – by which various individuals pursue their private interests and have diverse "lifestyles". In contrast, Arab-Islamic culture binds everyone to the substantive values prescribed in the Koran.

Sixth, whereas democratic societies are preoccupied with the present (PEACE NOW), Arab-Islamic culture exists under the aspect of eternity colored by events of the past and dreams of the future. This is one reason why the concept of revenge for past injuries is a dominant motif of the Arab mind. (A local proverb tells about a Bedouin who took revenge after forty years and said, "I was hasty.") Given their loyalty to the group, they are religiously bound to wreak vengeance on those who have slighted the honor of any Muslim. (Israel's very existence – its ruling over Muslims – is deemed an insult to Islam, for Jews are supposed to be *dhimmis*.)

Seventh, whereas democracy is steeped in secularism, Arab-Islamic culture is rooted in religion. Even Arab leaders who are not devout Muslims identify with the basic goals of Islam. The radical separation of religion and politics found in democracy is foreign to Islamic regimes.

Eighth, it bears repeating that the peaceful tendencies and publicity found in democracy stand in striking contrast to the militancy and dissimulation characteristic of Islam. Here let me quote the late Professor Yehoshafat Harkabi, a former head of Israeli Military Intelligence, a confidant of Shimon Peres and an advocate of a Palestinian state.

Writing when one did not have to fear the charge of racism, Harkabi refers to Islam as a "combatant", "expansionist" and "authoritarian" creed. He admits that "the idea of *jihad* is fundamental in Islam," in consequence of which "hatred", "hostility" and "conflict" are endemic to Arab culture.[196] Moreover, he quotes Arab sociologist Dr. Sonia Hamady, who writes: "The Arabs usually look for external causes of their frustrations; they prefer to put the blame on some scapegoats [like Israel or America, the "Great Satan"]. Similarly, as a rule, their aggressive feelings are not turned inward but directed towards others."[197] Furthermore, and of crucial significance, Harkabi acknowledges that "the use of falsehood", "distortions of the truth" and "misleading slogans" are typical of Arab political life. Harkabi goes so far as to suggest that mendacity is "second nature" to Arabs, and that one may rightly regard "falsehood as the expression of [Arab] national character". Again he quotes Hamady: "Lying," she writes, "is a widespread habit among Arabs, and they have a low idea of truth."[198]

The only rational conclusion one can draw from Harkabi's own analysis of Arab-Islamic culture is that *to expect genuine and abiding peace between Israel and her autocratic neighbors is not only a piece of folly but an insult to Islam.*

Finally, it must be reiterated that in dealing with Arab-Islamic regimes, Israel confronts not merely personal and transient dictatorships, but autocracies which, despite their differences, are part of a world civilization. Islamic civilization is animated by memories of former greatness and aspirations of future glory. This makes Muslims exceedingly proud, so much so that even an illiterate Arab, living in squalor and filth, feels naturally superior to the Jews, as English aristocrats would in olden days, feel toward Cockneys.

This analysis leads to a rather grim conclusion: All other things being equal, democratic diplomacy cannot compete well with martial and Islamic diplomacy. Of course, not all other things are equal, especially in the case of Israel. For Israel's Arab adversaries have the strategically and economically motivated support of the world's only superpower, the United States, a democracy committed to Israel's withdrawal to her pre-1967 "Auschwitz" lines. This suggests that democratic diplomacy in the Middle East is a destructive and, for Israel, a self-destructive, fraud. It also suggests that Israel's government had better learn a very different kind of diplomacy. But first, other aspects of Israeli diplomacy must be clarified.

The Irrational Dimensions of Israeli Diplomacy

Israeli diplomacy is fraught not only with many of the misconceptions of democratic diplomacy, but with fear of anti-Semitism and a compulsive adulation of democracy. This makes Israeli politicians across the political spectrum all the more obsequious when negotiating with other nations, especially democracies, *a fortiori* the United States. Many Jews, even among the religious, harbor the fear that if Israel's government were to act distinctively Jewish, it would irritate the nations and arouse their hostility. This is the real reason why they identify Judaism as democratic. Yet such antipathy toward Israel already exists despite the diluted Jewish character of various Israeli governments.

Recall the refusal of democratic Europe to allow the United States to use NATO landing fields to re-supply Israel during the Yom Kippur War. Recall, too, Washington's recognition of the PLO in 1974, even though its Covenant calls for Israel's destruction. To this add the UN General Assembly's 1975 resolution (recently rescinded) equating Zionism with racism, and the Security Council's frequent condemnations of Israel with or without the compliance of the United States. Perhaps most grotesque was the Security Council's precipitous condemnation of Israel for the opening of a new tourist door in the 2,000 year-old Hasmonean Tunnel which, apart from being Jewish and in no proximity to the Temple Mount – also Jewish – provided a pretext for the (previously planned) outbreak of Arab violence in September 1996.

Evident here is the old hydra of anti-Semitism, which secular Zionists thought they could escape by establishing a secular democratic state in the Land of Israel. True, the Nazi Holocaust discredited overt anti-Semitism, but as one writer has pointed out: "The Palestinian grievance has enabled latent anti-Semitism to be channeled discreetly into 'respectable' criticism of Israel – which was shrewdly distinguished from world Jewry."[199]

Contrary to prevailing notions, it is by no means obvious that Israel's situation would be worse under a government headed by "stiff-necked" Jews, to recall their biblical appellation. Oddly enough, modern Israel is also called stiff-necked – "intransigent" is the current label – even though her government has been pathetically yielding. Whatever one may think of its treaty with Egypt, for a Likud government to have surrendered the Sinai with its Israel-developed oil fields, strategic air bases and $15 billion infrastructure without being able to retain the small Jewish settlement of Yamit – to have sacrificed all this for what Anwar Sadat scornfully called a "piece of paper," is hardly a mark of intransigence. What shall we then say of a Labor Government that was anxious to surrender Judea and Samaria to the head of a mere terrorist organization? Benjamin Netanyahu once said that yielding control of Judea and Samaria – the inevitable consequence of the Israel-PLO agreements – would lead either to war or to Israel's annihilation. Yet he felt committed to implementing those agreements despite their having been repeatedly violated by the PLO. Remarkable manifestations of Israeli intransigence.

What incites the nations – unknown to themselves – is not Jewish intransigence so much as Jewish infirmity. To tell the nations, as did Menachem Begin and Yitzhak Shamir – reputed hawks – that "everything is negotiable," is to confess that nothing is sacred, indeed, that Israel can be bought. But then to enter the diplomatic arena and drag out negotiations when you have compromised your nation's honor must surely arouse not only contempt but irritation and hostility. Such self-abasement alienates friends, who admire strength, and incites enemies, who exploit weakness.

For Israel's government to cultivate a reputation for intransigence concerning its people's heritage and patrimony, and to be worthy of that reputation, need not arouse the enmity of democratic nations (certainly not if such intransigence is modulated with a measure of biblical wisdom). Consider: when the Government of France behaves distinctively French – cynical and condescending, some would say – no other nation is agitated by the fact. Nor is any foreign office disturbed by that which has long distinguished England's foreign policy: righteous hypocrisy. Again, in Saudi Arabia, when a Muslim's hands are cut off for theft, not a word of opprobrium will be heard from the American State Department. Cutting off the hands of thieves is recognized and accepted as the Saudi way.

One reason underlying such sublime indifference is this: Governments are expected to conform, more or less, to the tradition of their people. This is an obvious precondition of international understanding, of stable relations among independent and sovereign states. When any government fails to act authentically, that is, in accordance with its nation's basic beliefs and values – which the diplomatic corps of other nations study assiduously – this causes confusion and sometimes hostility in foreign capitals.

Contrast the government of Israel. Far from acting distinctively Jewish, it emulates democratic America. Only let it deviate one iota from the indiscriminate egalitarianism and unrestrained libertarianism of contemporary America than the wrath of Washington and of the news media is heaped upon the supposed-to-be Jewish state.

In Israel, the dogma of contemporary democracy – more immune to questioning than any religion – has produced the most ludicrous anomalies. Indiscriminate egalitarianism compels the supposed-to-be Jewish State of Israel to allow its Jew-hating Arab citizens to vote, such that now there are various Arabs in the Knesset – really PLO surrogates – who taunt Jews by speaking Arabic in that "Jewish" assembly. As for Israel's unrestrained libertarianism, the only place in the Middle East where the PLO has its own press is in Jerusalem. In fact, during the Persian Gulf War, a Likud Government allowed Israel's Arab press to publish pro-Iraqi and anti-American propaganda while Israel was being bombed by Scud missiles!

By exalting contemporary democracy, Israeli politicians and intellectuals have established, in the minds of American policy-makers and opinion-makers, a set of expectations which no democratic people would tolerate of their own government. Conversely, having from the outset failed to act authentically as a government whose policies and pronouncements are preeminently Jewish, Israel's leaders have laid the foundation for their country's humiliation and for much of the world's antagonism toward the so-called Jewish state.

To compound its folly, by emulating a democracy that pays lip-service to Christianity, Israel's government has unwittingly conditioned gentiles to expect the Jews to abide by the most unassertive or self-effacing Christian precepts: turn the other cheek, love your enemies, resist not evil. And to the extent that this government has adhered to these benign and apolitical precepts – unpracticed by any gentile nation – it has not only forsaken Judaism, it has also repressed the sense of outrage among Jews whose loved ones have been victims of Arab terrorists. Animated by an unmanly humanism, the government of Israel has been dehumanizing its own people. Even their instinct of self-preservation has been sacrificed on the altar of the secular democratic state.

Contrary to the expectations of Jewish politicians and intellectuals who, out of fear of anti-Semitism, mindlessly portray Israel as a democracy so as it endow it (and themselves) with legitimacy and respectability, it is precisely this lack of Jewish national authenticity – this adulation of decayed democratic values – that underlies international contempt for Israel.

Contrast Mr. Netanyahu's above mentioned address to the American Congress. When he spoke as a proud Jew he was applauded; when he declared that Jerusalem would ever remain Israel's undivided capital, he received a standing ovation. On the other hand, Mr. Netanyahu punctuated his address with the trite incantation of "democracy" – obviously to arouse sympathetic support from his audience vis-a-vis nasty Arab autocracies. This obsequiousness, so typical of Israeli politicians, is a *strategic error. For the more Israel is perceived as a democracy, the more it is expected to make concessions to Arab autocracies.*

A Jewish Alternative

To avoid the perils of democratic diplomacy, Israel's Prime Minister – but now let us say Israel's Jewish statesman or future President – will have to emphasize Israel's *raison d'être* as a *Jewish* state. This brings us back to a basic theme of this book. Israel's Jewish statesman will have to show that in Israel, the basic principles of democracy, freedom and equality, are derived from the Torah's conception of man's creation in the image of God. He will have to teach people here and abroad that *only from this conception of man can the unfettered freedom and indiscriminate equality of contemporary democracy derive ethical and rational constraints*. But this means that our Jewish statesman will have assimilated democracy to Judaism, not Judaism to democracy. It means that *democracy, however important, will not be the paramount principle of an authentic Jewish commonwealth*.

Strange as it may seem, Mr. Netanyahu unwittingly approached this position when he proudly declared: "*I am a Jew first and an Israeli second.*" And further: "*Israel is the state of the Jews, and not of its citizens.*"

If Israel were simply a state of its citizens it would be a conventional, pluralistic democracy. Any Israeli citizen, regardless of his religion or ethnicity, could then become – and by law he can become – Israel's President or Prime Minister. But how can this be if Israel is supposed to be a Jewish state? Obviously there is a basic tension between a Jewish state and a normless democratic one. So long as Israel's political leaders genuflect to democracy, they will the more readily succumb to the pitfalls of democratic diplomacy. Let me suggest how a future President of Israel can avoid such pitfalls and serve the cause of his country as well as of democracy, indeed, of mankind.

A Primer on Diplomacy

The question before us is this: How can democracies in general, and Israel in particular, negotiate effectively with dictatorships?

A study of autocratic regimes reveals that their methods of negotiating with democracies differ significantly with those they employ with other autocracies. Contrary to appearances, authoritarian politicians are not necessarily less politicians. They are, however, less amenable to compromise with democratic politicians, and precisely because they usually don't have to! Their "stall-and-rage" technique of dealing with democracies works well for them; it does not work well when dealing with fellow dictators, and is seldom used for that reason. Hence it is not only the character of dictatorships, but the cunning of dictators that produces the kind of negotiating tactics we always seem to experience; his tactics depend not only on his system of government, but on the tendencies of our own.

Bearing this in mind, suppose we were to write a handbook for democratic negotiators based on the current and simplistic assumption that dictators have an intrinsic antipathy to compromise. The manual might say something like this:

The nature of dictatorships makes it inherently difficult for rulers of such regimes to compromise. The autocrat himself is little used to political compromise and tends to view it, as he does all domestic opposition, as a challenge to his authority, perhaps to his very life. This personal hostility to compromise or meaningful give-and-take is reinforced by the inherent instability and vulnerability of all regimes resting on coercion rather than consent. The democratic statesman must take this into account, tempering his expectations and standing ready to take the first step, going the extra mile, and perhaps giving more than he gets.

Suppose, however, our manual for democratic negotiators were based on very different but generally more realistic assumptions about dictators. It might read like this:

The nature of autocratic political systems makes it inherently easy for rulers of such regimes to compromise. Successful autocrats are above all things calculating, possessed of a shrewd grasp of facts operative in the negotiating arena. They have no difficulty envisioning the kind of settlement that would be equitable or that would at least temporarily terminate disputes with other powers; and ruling over a society resting on coercion rather than consent, they have no difficulty in imposing such a settlement should they deem it necessary.

Negotiating problems arise exactly because the autocrat understands the propensities of democratic statesmen and the political system they represent. He knows that to the democratic mind compromise is often seen as a good in itself; that completed negotiations are frequently taken as successful negotiations serving to secure personal or domestic political advantage. The autocrat also knows that democratic politicians are impatient for results, especially during election years, in consequence of which he need only bide his time, remain obdurate, or threaten to break off negotiations in order to elicit gratuitous concessions intended to hasten and conclude the negotiating process.

He is particularly well attuned to the fact that democratic governments are greatly influenced by public opinion, that opinion is usually divided on all issues, and that opinions in democracies can be manipulated to his own advantage. He is also aware of the democratic antipathy to violence and therefore sees the threat of conflict working in his favor. If his democratic counterparts regard him as irrational or ideologically disinclined to compromise, or if they view his system of government as one that by its nature is unable to make significant concessions, he will know this too and take manifest advantage of it.

The democratic statesman must in no way encourage the dictator on any of these points or negotiations will degenerate into a tedious, counterproductive exercise in making unilateral concessions. He must know from the very outset what he wants out of the negotiations. He must let the dictator take the first step toward compromise and under no circumstances be willing to give more than he gets or give the slightest indication that this might be the case. It must never be forgotten that the autocrat will view all efforts to be "reasonable" – as this term is understood by democrats – as confirmation of his own understanding of democratic negotiating weakness, and he will press his claims unremittingly thereafter.

Would Israel's use of this type of diplomacy be effective with Arab-Islamic dictatorships? Perhaps, if fortified not only with military strength, but also with a due measure of Jewish wisdom and Jewish national pride – qualities respected by Muslims. Muslims are contemptuous of the democratic West, its materialism and nihilism. This materialism and nihilism have invaded Israel. To this extent Israel poses a threat to Islamic civilization. In other words, Israel, perceived as a secular democratic state, threatens the political-religious power structure of the Arab-Islamic world.

Arab despots have learned, however, that they can accomplish their objectives vis-a-vis Israel without war, that is, by means of diplomacy, and precisely because Israel's political and intellectual elites are secular democrats more or less devoid of Jewish wisdom and Jewish national pride. Only effete and bourgeois democrats would barter away their people's 3,500 year-old patrimony for peace, let alone for an ill-founded one. Only by virtue of his calculated understanding of such men would Anwar Sadat find the boldness to come to Jerusalem and demand Israel's complete withdrawal to its pre-1967 borders. Only to such men would he have the temerity to declare: "To speak frankly, our land [sic] does not yield to bargaining... We cannot accept any attempt to take away...one inch of it nor can we accept the principle of debating or bargaining over it."[200]

It will be objected that if Israel does not compromise with its Arab-Islamic neighbors – and this means the open-ended policy of "land for peace" – war is inevitable. There are basic flaws in this objection, and quite apart from the fact that "the history of man is," as Churchill said, "the history of war." First, Israel's elimination from the Middle East is a demonstrable goal of various Arab-Islamic regimes, whose spearhead is Arafat's PLO. Second, trading Jewish land for "peace" can only facilitate that goal. Third, and most important, why the ruler of any state ventures on the path of war depends on his perception of the enemy, and not only of the enemy's military power. If Israel were perceived as a truly Jewish as opposed to, a secular democratic state, this would certainly affect the attitudes and calculations of Arab regimes. Nothing thus far done or tried by any Israeli government – and all, to repeat, have been dominated by secularists – has altered the authoritarian and militant character of these regimes. Another approach is needed.

Taking the Initiative

A study by Harvard Professor Samuel P. Huntington indicates that between 1974 and 1990 more than thirty countries in Europe, Latin America, and East Asia shifted from authoritarian to democratic systems of government. The regimes that moved to or toward democracy, says Huntington, fall into three groups: "one party systems, military regimes, and personal dictatorships".[201] Conspicuously absent from his study is any reference to the Arab-Islamic world, whose twenty-one regimes, unlike those mentioned by Huntington, may be classified as "theopolitical" dictatorships.

Clearly, Islamdom is less susceptible to democratization than those studied by Huntington. Recall Algeria's experiment with multiparty national elections in 1992. The winning party consisted of Muslim fundamentalists! The capitals of the democratic world breathed a sigh of relief when the victors were promptly crushed by the junta hitherto in power.

The failure of Algeria's experiment in "democracy" suggests that, given the religiosity of the Muslim masses, successful democratization of any Arab-Islamic regime would have to conform to significant aspects of Islamic law, the *shari'ah*. It would have to be non-secular and moderately hierarchical. Consistent therewith, Islamic law embodies the concept of *shura* or "consultation". This concept could justify a religious constitutional system of government. In addition to Islamic courts, the constitution could prescribe an independent, unitary executive having the power to propose legislation, but which legislation would require the approval of a popularly elected assembly.[202] There are Islamic groups pressing for such reform.[203] Israel should indirectly encourage such groups by adopting for itself a Jewish constitution such as that proposed in the next chapter.

Now let us return to the theme of the Jewish statesman, and let us suppose that Israel has a unitary Executive, a President nominated by the Senate and elected by the people. The office itself will have greater dignity than that of a prime minister because our President will be the head of state and symbolize its unity and grandeur. In this age of the media – I almost said mediacracy – the President's primary task is to enlighten public opinion, and this must be done via the media. Accordingly, the President should remind the media that a "peace process" led to the Nazi conquest of democratic Czechoslovakia; that democratic England played "honest broker" in that peace process; that the same peace process, endorsed by the United States, led to the bloodiest war in human history including the Holocaust; that even diplomatic relations and commercial ties between the US and Nazi Germany and Imperial Japan did not prevent World War II; that it is *only because democracy was imposed on those dictatorships that peace now prevails between them and America*. The President should emphasize these facts at home and abroad.

He should convey a still more significant set of facts. He should remind men and women that the US did not recognize the Soviet Union until the Administration of Franklin D. Roosevelt – sixteen years after the Bolshevik Revolution. Four American presidents, including Woodrow Wilson, refused to recognize Communist Russia on the grounds that it was animated by a militant ideology and ruled by men whose signatures to international agreements were worthless.[204] Nor did recognition of the Soviet Union diminish its hostile designs on democratic America. (Recall General Ivri's remark regarding the sham peace between Egypt and Israel.) What our President should stress, however – again at home and abroad – is this: *It was no "peace process" but only the disintegration of the Soviet dictatorship and its taking the path of democracy that terminated the Cold War between the US and the USSR.* Only now can there be peace between Russia and America.

Similarly, Israel's Government should boldly affirm that no "peace process" but only the non-secular democratization of Arab-Islamic dictatorships can provide a basis for peace in the Middle

East. This truth should be made a *declaratory* principle of Israel's foreign policy. Consistent with this principle and with our "handbook" on diplomacy, Israel should not negotiate with any Arab-Islamic regime until it shows clear signs of democratic reform. One sign is the introduction of a market economy; another is a reduction of military expenditures. A market economy would decentralize the corporate power of Arab states and raise the living standards of their poverty-stricken people. Israel can hasten the non-secular democratization of the Middle East by adopting a Jewish democratic constitution and by privatizing, in a democratic way, its own economy. (Of this, more in a moment.)

Hindering democratization as well as peace in the Middle East is the concept of *jihad*, a basic Islamic tenet. And here I mean *political* as opposed to *personal* (or self-purifying) *jihad*. The former, understood as Holy War, has been the historical spearhead of Islam. This bellicose dimension of *jihad* is what energizes the nationalism of the Middle East's Sunni-Arab-Muslim majority of which the PLO is a part. This militant concept, which also animates the Shiites, is directed against the non-Arab as well as against the non-Muslim minorities of the Middle East, be they Kurds, Maronites, Copts, Berbers, etc. Hence the non-secular democratization of Muslim regimes, to be conducive to peace, especially with Israel, would necessitate the renunciation of the political dimension of *jihad* (hereafter understood as such). Insisting on its disavowal should be a cornerstone of Israel's Middle East foreign policy.

"This is impossible," it will be said. Perhaps. But much may be gained by admonishing Islamic dictatorships (via the media) that the concept of *jihad* contradicts the United Nations Charter and the Universal Declaration of Human Rights which prescribes "tolerance and friendship among all nations, racial, or religious groups".

Of course, to propose the "impossible", that Islamic renunciation of *jihad* should be the *sine qua non* for the establishment of diplomatic relations between Israel and any Muslim regime, is to go beyond politics. But as we have seen, the Arab-Jewish conflict transcends politics. Politics, defined as the art of the possible, has utterly failed to overcome that conflict. Needed, therefore, is the art of the "impossible" – of the *metapolitical*. And why not? Can politics explain the survival of the Jewish people? Was not Israel's rebirth "impossible"? Was not Israel's victory in the Six Day War "impossible"? Conversely, was not the virtual defeat of the Israel Defense Forces by stone-throwing Arab women and children "impossible"? Does it not defy logic and human experience – hence, does it not fall within the realm of the impossible – that a government of Israel should surrender its heartland to a gang of Arab terrorists and then arm 40,000 trained Jew-killers to secure peace in Judea, Samaria, and Gaza?

On the other hand, to reject as impossible a policy that insists on renunciation of *jihad* is tacitly to admit that peace is impossible and that Israel's participation in the "peace process" is an exercise in self-immolation. Unless *jihad* is honestly renounced, the true state of relations between Israel and any Muslim regime can only be, at best, the cease-fire mentioned by General Ivri, along with its sinister implications for the future. Israel should thus make *ideological* as well as political demands on its Islamic adversaries. The disavowal of *jihad* should be a precondition of any future peace process, for it is the litmus test of whether a Muslim regime is sincerely committed to peace with Israel.

I have no intention of disparaging Islam by singling out its militancy. In this century of triumphant secularism, barbarism armed by science has slaughtered more people than barbarism animated by religion. More people have been killed in the name of Karl Marx than in the name of Allah. The secular West, with all its fine phrases, can hardly preach morality to the Muslim East. Indeed, I contend that Israel will have to take seriously the Arab spokesman mentioned in the last chapter, who clearly suggest that nothing so arouses Islamic hostility than the "propagandists of secularism" prevalent among Israel's political and intellectual elites.

Israel will thus have to put its own house in order before making demands on others. Israel's Arab-Islamic neighbors have some justification for resenting a predominantly secular state in their midst, one that harbors aspects of decadence evident in contemporary America. *Secularism is a threat to Israel's neighbors, hence an incitement to Arab violence.*

Given a Government animated by Jewish pride and wisdom, it need not be provocative to make ideological as well as political demands on Arab-Islamic dictatorships. Israel would only be giving expression to some basic principles of Western civilization. Admittedly, there are certain flaws in the West which will not be found in Islamic civilization. I have in mind the disintegration of the family engendered by the secularism and moral relativism rampant in contemporary democracies.

Jews, more than others, should appreciate this fact, given the centrality of the family in Jewish history. Incidentally, Article 16 of the Universal Declaration of Human Rights proclaims: "The family is the natural and fundamental group unit of society and is entitled to protection by society and the State." The State thus has an obligation to secure what Article 29 terms the "just requirements of morality." Of course, these are pious platitudes. Nevertheless, they are infinitely more meaningful than the platitudinous peace process.

On the other hand, Israel, if true to itself, can initiate a new and genuine peace process because Judaism, properly understood, is the connecting link between East and West. By virtue of its unique synthesis of ethnic particularism and universalism, Judaism can simultaneously justify ethnicity and emphasize the one doctrine that can prevent ethnic conflict and bloodshed, again, the Seven Noahide Laws of Universal Morality, i.e., ethical monotheism. Moreover, because of its long-established affinity to science, Judaism can endow science – which has served despots as well as democrats – with ethical and conceptual constraints lacking in the West and urgently needed in the East whose stockpiling of weapons of mass destruction is not for purposes of deterrence.

A Homestead Act

It goes without saying that foreign policy cannot be severed from domestic policy. To alleviate poverty, facilitate the absorption of immigrants, and set an example to its neighbors in the Middle East,

Israel needs to engage in socio-economic renewal on a massive scale. Whatever areas of Judea and Samaria remain under Israel's control, the Government should pass a homestead act such as that enacted by the Congress of the United States in 1862. Small plots of land should be sold at low prices to Jews both in Israel and abroad with the proviso that they settle on the land, say for a period of six years. This would diminish the dangerous population density of Israel's large cities and, at the same time, encourage Jewish immigration to Israel. Model cities should be built, facilitated by foreign investment on terms favorable to investors. At the same time, the Government should formulate an economic policy that would encourage tens of thousands of Israelis living abroad to return to their homeland.[205]

In Chapter 4 we proposed a democratization of political power by making members of parliament accountable to the people in district or constituency elections. This democratization of political power must be paralleled by a democratization or diffusion of economic power. The Government along with the Histadrut owns or controls almost 90% of the country's resources and assets. The worker in this statist economy is merely a wage-earner, as he would be under a capitalist economy. Whether he derives from his labor a "living wage" depends primarily on others. He can no more influence the decisions of the economic elite than of the political elite.

To diffuse economic power, "privatization" is not enough. The predominant method of privatization today is first to select state-owned enterprises and then seek out existing investors, whether foreign or domestic, who can afford to purchase assets or shares of these enterprises.[206] However, most people have little or no savings to invest. Privatization automatically channels most of the future ownership of divested state-owned enterprises to economically privileged groups or foreign interests. Privatization may thus replace one set of elites with another.

Unless privatization is properly orchestrated, most people will still have to rely for their subsistence exclusively on wages and on other people's income redistributed by government taxation. It so happens, however, that technological advances and the mobility of capital in an increasingly globalized economy can play havoc not only with wage-earners, but with corporations and even nations.

"Labor saving" technology together with lower wage markets (for example, Asia) are now combining to diminish the relative economic value of human labor vis-a-vis capital or the means of production. Thinking computers will increasingly replace people and millions of jobs in many industries and offices. More people will find it difficult to gain an adequate income from wages or welfare. (One consequence of this trend, that is, of a "wage-based" economy, is that more and more mothers will have to find work outside the home to make ends meet.)

Simply raising the worker's wages is often not only impractical, but can be unjust as well. It may force a company to downsize, relocate its operations, or go out of business. To prevent the worsening gap between the rich and the poor, Israel will need to reform some of its basic economic institutions (e.g. capital credit, banking, and taxation) to promote economic empowerment and sustainable growth through broad-based capital ownership.

To this end, Israel should, to some extent adopt, in carefully orchestrated stages, Employee Stock Ownership Plans (ESOPs). By democratizing access to capital credit (to be repaid by *future* savings and company profits), workers could acquire ownership of income-producing assets in new, or expanding, or in the divestiture of state-owned or Histadrut-owned enterprises and land. Property income could then supplement income from wages. Also, faster rates of (non-inflationary) growth linked to expanded capital ownership would serve to overcome the resistance of Histadrut workers who fear that privatization will result in loss of job security, subsidized wages, and other benefits with little or nothing in exchange.

The object here is to fashion a Jewish economy that avoids the greed inherent in capitalism as well as the egalitarian envy manifested in socialism. Such an economy would appeal to Islamic modernists seeking to introduce a modicum of political and economic democracy in the corporate states of the Middle East.

Conclusion

The more Israel becomes *Jewish*, the more Arabs west of the Jordan will recognize the futility of their present war of attrition. They will see that their high birthrate will not overwhelm the Jews. Indeed, the more Jewish Israel becomes, the more Arabs west of the Jordan will emigrate to other countries. *Israel's problem is not to change any Arab-Islamic state. Israel's problem is to change itself.* Only if Israel undergoes a renaissance in Hebraic civilization will her Government be able to negotiate wisely and effectively with Arab-Islamic regimes. Such a renaissance might even hasten their transformation into peace-loving states. We offer in the next chapter the constitutional means of hastening that renaissance.

CHAPTER 10
A Jewish Democratic Constitution for Israel

Ask not if a thing is possible; ask only if it is necessary.
            The Alter of Kelm

A people may be unprepared for good institutions, but to kindle a desire for them is a necessary part of the preparation.
            John Stuart Mill
            Representative Government

The reader who has come with me thus far will understand that so profound are the causes of Israel's disintegration that no superficial reform will prevent this country's approaching collapse. Israel's entire system of government requires a drastic overhaul, and this can only be accomplished by means of a constitution, one based on Jewish principles. Only such a constitution can (1) provide the mechanism for Jewish statesmanship and the pursuit of Jewish national purpose, (2) overcome the divisive forces of Israel's existing political and judicial institutions, (3) ameliorate secular-religious discord, and (4) enable statesmen to deal effectively with the Arab demographic problem. Finally, only such a constitution can transcend the conflict between normless democracy and Judaism.

Objections to a Constitution Answered

Here let us anticipate and answer various objections to a constitution. First, it may be said that so imminent are the external dangers confronting Israel that to place a constitution on the public agenda would be a mischievous distraction. (That may very well be what is needed to derail the suicidal "peace process"!) But having shown that Israel's political institutions are very much responsible for her internal tensions, and seeing that these tensions enfeeble the country and magnify its external dangers, it logically follows that Israel will not overcome her precarious situation without fundamentally changing her system of government.

Nevertheless, it may be objected that Israel is so faction-ridden that a constitution, however desirable, is utterly impractical. For example, religionists may oppose a constitution, saying, "We have a constitution, the Torah." Such critics should be reminded of the religious parties that supported a draft constitution in 1949. (See Chapter 4.) Besides, religious people can hardly reject the constitution proposed in this chapter before they have studied it and questioned its author.

Still, if they persist in the facile remark, "We have a constitution, the Torah," it may then be said that few rabbinical leaders today are qualified to exercise the powers of government prescribed in the Torah, and fewer still command the recognition of most Jews in Israel. With all due respect to Israel's learned rabbis, how many fulfill the extraordinary qualifications of the Sanhedrin? The judges of that supreme body, according to the fourteenth book of Maimonides' *Mishneh Torah*, must not only be experts in the vast corpus of Jewish law, but well versed in many branches of science, including astronomy, mathematics, logic, anatomy, and medicine. All honor to Israel's halakhic authorities, but would investing them with the *legislative* as well as judicial powers of the Sanhedrin be acceptable to the majority of Israel's Jewish population – as it must be according to Jewish law? Moreover, on what prominent Jew would the people of Israel be willing to bestow the executive power and life-long tenure of a king? And where are the prophets who, like those of old, admonished kings who strayed from the high standards of the Torah?

Another objection, more likely from secularists, is that Israel has a constitution, or at least an "emerging constitution," in the form of its "Basic Laws". These so-called Basic Laws, however, have neither rhyme nor reason, having been enacted intermittently by the Knesset during the past four decades. A word about these laws is in order.

Israel's first Basic Law: The Knesset, was enacted in 1958, ten years after the founding of the State. Until then, there was no fixed term or tenure for the Knesset. Each session determined its own longevity! Basic Law: Israel Lands (1960), provides that ownership of state lands may not be sold or transferred to non-state owners. Since only about five percent of the land in Israel is private property (contrary to the rabbinical principle that "there is no Jew who does not own four cubits in the Land of Israel"), and since the law defines "lands" as including "houses, buildings, and everything that is permanently connected to the land", Jews are little more than tenants of the State. Indeed, judging from the manner in which various Israeli governments have surrendered Jewish land to Jordan and the PLO, it would seem that the Land of Israel belongs not to the people of Israel but to their rulers. So much for Basic Law: Israel Lands.

Some other Basic Laws and their initial dates are: The President of the State (1964); The Government (1968); The State Economy (1975); The Army (1976); Jerusalem, Capital of Israel (1980); The Judiciary (1984); The State Comptroller (1988). The important thing to emphasize about these ad hoc laws is that they have failed to imbue citizens with national unity or with any sense of national purpose.

Consider Basic Law: The Government, which stipulates that "The Government is competent to do in the name of the State, subject to any law, any act whose doing is not enjoined by law upon another authority." Hence the Government can declare war, make treaties, and change the exchange rate without ever consulting the Knesset!

Treaties are not "submitted to the Senate" or "laid before Parliament" for ratification, as is the case, respectively, in the United States and Great Britain. In Israel, treaties are merely announced by the Government and published within twenty days. The Knesset may pass a resolution in favor of a treaty, but this has no legal significance. True, a Knesset vote of no confidence could topple the Government, but this sort of thing has never happened.

Consider Basic Law: Human Dignity and Freedom, previously mentioned. Enacted in March 1992, this law seeks to "anchor in a basic law the values of the State of Israel as a Jewish and democratic state." This law has not only failed to resolve the fundamental normative contradiction that exists between the

Jewish state and contemporary democratic doctrine, but such is the law's vagueness that it has endowed the Supreme Court with enormous power contrary to the idea of a Jewish and democratic state! (Of this, more in a moment.)

Most remarkable about Israel's so-called Basic Laws is the ease with which they may be amended. No special majority protects them. Their continuity depends on absolute majorities of at least 61 members in Israel's 120-member Knesset. However, since the Government has the support of at least 61 MKs, the Government can change a Basic Law whenever it wishes! This is precisely what happened in 1999 when Prime Minister Ehud Barak had Basic Law: The Government, amended so as to enlarge his cabinet in order to provide additional posts for his Labor Party and coalition supporters.

Under this flawed system, Basic Laws are enacted by ordinary legislative procedures. Some have been sponsored by the Government, others by private members. Basic Law: The State Economy, was sent to the Knesset's Finance Committee, not the Law Committee!

What, then, is "basic" about a Basic Law? Not easy to say. Basic Laws are said to be "entrenched" because their amendment or repeal requires an absolute Knesset majority. But if the Knesset wishes, entrenchment can apply to ordinary laws. Lacking is any clear definition as to whether, when, and how Basic Laws are to be placed above ordinary legislation. Also lacking is any provision for their codification. No more need be said of Israel's "emerging constitution", except that it is not conducive to the rule of law, something Israel lacks.

The Rule of Law

The rule of law is a fundamental Jewish principle, as the Torah makes abundantly clear. But what do we mean by the "rule of law", and why is a constitution, in almost all cases, a precondition of the rule of law? At the simplest level, the rule of law renders those who make the laws subservient to the laws, like all other members of the community. But inasmuch as the laws may be changed by the legislature, the rule of law will be as mutable as the membership or majority of the law-making assembly.

In Israel, what is glibly referred to as the rule of law is little more than a facade for the rule of the Supreme Court. For example, until the mid-1980s, only someone directly harmed by a government decision could petition the Court against that decision. Since then, the law has not changed, but the Court has created a new norm: Anyone can petition the Court on anything at all, and no issue is beyond its purview. During the past thirteen years, the Supreme Court has declared Knesset Members unfit to be ministers or deputy ministers, revoked an Israel Prize, reversed attorney-generals' decisions not to indict various individuals, and struck down the closure of a street on the Sabbath – all with no backing in explicit written law, but merely on the grounds that these actions were "unreasonable". Prior to December 1998, the Court found wholesale draft deferments for yeshiva students reasonable. In that month, however, it found such deferments unreasonable, even though no new law had been passed. But if the law is no more than what a handful of judges consider "reasonable" at a given moment, why should it command anyone's respect and obedience? And if law is supposed to be made by Israel's elected representatives, why should an unelected judge's ideas of reasonableness have any more power than those, for instance, of rabbis who contend that draft deferments for yeshiva students help preserve Israel's Jewish character?[207] This is not to advocate unqualified draft deferments for such students, but surely the rule of law must be something more meaningful than the dictates of the Supreme Court.

Let us first consider the problem from a philosophical perspective. As I have elsewhere written:

The rule of law requires that the future shall resemble the past, that there be some presumption in favor of past arrangements. The rule of law thus exemplifies the moral order of the universe. For it belongs to the goodness of the universe that what men have struggled for and created in the past should have some relevance for the future. In these terms are we to understand why extraordinary majorities are required to amend [a] constitution... [Such a constitution] bears witness to a very simple truth of which statesmen would do well to remind their countrymen, namely, that the living do not possess a monopoly of wisdom. It is a vulgar conceit which violates the wisdom as well as the goodness of the universe to think that the present, by virtue of fortuitous and evanescent majorities, should possess the power and the right to nullify the works of the past. On the other hand, the same reason and goodness of the universe...denies to the past the power and the right to stifle the creative energies of the present. Somewhere Whitehead has said that the pure conservative is fighting against the essence of the universe – and so he is, as might also be said of the pure liberal. The one desires permanence, the other change, while the universe requires both. It is the same with the rule of law, of rational development.[208]

Descending to the political level, the rule of law requires that there be a *fundamental* law, one superior to ordinary legislation. By a fundamental law I mean one that prescribes the paramount principles of political rule. By "paramount principles" I mean (1) those which are not *ordinarily* subject to question, and (2) those which fix the general course and character of public life. By "political rule" I mean (1) those institutional functions and electoral procedures which determine the relationship between government and the governed, and (2) the ends for which these institutions and electoral procedures were established. Accordingly, the fundamental law (1) enunciates rights and duties, (2) empowers institutions and provides standards for the conduct of public affairs, (3) facilitates rational inquiry and cooperative effort for the solution of public problems and satisfaction of public needs, and (4) enables men to rise above necessity, anticipate future problems, introduce ordered change, and, ultimately, enhance and elevate the quality of individual and community life.[209]

Obviously, a fundamental law to be such, must not only be superior to ordinary legislation; it must also be relatively permanent or not subject to frequent change. Supreme Court President Aaron Barak thinks otherwise. Referring to Israel's Basic Laws, he has said they must be easily amendable to allow them to properly reflect the nation's "changing values". If so, what need is there of a Supreme Court or of judges with a virtual life tenure? Indeed, the primary reason why judges, generally speaking, are not made subject to popular election is precisely to secure their detachment from the shifting winds of public opinion. The rule of law requires such detachment.

Justice Barak's attitude stands in striking contrast to that of James Madison, the father of the American Constitution. Madison warned against frequent change even of ordinary legislation, let alone a nation's fundamental law or constitution. Writing in *Federalist 63*, Madison points out that "a continual change even of good measures is inconsistent with every rule of prudence and every prospect of success." Why? Because "it forfeits the respect and confidence of other nations, and all the advantages of *national character*." I emphasize "national character" for that is the one thing lacking or now being undermined in Israel and which a constitution must correct.

Madison warns that, "It will be of little avail to the people, that the laws are made by men of their own choice, if the laws...undergo such incessant changes that no man, who knows what the law is today, can guess what it will be tomorrow. Law is defined to be a rule of action; but how can that be a rule, which is little known and less fixed." How much more so does Madison's reasoning apply to a nation's basic or fundamental laws, embodied in its constitution?

There is a more subtle matter alluded to earlier. Madison points out that the effect of mutable laws is the advantage it gives to clever "insiders" over the uninformed mass of the people. (Which insiders, while intoning such soporifics as "democracy," "freedom", and "human dignity", can impose their will on the people.) "This," says Madison, "is a state of things in which it may be said with some truth that the laws are made for the *few*, not for the *many*."

Our philosophic statesman concludes:

But the most deplorable effect of all is the diminution of attachment and reverence which steals into the hearts of the people, towards a political system which betrays [by easy and frequent changes in the law] so many marks of infirmity... No government, any more than an individual, will long be respected without being truly respectable; nor be truly respectable, without possessing a certain portion of order and stability.

Now, having said that the rule of law requires (1) that there be a fundamental law, (2) that this law be superior to ordinary legislation, and (3) that it be relatively permanent, the question arises, "Who is to be the final interpreter of this fundamental law?" For the law to be fundamental, there must be a single, final arbiter, and that can only be the Supreme Court. For the judges of the Court, by virtue of their legal education and relative insulation from politics, are best qualified and situated to serve as guardians of the fundamental law – say a constitution. However, no decision of the Supreme Court should be deemed final from a *Torah* point of view. To repeat what was said in Chapter 7: "...any legislation [or ruling] enacted by a court but not accepted by the majority of the public is no law" (*Avoda Zara* 2:8). The constitution proposed below adheres to this Jewish principle.

The Design of Constitutions

After studying various constitutions, the present writer has reached the conclusion that a constitution should be written primarily for people, not for lawyers. Hence it should be brief, like the American Constitution. The powers of the Legislative, Executive, and Judicial branches should be balanced as well as limited. The constitution should have a Bill of Rights, but not a long one, else it will multiply litigation. This means that the constitution should be designed as an *educational* as well as a legal document. Thus crafted, the constitution's prescribed system of government will be more comprehensible to laymen and thus facilitate government by the consent of the governed, a principle of Jewish law. Surely if the people are to influence the laws affecting their lives, they must have adequate knowledge of the general structure and purposes of the three mentioned branches of government, something a concise constitution can provide for secular and religious students alike. Such a constitution, more clearly and coherently than Israel's uncertain, uncoordinated, and intermittent Basic Laws, can delineate and interrelate the powers of government, define the basic rights and duties of citizens, prescribe criteria by which to remove corrupt public officials, and thereby promote public morality and the rule of law.

To be sure, no constitution – not even the Torah – can guarantee honest government and ensure its efficient operation. Nevertheless, a well-designed constitution can increase the *probability* of obtaining such a government. It can therefore facilitate the development of consistent, comprehensive, and resolute national policies and thus contribute to national unity and security as well as national dignity and prosperity.

Every sensible and unbiased Jew, whether religious or not, will support such a constitution, provided he is fairly confident that it will help remedy the manifest flaws of Israel's existing form of government, while safeguarding his personal, civil, economic, and religious rights. No well-informed and civic minded Jew can be happy with a parliamentary system which makes Israel the only one of seventy-five reputed democracies that lacks constituency elections! Surely he would prefer to vote for an individual candidate familiar and accountable to him, rather than vote for an obscure, self-perpetuating oligarchy, i.e., some party list that gives politicians safe seats and enables them to ignore Jewish public opinion with impunity. Who can be content with a parliamentary system whose electoral threshold spawns political parties like weeds, fills the Knesset with party-hopping job seekers, fosters egotism and venality, fragments and paralyzes the Government, sullies public life and undermines any sense of national purpose? True, a constitution cannot of itself make men virtuous, but it can mitigate rather than magnify their vices.

The present writer has no illusions about the tremendous obstacles that the adoption of a constitution needs to overcome, especially a Jewish one: entrenched interests, intellectual complacency, bigotry, downright ignorance, and preoccupation with the "peace process". Prudence therefore prompts me to urge, as a practical preliminary measure, the immediate reform of Israel's parliamentary electoral system. The adoption of multi-district elections, using either the "Personalized" Proportional

Representation or the Preferential Vote system discussed in Chapter 5, would mitigate the basic causes of Israel's disintegration. Making Knesset members accountable to the people in constituency elections and diminishing the number of parties in that assembly by means of a 5% threshold would augment the Knesset's power and dignity. The Knesset could then (1) streamline the cabinet, (2) require an extraordinary Knesset majority for ratification of any treaty or agreement with foreign powers, (3) reform the judiciary as hitherto recommended, (4) remove the parliamentary immunity of seditious MKs, (5) require the Attorney General to enforce the law prohibiting any party that negates the Jewish character of the State, (6) revise the loyalty provision of the Citizenship Law as recommended in Chapter 4, and (7) establish a high-toned constitutional committee representative of Israeli society to draft a constitution for the Jewish commonwealth.

The importance of a newly constituted Knesset cannot be exaggerated. Paradoxical as it may seem, *nothing so weakens this country as the absence of a Legislature independent of the Executive, one whose members are directly accountable to the voters (and not simply to a party).* Precisely because a prime minister may lack the courage to resist foreign pressure, an independent legislature is necessary to compensate for his frailty either by the threat of decisive opposition to his foreign policy, or, conversely, *by rallying to his support to neutralize intimidation from abroad.*

We have shown that, such is the impotence of the Knesset vis-a-vis the cabinet on the one hand, and such is the enormous and unchecked power of the Supreme Court on the other, that Israel, despite periodic multiparty elections may well be described as an ersatz oligarchy. Indeed, Israel has the worst of two worlds. Her people not only live under an alternating oligarchy, but the oligarchy is dignified and thereby fortified by the veneer of democracy, which renders the people of Israel all the more powerless. Moreover, because Israel is perceived as a democracy, her Government is expected by the democratic world to make gratuitous concessions to Arab despots, indeed, to take "risks for peace" which no democratic government would dare ask of its people. Israel's form of government is a disaster. The one measure, more than any other, that can *begin* the process of political salvation is this: curtail the pernicious power of the parties by making Knesset members accountable to the people in constituency elections. In other words: POWER TO THE PEOPLE!

Of course I am speaking of the *Jewish* people. It goes without saying that Israel's Arab inhabitants do not feel part of the Jewish people. But what is more, they understandably resent living in a Jewish state, one ruled by a Jewish majority. Allow me a brief digression.

Arab resentment was shockingly evident in a 1994 symposium held by the Dayan Institute of Tel Aviv University. Participating in that conference were prominent Arab citizens who spanned the entire spectrum of political opinion, from those who were members of the Labor Party to those who were undisguised supporters of the PLO. Without an exception, these Arabs declared that even if a Palestinian state were created, that would be insufficient because a million Arabs in Israel would still be living under "foreign" domination. The claim of the Arabs was that, if the Jews truly wanted peace, they would have to change the name of the state so as to reflect the entire population rather than merely the Jewish majority. The state would have to become a bi-national one with a new flag and a new national anthem. This is not all.

Inasmuch as the Arab participants in that Tel Aviv University conference also insisted on the enactment of an Arab "law of return" to admit all Arabs who fled from the land as well as their descendants – the number might be inflated to exceed four million! It should be obvious to any candid observer that the participants of this conference have nothing less in view than Israel's disappearance in an Arab-Islamic sea. The statements of various Arab Knesset members cited in Chapter 4 make this even more transparent.

The moment of truth is approaching, and the Jews of Israel had better look to their own cultural and national self-preservation. This will ultimately require a Constitution whose Legislative, Executive, and Judicial institutions are distinctively Jewish. Those who exercise the powers of those institutions must of necessity be Jews, be they religious or not. At stake here is not only the Jewish people's cultural and national self-preservation but *distributive justice*. Distributive justice is giving to each his due: giving equal things to equals and unequal things to unequals in proportion to their inequality, i.e. in proportion to their merit or contribution to the common good. Hence it is simply unjust to give equal *political* rights to those who work and fight for Israel's welfare and to those dedicated to Israel's demise.

Accordingly, the present writer proposes a four-branch system of government in which only Jews are eligible to vote for, and be members of, the Legislative, Executive, and Judicial branches, while the fourth branch, to be described below, will be open to Jews and non-Jews alike.

General Structure and Principles of a Jewish Constitution[210]

A Presidential-Parliamentary System

Given Israel's precarious situation in the Middle East, unity in the Executive branch is utterly essential, and for reasons delineated in Chapter 7. A President whose cabinet shares his convictions will best serve this purpose.

The Parliament should be bicameral. While the function of law-making will be assigned to the upper branch, the "Senate", the function of administrative scrutiny will be assigned to the lower branch, the "House of Representatives". To anticipate objections to a second branch of Parliament without law-making power, let us compare it with the existing Knesset.

Although the Knesset, in theory, has absolute power, in practice it is little more than a rubber-stamp for the cabinet. It does not legislate so much as affirm legislation initiated by the coalition of party leaders heading the cabinet ministries. Subservient to the cabinet, the Knesset is incapable of exercising the important function of administrative overview – *which is why corruption in government is so widespread in Israel.* Second, whereas members of the Knesset are utterly dependent on their parties, members of the proposed House of Representatives will be accountable to their constituents. Representatives will have a base of independent power, while constituents will have their own representatives. Since Representatives will be excluded from the cabinet, they will not be deterred from scrutinizing the bureaucracy to see whether the laws are being faithfully and efficiently administered. This will minimize corruption.

A Draft Constitution

A. The Preamble

[It would be perverse and ignominious that the People who gave mankind ethical monotheism should omit reference to God in the Preamble of its Constitution when God is mentioned in various constitutions of the democratic world. Hence the following is suggested.]

We the People of Israel, grateful to God for preserving us as a Nation and for returning us to the Land of our Fathers, mindful of our sacred responsibility to Mankind as the Torah-bearing Nation, dedicated to Truth, Justice, and Peace, do solemnly establish this Constitution. Accordingly, nothing in this Constitution is to be construed as derogating from the Wisdom of our Prophets and Sages. To the contrary, this Constitution is intended to preserve the Jewish heritage and to hasten the day when Israel will present the example of a Nation in which Freedom dwells with Righteousness, Equality with Excellence, Wealth with Beauty, and the here and now with Love of the Eternal.

B. Institutions of Government

[Inasmuch as Judaism is a nationality, indeed, a 3,500 year-old culture, to preserve the integrity and continuity of this culture, only Jews, be they religious or not, are eligible to vote for, or be members of, the Senatorial, Executive, and Judicial branches of Government.]

The Senate

(1) The Senate shall be composed of seventy-two members having a six-year tenure. One-third will be chosen every second year.

(2) To be eligible for membership in the Senate, a person must have knowledge of the Hebrew Bible, Jewish history and customs. This knowledge must be certified by secular and/or religious institutions of learning prescribed by law.

(3) The "Personalized" Proportional Representation system (see Chapter 5) will be used to constitute the Senate. The country will be divided into forty-eight districts. The district boundaries will be determined by a non-partisan committee prescribed by law and presided over by a former member of the Supreme Court. The forty-eight districts will be based on single-member plurality rule. Those parties which did not receive in the single-member districts the seat share proportional to their nationwide vote share will receive the remaining twenty-four Senate seats.

(4) The electoral threshold shall be prescribed by law, but shall not be less than five percent.

(5) A majority of the members of the Senate may, by a petition addressed to the President, request the President to decline to sign and promulgate as a law any Bill (other than those affecting defense and appropriations) on the ground that it contains a provision of such national importance that the will of the people thereon ought to be ascertained.

(6) No treaty or agreement with any foreign power or entity shall become law prior to thirty days after its submission to the Senate. One-third of the Senate's membership can prevent any treaty or agreement with a foreign power from becoming law immediately, by setting it aside until the next senatorial election. Such a pending bill comes into effect only if the new Senate, too, adopts it without changes after the election.

(7) The Senate shall have the power to declare war, provide for the common defense, and make all laws which shall be necessary and proper to promote the welfare and dignity of the Jewish Commonwealth.

(8) No Senator may change his party affiliation during his term in office.

The House of Representatives

(1) The House of Representatives shall consist of seventy-two members having a tenure of four years. One-half shall be chosen every two years.

(2) The "Personalized" Proportional Representation system will be used to constitute the House. The districts used for electing Representatives shall be the same as that for Senators, as will the number of single-member plurality districts as well as the number of compensatory seats for parties which did not receive, in the single-member districts, the seat share proportional to their nationwide vote.

(3) The electoral threshold for Representatives shall be the same as that for Senators.

(4) Excepting classified security matters, the House will inspect the State administration, including the ministries, the army, and every institution or enterprise in which a State authority participates, whether managerially or financially. Inspection shall include accountancy, legality, and appropriateness of the practices examined.

(5) The House will conduct public hearings, investigate public complaints regarding the State administration, and suggest measures to remedy any administrative shortcomings and abuses. [The House's investigatory powers render it a formidable body, as would be appreciated by those familiar with the power wielded by any investigating committee of the American Congress.]

(6) The House may recommend legislation to the Senate, which the Senate may simply reject or amend as it sees fit. But if such recommendations are enacted into law, their juridical authority will be derived from the action of the Senate.

(7) No Representative may change his party affiliation during his tenure in office.

The President

(1) The executive power shall be vested in a President. The President shall hold office for four years, and, together with a Vice-President chosen for the same term, shall be chosen as follows:
  a. Forty days prior to the prescribed date for national elections, the Senate shall convene to nominate at least two presidential candidates. Any group of 20 or more Senators may nominate a presidential (and vice-presidential) candidate, but no Senator may nominate more than one presidential and vice-presidential candidate.
  b. The names of the presidential candidates (and their respective vice-presidential candidates) shall be placed on a national ballot. The candidate receiving a majority of the votes cast shall be President. If no candidate receives a majority, the two receiving the highest number of votes shall compete in a run-off election.
  c. An incumbent President will be automatically eligible for re-election (if he so desires), in which case the Senate will nominate two additional presidential candidates.

(2) To retain the services of a wise and experienced President, he will be eligible for re-election for three successive terms after his initial election to the Presidency.

(3) The President shall recommend legislation to the Senate, have the power, with the consent of the Senate, to make treaties, be commander-in-chief of the Israel Defense Forces, and be responsible for the administration of the laws.

(4) The President will have a suspensive veto over Bills submitted by the Senate, which veto may be overridden by a majority plus one vote of a Senate plenum.

(5) The President shall nominate the members of his Cabinet. The names shall be submitted to the Senate for confirmation by a majority plus one vote of the plenum.

(6) The President shall nominate the Justices of the Supreme Court. The names shall be submitted to the Senate for confirmation by a majority plus one vote of the plenum.

(7) The President will be subject to impeachment for malfeasance of office by a two-thirds vote of a Senate plenum.
(8) The Vice-President shall preside over the Senate and vote only in the event of a tie.

The Judiciary

(1) The judicial power shall be vested in a nine-member Supreme Court and in such inferior courts which the Senate may from time to time establish.
(2) The membership of the Supreme Court will include three professorial and three rabbinical experts in Jewish law, all of whom, however, must be knowledgeable of secular law. Two of the remaining three members will be attorneys certified by the Israel Bar Association. The remaining member will be a former Attorney General, or, if one is not available, a former chairman of the Knesset Law Committee.
(3) The Supreme Court shall be the final interpreter of the Constitution, except as otherwise provided by this Constitution. However, any law nullified by the Court will be submitted to a popular referendum.
(4) Among the diverse systems of law operative in Israel, Jewish law shall be "first among equals" in every case where an Israeli statute is ambiguous or uncertain, except only where the Israeli statute explicitly differs from Jewish law. [This conforms to the Foundations of Law Act of 1980, which provided: "Where a Court finds that a legal issue requiring decision cannot be resolved by reference to legislation or judicial precedent, or by analogy, it shall reach its decision in the light of the principles of freedom, justice, equity, and peace of the Jewish heritage." The term "heritage" will be construed to include Jewish law.]
(5) Questions of personal status (e.g. marriage, divorce, and conversion) shall be decided solely by Rabbinical Courts.

Amendments

Amendments to the Constitution shall require the approval of two-thirds of a Senate plenum followed by a referendum requiring a three-fifths vote for confirmation by those eligible to vote for members of the Senate.

Other Constitutional Provisions

(1) All elected officials and civil servants shall duly affirm Israel's *paramount* governing principle as a *Jewish* state.[211]
(2) Any party that negates the Jewish character of the State will be excluded from participation in any national or local election and will also be subject to the penalties of the law.
(3) No person holding office under this Constitution shall, during his tenure, be eligible for any other public office. Nor shall he be a member of, or receive any emolument from, any profit-making enterprise, or appoint any personnel employed therein.
(4) Election campaigns shall be confined to thirty days and be financed solely by public funds. Per capita expenditures for such campaigns will not exceed that of other democracies. Any expenditure that exceeds the statutory limitations will not be financed by subsequent legislative appropriations.
(5) No person shall vote in any national election unless he has been a resident of Israel for one year.
(6) Hebrew shall be the only official language of the State.

A Constitutional Bill of Rights

(1) The Land of Israel, of which the State is only the custodian, belongs exclusively and eternally to the Jewish People. Hence, except for public purposes defined by law, the State shall foster private Jewish ownership and development of the Land of Israel.
(2) *Force majeure* aside, no land under Israel's sovereignty may be surrendered to any foreign power or entity.
(3) No law of the Senate, and no decision of the Supreme Court, shall be promulgated without due respect for the abiding beliefs and prevailing practices of the Jewish People.
(4) The right of workers to strike is inviolable, except to the extent that it deprives the community of its right to essential services.

(5) No Israeli national or citizen living abroad shall be denied the right to vote in elections for which he is qualified.

(6) All residents of Israel will be guaranteed freedom of religion and freedom of speech and press. All residents of Israel shall have the right to establish their own religious and educational institutions, provided these are consistent with loyalty to the Jewish State.

(7) No resident of Israel shall be compelled in any criminal case to be a witness against himself, nor be deprived of life, liberty, or due process of law.

(8) In all criminal prosecutions the accused shall enjoy the right to counsel, to a speedy and public trial, to be informed of the accusation for which he is been charged; to be confronted by witnesses against him; to have compulsory process for obtaining witnesses in his favor, and to have the assistance of counsel for his defense.

(9) The right of all residents of Israel to be secure in their persons, houses, papers, and effects, against unreasonable searches and seizures, shall not be violated.

(10) The enumeration in this Constitution of certain rights shall not be construed to deny or disparage others retained by the Jewish People or affirmed by the Torah respecting Jews and non-Jews.

Conclusions

The above constitutional provisions are tentative and by no means complete. The modes of constituting the various branches of government will have to be further elaborated, as will their respective powers and procedures. Nevertheless, this proposed Constitution would: (1) enhance Israel's dignity; (2) facilitate the wise formulation and execution of national policies; (3) elevate the moral and intellectual character of Israeli politics; (4) enable the Government to negotiate more effectively with foreign powers; and (5) promote Jewish unity and Jewish national pride.

In short, the proposed Constitution would counter the basic causes of Israel's disintegration and thus prevent this country's collapse.

EPILOGUE

This Epilogue will convey a yet deeper level of understanding of why the State of Israel is disintegrating, and *must*, if Israel, itself eternal, is to achieve its complete redemption as a Torah nation. Allow me to quote at length from Rabbi Matis Weinberg, whose, *FrameWorks* (*Exodus*), is a masterpiece of Torah philosophy interfaced with extraordinary secular erudition:[212]

Every *ge'ula* [redemption] begins as an "appointment" [*pacode*], as if with a future that can be grasped and defined. Every *ge'ula* moves on to *dis*appointment, when the presumptions are exposed and the spurious beliefs are debunked. The simplistic nationalism that fueled the early messianism in Egypt, the emotional quest for roots and significance that drove the young Moshe to identify with the enslaved children of Yisrael – these cannot drive true *ge'ula*. [Recall Moshe's initial failure in Exodus 2:11-14, 5:22-23.] But the disappointment comes only of the appointment itself! If not for *pacode* [appointment] there would be only apathy, an endless grinding on of slavery... *Pacode* catalyzes the search for the real thing, for a *ge'ula* that can stand. *Shemot* [Exodus] reveals the real thing...

Ge'ula is never the product of nationalism or messianism. It is the product of Covenant, of Brit, the commitment to the building of the world and the perfection of Creation [by the establishment of a Torah nation]. There alone lies the significance that begins to glow when all the veneer has peeled away from the wishful and childish ideologies of the early *pacode* [appointment]...

The first *ge'ula*, the first *pacode* in Egypt, is the model for the future – not only for freedom from Babylon, but for freedom from Edom [the Christian world] and Yishma'el as well. In each *ge'ula* there is that first shock of recognition, followed by despair – a despair that gives way to the freedom of reality, the recognition of truth.

So hopeless will be that period of the final *go'el*, the time called "the birthpangs of the Mashiah"... that there were great teachers in Israel who said: "Let him come, but let me not [live to] witness it..."

Yisrael stands now, once again, near the close of exile – and the pattern reasserts itself. Once again, the last awful years of foreign subjugation and atrocities seem to end in an impressive declaration or two [i.e., the UN Resolution of November 29, 1947 and Israel's Declaration of

Independence of May 14, 1948], and the future appears bright. The rebuilding of the land, and finally of Yerushalyim herself, proceeds apace. But the potential redemption then loses its way. It becomes entangled in bloodshed, pettiness, political scheming, and moral decay. The bright dreams lose their shine, and the children of Israel begin, once again, to "despair of the *ge'ula*".

Conception is complete. But the embryonic *ge'ula* still needs to grow beyond its childish ideologies [political and even religious Zionism, socialism, and democracy], the national dreams now being debunked one by one.

There never really was any way to exchange the Covenant for mere love of the soil. There never really was any way to satisfy the Jewish yearning for significance with puerile nineteenth-century nationalism. There never really was a way to infuse with an indigenous culture a society deprived of its roots. There never really was an way to excuse the Jewish claim of uniqueness without Sinai...

Yet those ideologies are the rightful progeny of a new *pecida*. Many people today are painfully hurt to find that they have thrown in their lot and their lives with the wrong dreamers...

The lovers of the soil have turned to foreign workers and industrial investments. The original builders of *Eretz Yisrael* now view Jewish settlers in Judea and Samaria as unenlightened embarrassments. Those who would once have given their right arm for an exclusive "Hebrew" culture watch CNN and Eurovision... "Economic Zionism" [or "Post-Zionism"] now espouses a sanitized dream: a grand vision a children of Israel who have achieved at last a standard of living comparable with that of the United States.

All this is how it must be – the crunch has come, the dreams have dissolved, and the real choices need to be made. We must either choose the kind of bare and awkward truth to which *ge'ula* must lead, or we must accept the maudlin emptiness suggested recently by an honest Israel publicist who looks straight into the reality that others refuse to acknowledge:

"Most of the world's Jews, led by the US, will disappear among the non-Jewish populations... The State of Israel will become a state of its citizens, enlightened...open, its borders merely lines on a map. Israelis of Jewish origin will marry Arabs, Arabs will marry them, both sons of the land...whose inhabitants will live not in the past but in their own lives."

Events now conspire to force us to confront the essence of Jewish identity, unclouded by silliness. We either unabashedly confirm the commitments of Yisrael, or we must accept an honorable oblivion.

Yet in reality there is only one choice and eventually it must be confirmed. We are sustained still by... a covenant that will not die, and by a history that will not leave us alone. But there can be nothing counterfeit in *ge'ula*, and that is why it takes so long. It has taken us a very long time to run out of ideologies, both religious and secular. There are still some myths that must run their course, do their damage, and expose their sham.

The process has begun, and gestation proceeds beneath the surface...

"*'Would I bring to the labor room and then not deliver!?' says the Lord.*"
        (Isaiah 66:9)

ENDNOTES

[1] Eighteenth-century scholars saw in the American Constitution principles rooted in the Torah. See Abraham I. Katsh, *The Biblical Heritage of American Democracy* (New York: KTAV Publishing House, Inc., 1977), ch. 2. See also Paul Eidelberg, *The Philosophy of the American Constitution: A Reinterpretation of the Intentions of the Founding Fathers* (New York: Free Press, 1968; reprinted in 1986 by the University Press of America), chs. 7 and 8.

[2] See Paul Eidelberg, *Demophrenia: Israel and the Malaise of Democracy* (Lafayette, LA: Prescott Press, 1994), p. 43.

[3] See Mordechai Nisan, *Minorities in the Middle East* (Jefferson, NC: McFarland & Co., 1991), pp. 7-11.

[4] For a refutation of the German bible critics, see Paul Eidelberg, *Judaic Man: Toward a Reconstruction of Western Civilization* (Middletown, NJ: Caslon Co., 1996), pp. xviii-xx, 163-178.

[5] David Ben-Gurion, *Memoirs* (New York: World Publishing Co., 1970), pp. 18-19: "Of course, speaking personally, I believe that theology reverses the true sequence of events. To me it is clear that God was 'created' in the image of man as the latter's explanation to himself of the mystery of his own earthly presence."

[6] See Paul Eidelberg, *On the Silence of the [American] Declaration of Independence* (Amherst, MA: University of Massachusets Press, 1976).

[7] See *Peretz v. Kfar Shmaryahu Local Council* (1962), 16 P.D. 2101.

[8] Leo Strauss, *Liberalism Ancient and Modern* (New York: Basic Books, 1968), p. 228.

[9] Ibid., p. 229. It should be noted that the term Zionism is derived from Zion, one of the most sacred words in the dictionary of authentic Judaism. Zion is the dwelling place of God's glory. It is the Sanctuary of the Torah, the Holy City which surrounds it, the Holy Land of which Jerusalem is the eternal capital. From Zion, from Jerusalem, the word of God – the Truth – shall come forth.

[10] Sir Herbert Samuel, an English Jew who became the first civilian high commissioner of Palestine, declared that the idea of a Jewish State "is not contained in the Balfour Declaration", which he helped to frame. Cited in Henry Cattan, *Palestine and International Law* (London: Longman, 1973), p. 56. Cattan's anti-Jewish bias – he called for Israel's dismantling – does not negate his legal conclusions.

[11] Cited in ibid., p. 58.

[12] Ibid., p. 67.

[13] Ibid., p. 75. Others have written, "Although the General Assembly may make recommendations both to Members of the United Nations and the Security Council, it should be kept in mind that recommendations have no obligatory character... ", ibid., p. 73.

[14] In Chapter 12 of *The Prince*, Machiavelli cleverly indicates that "arms", i.e., force, is the ultimate foundation of law. Therein is the modern origin of legal positivism or, as it is also called, legal realism.

[15] Distracted and debilitated by inevitable Arab obstructionism and violence, the fledgling and economically impoverished Jewish state could hardly have absorbed the 700,000 Jews who immigrated to Israel from the Arab world between 1948 and 1951.

[16] See Eidelberg, *Philosophy of the American Constitution*, Appendix 2.

[17] Alfred North Whitehead, *Science and Philosophy* (New York: Philosophical Library, 1948), p. 75.

[18] Writing in the *New York Post*, Oct. 17, 1999, David Bar-Ilan, who served as policy and communications director in the Government of Benjamin Netanyahu, warns: "today the only regimes that officially and openly promote and propagate anti-Semitism are not in Europe but in the Middle East. In Syria, Defense Minister Mustafa Tlass prides himself on a book he wrote about how Jews use the blood of Christian children in Passover matzahs. Hitler's *Mein Kampf* and the anti-Semitic Czarist forgery, *The Protocols of the Elders of Zion* are the best sellers there, as they are in the rest of the Arab world. In Egypt's [government-controlled] press, Jews are caricatured the way they were in Hitler's *Der Stürmer*: as slimy, hook-nosed, greedy, malevolent monsters whose blood-drenched tentacles control the world's power centers. And all the sickening anti-Semitic canards – from Holocaust denial to equating Jews with Nazis and charging Israeli scientists with spreading AIDS among Arabs – are featured regularly in the mainstream press. Egypt's anti-Semitic themes are faithfully parroted in the controlled Palestinian media. The Palestinian media also consistently deny the historic connection between the Jews and Jerusalem and the right of the Jews to nationhood. Even more troubling is the anti-Semitic incitement in Palestinian schoolbooks. A recent study of 140 Palestinian textbooks shows that anti-Semitism is all-pervasive in Palestinian texts. Jews are invariably depicted as robbers, aggressors, wild animals, locusts and treacherous cheats who have faked their history and stole Palestinian land. Nowhere in the Palestinian texts is there a single mention of the State of Israel or the peace agreements. The list of the world's countries in the standard Palestinian geography

book omits Israel, but a state named Palestine whose capital is Jerusalem is included. No Palestinian maps ever mention Israel. All the land between the Jordan River and the Mediterranean is "occupied Palestine", to be liberated in holy war.

This kind of brainwashing in the media and the classroom cannot be viewed merely as a gross violation of all Arab-Israel agreements. It is "a calculated, all-encompassing indoctrination campaign, in preparation for war." This article is perfectly consistent with the PLO's Fateh's Constitution, as may be seen in the Appendix to Chapter 8.

[19] See Strauss, *Liberalism Ancient & Modern*, p. 244. As Strauss notes, Spinoza hated Judaism as well as Jews, an attitude Hermann Cohen deemed "unnatural" and even as a humanly incomprehensible act of treason." I mention this in passing because one may find a similar phenomenon among certain Jews in Israel today.

[20] *The Chief Works of Benedict de Spinoza* (Dover: 1951), I, pp. 207, 257, 263, 265.

[21] For a critique of Spinoza's Ethics, see Eidelberg, *Judaic Man*, ch. 2.

[22] Henri Baruk, *Tsedek* (Binghamton, NY: Swan House Publishing Co., 1972), pp. 80, 133-140.

[23] Samson Raphael Hirsch, *The Pentateuch* (6 vols.; Gateshead: Judaica Press, 1982), on Gen. 11:7.

[24] As quoted in Mordechai Breuer, *The "Torah-Im-Derekh-Eretz" of Samson Raphael Hirsch* (Jerusalem/New York: Feldheim, 1970), p. 22.

[25] Exod. 23:2 actually refers to judicial proceedings in criminal cases. The plain meaning of the verse is, "Do not go with the [bare] majority to do evil [that is, to convict, but otherwise] incline toward the majority." On this verse, see Hirsch's commentary in *The Pentateuch*.

[26] See Louis Jacobs, *The Talmudic Argument: A Study in Talmudic Reasoning and Methodology* (Cambridge: Cambridge University Press, 1986), p. 50. An oft-cited example of the probability principle is the town in which nine butcher shops sell kosher meat and one sells non-kosher meat (*Hullin*, 11a). Any meat found in the town is halakhically kosher. What determines the status of the meat is not its physical properties, i.e., whether it was ritually slaughtered, but the supervening halakhic principle under discussion. This corresponds to Einstein's view of physical reality: "It is the theory that decides what we observe," or determines what is real. Cited and elaborated in Paul Eidelberg, *Jerusalem vs. Athens: Toward a General Theory of Existence* (NY: University Press of America, 1983), p. 195.

[27] See *Berakhot* 37a, *Kiddushin* 59b, *Yevamot* 108b, *Gittin* 15a, 47a.

[28] For a critique modern psychology, see Paul Eidelberg, "The Malaise of Modern Psychology," *Journal of Psychology*, Vol. 126, No. 2, Mar. 1992, pp. 109-130.

[29] To appreciate the exalted role of the woman in Judaism, see Samson Raphael Hirsch, *Judaism Eternal* (2 vols.; London: Soncino Press, 1956), II, 49-89.

[30] See below, p. 144, referring to Supreme Court's September 1999 ruling that the use of "moderate pressure" in the interrogation of terrorists violates Israel's Basic Law: Human Dignity and Freedom.

[31] Raba ben Huna was Rav's student and succeeded his master as the head of the great Sura Academy in Babylon.

[32] Hirsch, *Judaism Eternal*, II, 134. For a comparable incident recorded in the Jerusalem Talmud, as well as a different assessment of its legal status, see Eliezer Berkovits, *Not in Heaven: The Nature and Function of the Halakha* (New York: Ktav Publishing House, Inc., 1983), p. 27.

[33] Hirsch, *Judaism Eternal*, II, 133.

[34] Ibid., p. 103.

[35] Commenting on the scriptural verse "You will be a kingdom of priests and a holy nation unto Me" (Exod. 19:6), Eliezer Berkovits writes: "This kingdom of priests is not a society in which a priestly caste rules over an unpriestly populace in the name of some god. A holy nation is a realm in which all are priests. But where all are priests, all are servants – and God alone rules. 'A kingdom of priests and a holy nation' is not a theocracy, but a God-centered republic."

God, Man and History (New York: Jonathan David Publishers, 1965), p. 136.

[36] See Y. Harkabi, *Arab Attitudes to Israel* (Jerusalem: Keter, 1973), almost every page of which documents Arab hatred of Jews.

[37] See M. D. Gouldman, *Israel Nationality Law* (Jerusalem: Alfa Press, 1970), p. 13 (italics added). Although this book was published in 1970, no subsequent change in the laws of Israel affect the validity of my thesis regarding the reversion of Israel to Palestine in terms of the crucial concept of citizenship. It should also be noted that the provision in question was violated by the British White Paper of 1939 which terminated Jewish immigration to Palestine, rendering it virtually impossible for Jews to escape the Nazi Holocaust.

[38] Ibid.

[39] Ibid.

[40] Ibid., pp. 134-136.

[41] Cited in ibid., p. 55.

42 Ibid., p. 15.
43 It should be noted that, under Part II, section 10 of the Nationality Law, a person can become stateless by renouncing his Israeli nationality. By so doing he would still enjoy his personal, economic, social, and religious rights, but not his political rights.
44 Ibid.
45 Ibid., p. 16, (italics added).
46 See Aaron Cohen, *Israel and the Arab World* (London: W. H. Allen, 1970), p. 229. And so it was after 1967 when Israel gained control of Judea, Samaria, and Gaza. Thanks to Israel's economic and technological assistance, not only did Arab income in these areas multiply four-fold, but the government established new hospitals, health centers, primary and secondary schools and universities. Predictably (except to paraMarxists and naïve capitalists), these schools and universities became hotbeds of insurrection. See Chapter 8 on paraMarxism and capitalism.
47 This was the Supreme Court's stated position in the previously cited case of *Peretz v. Kfar Shamayarhu*, Local Council, 1962. Nevertheless, the Court has issued several ruling based on the equality principle of the Declaration. It thus appears that the Court's *obiter dictum* now has the status of constitutional law.
48 Gouldman, p. 69
49 *Jerusalem Post*, Jul. 20, 1998, p. 4.
50 *Jerusalem Post*, Jul. 22, 1998, p. 4.
51 Reported by Israel Radio, Channel 7.
52 Reported by Israel Radio, Channel 7, Oct. 7, 1999.
53 *Jerusalem Post*, Feb. 16, 1999, p. 16.
54 *Jerusalem Post*, Jan. 7, 1993.
55 For a theoretical analysis, see Eidelberg, *Demophrenia*, ch. 5.
56 Yitzhak Rabin saw this, as is evident in his May 1976 statement quoted earlier. That statement, to repeat, was made when Labor was in power, as it had been since the founding of the State. In 1977, however, the Likud gained control of the Government, joined by the religious parties which abandoned their twenty-nine year alignment with Labor. Thereafter Labor became increasingly dependent on the Arab vote, hence on Arab citizenship. This dependency eventually produced a profound change in the political tactics and even mentality of Rabin and his Labor colleagues and goes a long way toward explaining their appeasement of the PLO on the one hand, and the surfacing of their scornful statements about Judaism and religious Jews on the other.
57 Quoted in Gouldman, pp. 19-20 (italics added).

[58] The same may be said of a 1970 amendment to the Law of Return! According to this amendment, the rights of a Jew to automatic citizenship are also given to a child and grandchild of a Jew, to the spouse of a Jew, the spouse of a child and grandchild of a Jew even if they are not halakhically Jewish, i.e., born of a Jewish mother! It does not even matter whether the Jew, by whose right a claim is made to enter the country, is alive or not. Neither does it matter whether he himself enters the country. Countless gentiles can thus become citizens even though the only justification for Israel's re-establishment in 1948 is that it be a Jewish state. Meanwhile the Supreme Court's liberal interpretation of the Nationality Law has facilitated the process of deJudaizing Israel. See Gouldman, p. 72.
[59] Cited in ibid., p. 9.
[60] Cited in ibid., p. 117.
[61] Ibid., pp. 117-118.
[62] See Shlomo Levy, et al., *Beliefs, Observations and Social Interaction Among Israeli Jews* (Jerusalem: Louis Guttman Israel Institute of Applied Social Research, 1993), ch. 14, p. 101, Table 38.
[63] See Yochanan Peres, "Religious Adherence and Political Attitudes", Sociological Papers, Bar-Ilan University, Vol. 1, No. 2, Oct. 1992, p. 4. Professor Peres is neither religious nor "right-wing".
[64] See Eidelberg, *Demophrenia*, pp. 39-40, 65-66.
[65] Consider the famous "Brother Daniel" case. In 1942, during the German occupation of Poland, Rufeisen, born to Jewish parents in that country, converted to Christianity (probably to save his life). In 1945 he joined the Carmelite Order of monks. In 1958 he came to Israel and applied for an immigrant's certificate under the Law of Return. The application was denied by the Minister of Interior. The decision of the latter was upheld by Israel's Supreme Court, contrary to Jewish law, but conforming to the Court's conception of citizenship. See Gouldman's discussion, pp. 23-26.
[66] See Eidelberg, *Judaic Man*, ch. 10, summarizing the research of Dr. Moshe Katz, *CompuTorah: On Hidden Codes in the Torah, (Jerusalem: privately published, 1996),* and *Doron Witztum, The Additional Dimension* (Jerusalem: privately published, 1989, in Hebrew).
[67] See Eliyahu Meir Klugman, *Rabbi Samson Raphael Hirsch* (Brooklyn, NY: Mesorah Publications, 1996), p. 137.
[68] Cited in *Pathways to the Torah* (Jerusalem: Aish HaTorah Publications, 1988), p. A6.2.

69 Friedrich Nietzsche, *The Joyful Wisdom* (New York: Frederick Ungar Publishing Co., 1960), p. 289. T. Common, trans.

70 See Isaac Herzog, *Judaism: Law and Ethics* (London: Soncino Press, 1974), pp. 213-214.

71 Harvey Cox, *Making Votes Count: Strategic Coordination in the World's Electoral Systems* (Cambridge University Press, 1997), p. 19. Much of the quantitative data in this chapter is drawn from Cox's book, and some of the electoral concepts developed therein will be applied to Israel. The judgments and conclusions, however, are solely those of the present writer.

72 The threshold will almost certainly be raised before the next election.

73 One other religious party, Meimad, was a coalition partner in Ehud Barak's "One Israel" list, which included Labor and Gesher. Meimad received a ministry in the Barak cabinet. As for the other three religious parties, Shas and the National Religious Party received cabinet posts, whereas United Torah Judaism, as in the past, declined that honor.

74 Rein Taagepera & Matthew Shoberg Shugart, *Seats and Votes: The Effects and Determinants of Electoral Systems* (New Haven: Yale University Press, 1989), pp. 1-2.

75 Ibid., p. 3.

76 See Asher Arian, *Politics in Israel* (Chatham, NJ: Chatham House, 1989), 2d ed., pp. 276, 284-285.

77 The exceptions, besides Israel, are the Netherlands and Namibia. As already noted, however, the Netherlands is a homogeneous country, where the Dutch constitute 96% of the population. As for Namibia, its 1998 population was only 1.62 million (compared to Israel's 6.1 million).

78 Although the following discussion ignores our proposed bicameral parliament, it can be relevant to both branches depending on their respective modes of election.

79 Cox, *Making Votes Count*, p. 92.

80 Ibid., p. 93.

81 This is the position of Abba Eban in "A Disastrous Process", *Jerusalem Post*, Jul. 10, 1998, p. 8. He there states: "The direct election of the prime minister has violated every principle of decent international order." A remarkable non sequitur. Eban even has the audacity to declare that so long as direct, popular election of the prime minister prevails, "Israel will have no right to call itself a democracy!"

82 The 1990 government of national unity was toppled, when, in a bid for power (which failed), Labor chairman Shimon Peres persuaded Shas to desert the national coalition.

[83] See note 77 above.

[84] See Taagepera & Shugart, *Seats & Votes*, pp. 25-26.

[85] Shortly after the manuscript of this book was completed, it was reported that Prime Minister Ehud Barak favored the adoption of the German electoral system for the Knesset. Half of the Knesset's membership would be based on single-member plurality districts and half based on proportional representation. See *Jerusalem Post*, Oct. 29, 1999, p. 1.

[86] District elections will of course generate local parties. How these would relate to national parties in Israel is problematic. Since a winner-take-all election for the premiership will tend to generate a national two-party system, over the years, a two-party system on the national level may diminish the number of parties on the local level. Much will depend on campaign financing laws, distinctive sectional interests, civic education, and the felt sense of national priorities.

[87] Notice how President Bill Clinton, a Democrat, adopted conservative policies after the Republican Party gained control of both houses of Congress after the 1994 midterm elections. In fact, Clinton won the 1996 presidential election because he very much campaigned on the party platform of his Republican opponent!

[88] A blatant example of the Labor Government's contempt for Jewish public opinion is the following. In various 1992 pre-election polls, an overwhelming majority of 80 to 90% opposed any withdrawal from the Golan Heights. Accordingly, the Labor Party's official platform proclaimed: "Israel sees in the Golan Heights an area of great importance for its security, its safety and the ensuring of its water resources, even in times of peace. Consequently, in every peace agreement with Syria and in the security arrangements, Israel's settlements and military control will be maintained on the Heights – on which Israel's jurisdiction, law and administration have been applied."

Labor leader Yitzhak Rabin himself declared to a Golan audience: "As for the future, it is inconceivable that even in peace time we should go down from the Golan. Whoever even thinks of leaving the Golan wantonly abandons the security of Israel." (See *Jerusalem Post*, Dec. 3, 1993, p. 6.) Nevertheless, Mr. Rabin betrayed his pledge to the nation once he became Prime Minister. He publicly proclaimed his willingness to withdraw from the Golan Heights in exchange for a peace agreement with Syria.

[89] Although the Netherlands appears to be an exception, that country is not only a constitutional democracy, but it also has a bicameral legislature.

[90] See Exod. 18:19: "...seek out from among all the people men with leadership ability, God-fearing men – men of truth who hate injustice." Similar qualifications are prescribed in the original constitutions of Maryland, Massachusetts, New Hampshire, and Rhode Island. See Eidelberg, *The Philosophy of the American Constitution*, pp. 266-270.

[91] See Hirsch, *The Pentateuch*, on Deut. 16:18.

[92] Law and Administration Ordinance, 1948, Section 42, Explanatory Note.

[93] Menachem Elon, *Jewish Law* (4 vols.; Philadelphia/Jerusalem: Jewish Publication Society, 1994), IV, 1606, Bernard Auerbach and Melvin J. Sykes, trans.

[94] Alexis de Tocqueville, *Democracy in America* (2 vols.; New York: Vintage Books, 1945), II, 159.

[95] Friedrich Nietzsche, *The Dawn of Day* (London: T. Fisher Unwin, 1903), pp. 203-206, J. Volz, trans.

[96] See Matis Weinberg, *FrameWorks* (Boston: Foundation for Jewish Publications, 1999); Nossom Slifkin, *Seasons of Life: The Reflection of the Jewish Year in the Natural World* (Jerusalem: Targum Press, 1998); Joshua Berman, *The Temple: Its Symbolism and Meaning Then and Now* (Northvale, NJ: Jason Aronson, 1995); Eidelberg, *Judaic Man*, ch. 6, ("The Malaise of Modern Psychology").

[97] See Nathan Aviezer, *In the Beginning: Biblical Creation and Science* (Hoboken, NJ: Ktav, 1990); Gerald L. Schroeder, *Genesis and the Big Bang: The Discovery of Harmony Between Modern Science and the Bible* (New York: Bantam Books, 1990); Akiva Tatz, *Living Inspired* (New York: Targum/Feldheim, 1993); Akiva Tatz, *Worldmask* (New York: Targum/Feldheim 1995); and Lawrence Keleman, *Permission to Believe: Four Rational Approaches to God's Existence* (Jerusalem: Targum/Feldheim, 1990), pp. 54-65, on biologists, mathematicians, and physicists who refute the neo-Darwinian doctrine of evolution of chance mutation and natural selection.

[98] Montesquieu, *Considerations sur les Causes de la Grandeur des Romains et de leur Decadence* (Paris, 1899), p. 4 (my translation).

[99] David Ben-Gurion, *Israel: A Personal History* (Tel Aviv: Sabra Books, 1972), p. 552.

[100] Addressing the Knesset in the summer of 1989, then Prime Minister Yitzhak Shamir declared: "I see documents and from them I learn that there are those amongst us who talk about peace but practice treason." Mr. Shamir was alluding to leaders of the Labor Party who, in violation of the law, were meeting with PLO chief Yasser Arafat. See *Ma'ariv*, Aug. 1, 1989. For an elaboration, see Eidelberg, *Demophrena*, p. 219, n. 50.

[101] This happened in 1990 when Labor Party leader Shimon Peres conspired with Shas – it has been called the "stinking maneuver" – to bring down the national unity government headed by Yitzhak Shamir.

[102] In his notes on the debates of the Federal Convention that drafted the American Constitution, Hamilton referred to wisdom along with self-confidence as creative of energy. See Paul Eidelberg, *The Philosophy of the American Constitution*, p. 192.

[103] Henry Taylor, *The Statesman* (New York: Mentor Books, 1958), p. 64.

[104] This calls to mind what Yitzhak Rabin says of Shimon Peres in *The Rabin Memoirs* (London: Weidenfeld & Nicolson, 1979), pp. 186, 223, 226, 242-243. "Peres," he writes, "let personal conflicts foment and seemed to take advantage of human foibles to place his adversaries under pressure" (p. 46). Rabin also accused Peres of using the media to disrupt the smooth running of government when it serves his personal interests (p. 218). Rabin claimed that Peres, "on a number of occasions…behaved as if he were out to challenge the cabinet's authority." But so did Mr. Rabin. Thus, in April 1989, while serving as Defense Minister under Prime Minister Shamir, Rabin prompted MK Abdel Wahab Darawshe to convey his (Rabin's) own peace plan to PLO chief Yasser Arafat (then in Cairo), a plan that deviated significantly from that of the Government. See *Yediot Aharanot*, May 30, 1989 (in Hebrew).

[105] See Howard Grief, "A Petition to the Supreme Court of Israel Challenging the Legality of the Oslo Accords", *International Journal of Statesmanship* (Jerusalem: Foundation for Constitutional Democracy), Vol. I, No. 2, Summer 1996, pp. 1-78. This article is a slightly condensed version of the petition submitted to the Supreme Court sitting as the High Court of Justice: HC 3414/96.

[106] Peres' efforts may have contributed to the Middle East international peace conference held in Madrid in October 1991, attended by Prime Minister Shamir. The Madrid Conference eventually led to Oslo.

[107] For a detailed analysis of the constitutional debates on this issue, see Eidelberg, *The Philosophy of the American Constitution*, ch. 9.

[108] See Cox, *Making Votes Count*, p. 38.

[109] "The Halakhic Status of the Israeli Court System", *Crossroads, Halakha and the Modern World* (Zomet Institute, Alon Shvut-Gush Etzion, 1988), Vol. 2, p. 207. Page references will hereafter appear between parentheses in the text.

[110] Although the term "laymen" includes unordained judges, the primary reference is to Jews unlearned in Jewish law.

[111] See *Jerusalem Post*, Mar. 31, 1996, p. 6. While this Basic Law was being considered by the Knesset Law Committee, Justice Aaron Barak, in contravention of the separation of powers, wrote a letter to the committee's chairman, Dedi Zucker (Meretz) recommending various changes in the Law. Legal experts stated that one of the changes Barak suggested would force the Government to allow the import of non-kosher meat. The Barak Court ruled to this effect in a case subsequently coming before it. The Court's ruling induced the Knesset to amend the law! For Barak's intervention, see *Jerusalem Post*, Jan. 28, 1994, p. 12.

[112] Cited in Yonason Rosenblum, "He Who Judges Too Much Judges Not At All: The Controversial Course Pursued by Israel's Supreme Court", *The Jewish Observer*, Nov. 1996, p. 8. It should be noted that thoughtful secularists such as former Supreme Court President Moshe Landau and Professor Ruth Gavison (see Appendix) deplore the Court's "judicial activism" and regarded many of its decisions as contrary to democracy.

[113] See *Jerusalem Post*, Dec. 1, 1994, p. 1; Dec. 13, 1993, p. 3.

[114] See Elon, *Jewish Law*, IV, 1685. Volume and page references will hereafter be cited in the text between parentheses.

[115] "Secular Courts in the State of Israel", *Halakha and the Modern World* (Zomet Institute, Alon Shvut-Gush Etzion, 1988), Vol. 2, p. 213. Page references will hereafter appear between parentheses in the text.

[116] See Rabbi Hershel Schachter, "Dina D'Malchusa Dina: Secular Law as a Religious Obligation", *The Journal of Halakha*, p. 104, for halakhic references.

[117] See Elon, I, pp. 133-135.

[118] Rav Ariel's argument resolves apparent contradictions in the Ran, the Rambam, and the Shulkhan Arukh, and one cannot do justice to his penetrating analysis without reproducing it in its entirety. Nevertheless, this chapter will adduce evidence supportive of Ariel's conclusion.

[119] See Salo W. Baron, *The Jewish Community* (3 vols.; Philadelphia: Jewish Publication Society, 1948), II, pp. 215, 239.

[120] Ibid., II, pp. 210-211.

[121] Ibid., I, pp. 212-213, 285-290. See Emanuel B. Quint and Neil S. Hecht. *Jewish Jurisprudence: Its Sources and Modern Application* (2 vols.; New York: Harwood Academic Publishers, 1980, 1986), 1, pp. 82-83, citing *Baba Kamma* 84b, which holds that non-ordained judges may hear only cases that occur frequently and involve a loss of money. "From the earliest Geonim to the present, all [halakhic authorities] agree that the twofold test [frequency of the case and loss of money] is the basis of jurisdiction [for lay judges]."

[122] Bernard Meislin, *Jewish Law in American Tribunals* (KTAV Publishing House, 1976), p. 125.

[123] The *Journal of Halakha and Contemporary Society*, Vol. III, Fall 1981, p. 35. Page references will hereafter appear between parentheses in the text.

[124] Kopel Kahana, *The Case for Jewish Civil Law in the Jewish State*, (London: Soncino Press, 1960). Page references will hereafter appear between parentheses in the text.

[125] Elon, IV, 1629-1634, 1642, 1856-1860.

[126] See ibid., I, 105-106 for a more elaborate definition of "Mishpat".

[127] Moshe Silberg, *Talmudic Law and the Modern State* (New York: Burning Bush Press, 1975), more extensively discussed in Paul Eidelberg, *Beyond the Secular Mind* (New York: Greenwood Press, 1989), pp. 154-156.

[128] Abraham H. Rabinowitz, *The Jewish Mind* (Jerusalem: Hillel Press, 1978), p. 64. See Moshe Avigdor Amiel, *Ethics and Legality in Jewish Law* (Jerusalem: The Rabbi Amiel Library, 1992), p. 3, and Meislin, p. 34, n. 51.

[129] Cited in Kahana, p. 86, n. 1.

[130] See Hirsch, *The Pentateuch*, on Num. 35:28.

[131] For a talmudic analysis of *lifenim mi-shurat ha-din*, see Elon, I, 156-159, and contrast Eidelberg, *Beyond the Secular Mind*, p. 78.

[132] See *Garrity v. New Jersey* 17 L. Ed. 2d 562 (1967), and *Spevack v. Klein*, 17 L Ed. 574 (1967). The Senate's failure to impeach President Clinton on charges of perjury and obstruction of justice should be viewed in this light.

[133] See Steven Plaut, "Affirmative Stupidity", *Jerusalem Post*, May 1, 1996, p. 3. Plaut shows that "affirmative action" has everywhere proven to be an abysmal failure, that it has not narrowed social gaps, that it often harms those it purports to benefit, and that its main victims are the most gifted members of the "beneficiary" group.

[134] To fully appreciate the consequences of the Supreme Court's egalitarianism, consider the following. In April 1996, the Court rejected a petition against the registration of Ahmed Tibi's Arab Movement for Renewal Party in the Knesset's May elections. Plaintiff charged that there was a conflict of interest between a party's obligation of loyalty to the State and Tibi's role as an adviser to Yasser Arafat, the head of a foreign power, and one that has openly called for Israel's piecemeal destruction. It was further argued that Tibi's party platform seeks to redefine Israel as "a state of its citizens", rather than as a Jewish state. Nevertheless, the Court ruled that since the right to establish a party is so fundamental to a democracy, a party could only be disqualified for reasons explicitly listed in the Party Law: denying Israel's existence as a Jewish and democratic state, inciting racism, or serving as a front for criminal activity. See *Jerusalem Post*, Apr. 30, 1996, p. 3. Some may say that the Court in the Tibi case manifested a lack of intellectual integrity or moral courage. Be this as it may, contrary to Judaism and Jewish law, the Court typically emphasizes rights and is virtually silent about duties (such as loyalty to the State that protects those rights).

[135] Cited in Elon, IV, 1592.
[136] Ibid., IV, 1594.
[137] Ibid., IV. 1590.
[138] Ibid. See Arnold Cohen, *An Introduction to Jewish Civil Law* (Jerusalem/New York: Feldheim, 1991), pp. 11-12, who writes: "Attempts to revive Jewish Civil Law in the twentieth century have failed because the proponents were not prepared to accept the Commandments and the Statutes" [which are inseparable from Judgments, i.e. Mishpatim].
[139] Elon, IV, 1828.
[140] Cited in Elon, IV, 1867.
[141] See Eidelberg, *Philosophy of the American Constitution*, pp. 229-232, discussing *Federalist 49*.
[142] See *Jerusalem Post*, Dec. 20, 1995, p. 3.
[143] Baron, *The Jewish Community*, II, 168.
[144] Ibid., IV, 1896-1897.
[145] Justice Barak has acknowledged this in a meeting with the Knesset Law Committee. See *Jerusalem Post*, Dec. 20, 1995, p. 3.
[146] *Jewish Law*, II, 539-540.
[147] See Jonathan Rosenblum, "A Court of One", *Jerusalem Post*, Oct. 15, 1999, p. B9.

[148] See Paul Eidelberg, "Israel 1994: Democratic Despotism", *Nativ, A Journal of Politics and the Arts*, Sep. 1994 (Hebrew).

[149] For a critical but balanced analysis of this view based on a survey of the economies of Middle Eastern states, see Patrick Clawson, "Mideast Economies After the Israel-PLO Handshake", *Journal of International Affairs*, 48:1, Summer 1994, pp. 141-145, who writes: "Politics, not economics, will be both the main goal and the main determinant of economic cooperation" (p. 164). See also E.G.H. Joffé, "Relations Between the Middle East and the West", *Middle East Journal*, 48:2, Spring 1994, pp. 265-266.

[150] See Shimon Peres, *The New Middle East* (New York: Henry Holt, 1993), pp. 95, 99.

[151] See Leo Strauss, *The Political Philosophy of Hobbes* (Chicago: University of Chicago Press, 1952), pp. 76-77.

[152] See Hobbes, *Leviathan* (Oxford: Basil Blackwell, 1956), pp. 82, 84 (originally published in 1651); Strauss, pp. 118-128, 152. Although Hobbes deemed absolute monarchy the best regime, his mentality is thoroughly democratic. See ibid., ch. 7 passim.

[153] Hobbes, pp. 34, 59.

[154] See Mahmud Abbas (Abu Mazen), *Through Secret Channels*, first reported in the *Jerusalem Post*, Jan. 13, 1995, p. 8, and subsequently in the *Jerusalem Post Magazine*, Apr. 7, 1995, p. 25. Abu Mazen led the PLO delegation in the Oslo talks. See also Mark Perry & Daniel Shapiro, "Navigating the Oslo Channel", *Middle East Insight*, Sep.-Oct. 1993, pp. 9-20.

[155] Lewis S. Feuer (ed.), *Marx and Engels: Basic Writings on Politics & Philosophy* (New York: Doubleday Anchor, 1959), p. 28 (re the program of the Communist Manifesto), p. 119 (re Marx's Critique of the Gotha Program).

[156] See Lloyd D. Easton & Kurt H. Guddat (eds.), *Writings of the Young Marx on Philosophy and Society* (New York: Doubleday Anchor, 1967), pp. 304, 294.

[157] See G. E. Von Grunebaum, *Modern Islam: The Search for Cultural Identity* (Berkeley: University of California Press, 1962), pp. 130, 204n10, 226, 231; and pp. 15, 40, 64, 215-218, 225n12, 229-230, 235, 255, 259. For a contrary, but not an entirely consistent view, see Bassam Tibi, *The Crisis of Modern Islam: A Preindustrial Culture in the*

Scientific-Technological Age (Salt Lake City: University of Utah Press, 1988), pp. 3-8, 22, 25, 37, 50-51, 106, 111. For diverse Islamic views, see John D. Donohue & John L. Esposito (eds.), *Islam in Transition: Muslim Perspectives* (New York: Oxford University Press, 1982).

[158] Karl Marx & Frederick Engels, *The German Ideology*, (New York: International Publishers, 1947), p. 14. For an analysis and refutation of Marx, see Paul Eidelberg, *Beyond Détente: Toward an American Foreign Policy* (LaSalle, IL: Sherwood Sugden, 1977), pp. 65-75, and *Demophrenia*, pp. 29-32.

[159] Hobbes, p. 46.

[160] Ibid., p. 32

[161] See Allan Bloom, *The Closing of the American Mind* (New York: Simon & Schuster, 1987); Dinesh D'Souza, *Illiberal Education* (New York: Free Press, 1991); and Paul Eidelberg & Will Morrisey, *Our Culture "Left" or "Right": Littérateurs Confront Nihilism* (Lewiston, NY: Edwin Mellen Press, 1992), which reveals the relativism of higher education in general, and of economists Milton Friedman, Paul Samuelson, and John Kenneth Galbraith in particular.

[162] See ibid., ch. 2, which reveals the relativism of Senator J. William Fulbright and of professor Zbigniew Brzezinski and how this relativism influenced the foreign policy of the Carter Administration.

[163] See C. S. Lewis, *The Abolition of Man* (New York: Macmillan, 1947), ch. 1. Lewis shows how relativism engenders hedonism and "men without chests" – precisely the tendency of Hobbes's emasculating principle that violent death is the greatest evil.

[164] See Seyyed Hossein Nasr, *Islam and the Plight of Modern Man* (London: Longman, 1975), ch. 1.

[165] The author is here indebted to Dr. Rael Jean Isaac, speech to a national conference of Americans For a Safe Israel, Mar. 3, 1995, pp. 1, 13.

[166] See Daniel Bell, *The End of Ideology* (New York: Free Press, 1961), rev. ed., Epilogue.

[167] See Nikolai Berdyaev, *Slavery and Freedom* (New York: Charles Scribner's Sons, 1944), p. 188. Even earlier, Nietzsche described socialism as egoism disguised as altruism. See his *The Will to Power* (New York: Random House, 1967), pp. 202, 412.

[168] Shimon Peres, *David's Sling* (New York: Random House, 1970), p. 169.

[169] Cited in Clawson, p. 141.

[170] See *Nativ, A Journal of Politics and the Arts*, 42:1, p. ii.

[171] Ibid., p. iii.
[172] See *The Jewish Press*, Apr. 14, 1995, p. 52. Clawson, cited earlier, points out that Egyptian-Israel trade in 1992 was a mere $13.3 million, representing 0.07% of Egypt's trade and 0.04% of Israel's (p. 145).
[173] *Jerusalem Post*, Apr. 14, 1992.
[174] Cited in Arieh Stav, "The Israeli Death Wish: A Study in the Jewish Attitude Toward National Sovereignty", Ariel Center for Policy Research, Policy Paper No. 53, Apr. 1999.
[175] *Teheran Times*, Oct. 23, 1991; *Time* Magazine, Nov. 4, 1991.
[176] See Peres, *David's Sling*, who once held this opinion of Arabs: "No compromise can satisfy them. It is the Arab goal to abolish Israel, not to change a political situation" (p. 10). Referring to King Hussein – and this applies to his successor – Peres admits that while Jordan has a vital interest in avoiding war, its monarch's authority is problematic. "A king is not a president or a prime minister. His authority does not spring from popular elections...but from a title inherited from his father... [M]ost of his thoughts and energies are inevitably concerned with how to preserve it" (p. 259).

In addition to potential threats from Syria and Iraq, Jordan's monarch cannot even count on the backing of the bulk of his population, two-thirds of which are "Palestinians". Far more than in 1970, Jordan is threatened by an irredentist movement fomented by the PLO ensconced in Jericho.

Finally, before Peres engaged in the "politics of peace", which, thanks to Arab voters and five Arab Knesset Members, brought his party to power in 1992, he warned: "Kingship may be a life job, but monarchs are not immortal. Jordan may be able to base her security on the words of a document, but Israel cannot base hers on a king" (pp. 260-261).
[177] See Eidelberg, *Demophrenia*, p. 43.
[178] Ibid., pp. 92-93.
[179] See Clawson, p. 162.
[180] Ibid., p. 144.
[181] Cited in Harkabi, *Arab Attitudes to Israel*, p. 98.
[182] See Y. Harkabi, *Arab Strategies and Israel's Response* (New York: Free Press, 1977), p. 55.
[183] *The Egyptian Gazette* (Cairo), Apr. 16, 1980. See also Paul Eidelberg, *Sadat's Strategy* (Montreal: Dawn, 1979), pp. 78-80, for more explicit statements of Sadat's objectives vis-a-vis Israel.
[184] Interview with the Egyptian magazine *October*, Jan. 14, 1978, as quoted in Shmuel Katz, *The Hollow Peace* (Jerusalem: Dvir, 1981), pp. 231-232.

185 See de Tocqueville, *Democracy in America*, II, pp. 282-285.
186 See Pitirim A. Sorokin, *The Crisis of Our Age* (New York: E. P. Dutton, 1942), p. 213.
187 See Eidelberg, *Demophrenia*, pp. 111-112, 133 on the hostility of Israel's own Arab citizens toward the existence of a sovereign Jewish state.
188 Cited in Joseph B. Schechtman, *The Life and Times of Vladimir Jabotinsky* (2 vols.; Silver Spring, MD: Eshel Books, 1956), II, p. 65.
189 See *Jerusalem Post*, Dec. 3, 1993, p. 6.
190 Harold Nicholson, *Diplomacy* (Oxford University Press, 1970), pp. 25-26.
191 *Pennsylvania Gazette*, Nov. 1994, p. 17; *The Jewish Week*, Jun. 2, 1994.
192 Henry Kissinger, *American Foreign Policy* (New York: W. W. Norton, 1974), p. 37.
193 Hasannin Heykal, *The Road to Ramadan* (New York: Quadrangle Press, 1975), pp. 260-261. Contrast Shimon Peres: "I have become totally tired of history because I feel history is a long misunderstanding." Which recalls Santayana: "Whoever forgets the past is condemned to repeat it."
194 What is remarkable about the Netanyahu Government was its almost daily reports of PLO violations of the so-called Oslo agreements, which violations, however, did not prompt the Government to abrogate those agreements.
195 See Arieh Stav, *Peace – The Arabian Caricature: A Study of Anti-Semitic Imagery* (Jerusalem: Gefen Publishers, 1999). See endnote 18, for examples of anti-Semitism in Egyptian, Syrian, and Palestinian media.
196 Y. Harkabi, *Arab Attitudes to Israel*, p. 133.
197 Ibid., p. 126.
198 Ibid., p. 348.
199 Cited in Gabriel Ben-Dor (ed.), *The Palestinians and the Middle East Conflict* (Ramat-Gan, Israel: Turtledove Publishing, 1978), p. 304.
200 See Eidelberg, *Sadat's Strategy*, p. 34.
201 See Samuel P. Huntington, "How Countries Democratize", *Political Science Quarterly*, Vol. 106, No. 4, pp. 91-92.
202 It should be noted that representative assemblies did not acquire their legislative functions until the seventeenth and eighteenth centuries. Democracy need not depend on their exercising those functions today. In fact, one can go back to classical antiquity and find examples of popular assemblies whose function was not to make laws but to approve or reject

proposed legislation submitted by magistrates and to hold the latter to account for any malfeasance in office. As John Stuart Mill has written, a "numerous assembly is as little fitted for the direct business of legislation as for that of administration." The primary work of legislation must be done, and increasingly is being done, by the executive departments and administrative agencies.

[203] Although Tunis, Egypt, Morocco, Jordan, and Yemen have recently experienced multiparty electoral competitions, these hardly warrant the label "democratization" in the sense of allowing for popular or majority rule. These reforms are very much attempts to stem the disaffection of key merchant, professional, and political families resulting from falling living standards and government corruption. According to some commentators: "In virtually every case, these reforms have been abetted by the intervention of institutions representing international capital, notably the International Monetary Fund and the World Bank." See "The Democracy Agenda in the Arab World", *Middle East Journal*, Vol. 46, No. 1, Winter 1992, p. 3; As'ad Abu Khahil, "A New Arab Strategy? The Arab Rejuvenation of Arab Nationalism", ibid., p. 31.

[204] See Eidelberg, *Beyond Détente*, ch. 5, which shows how moral relativism facilitated US recognition of the "Evil Empire".

[205] Had such policies been implemented shortly after the Six-Day War, many Arabs, without any prompting by the Government, would have emigrated to Jordan and the Persian Gulf states. Having formed no distinct culture or solid infrastructure in Judea and Samaria, their attachment to the land is superficial – avowals to the contrary notwithstanding. Indeed, while Jordan ruled the area from 1949 to 1967, about 400,000 Arabs moved from Judea and Samaria to the eastern side of the Jordan River. During and immediately after the 1967 war, 200,000 more Arabs – roughly one of every five inhabitants – moved to the East Bank. The move involves no great inconvenience. The distance from Nablus (Shechem) to Amman is only 46 miles. Which means that the Arabs of Judea and Samaria can move to Jordan as readily as they can drive to and work in Israel. If Israel's Government had also moved some of its ministries to Judea and Samaria, the idea of a Palestinian state would have died before it was born.

[206] I am indebted to Norman Kurland for this discussion of economic democracy. See John H. Miller (ed.), *Curing World Poverty: The New Role of Property* (St. Louis, MO: Social Justice Review, 1994), ch. 8.

[207] See Chapter 7, Appendix.

[208] Paul Eidelberg, *A Discourse on Statesmanship: The Design and Transformation of the American Polity* (Urbana/Chicago, IL: University of Illinois Press, 1974). p. 437.
[209] For a more extensive analysis, see Eidelberg, *The Philosophy of the American Constitution*, pp. 217-234.
[210] Based on a paper presented by the author at the American Political Science Association annual conference in Washington, DC on Aug. 31, 1997. The paper was translated into Hebrew and published in *Nativ*, Jan. 1998.
[211] See Shlomo Sharan, "State and Religion in Israel", *The Religious-Secular Conflict in Israel* (Israel: ACPR Publishers, 1999), p. 29, who writes: "...Israel is only one of the many 'ethnic democracies' in the world where a particular ethnic group is the majority and where minority groups automatically have their national identity submerged or highly limited... Among these can be mentioned countries such as Finland, Greece, Sweden, Denmark, Holland, Belgium, Japan, Korea, Switzerland... Furthermore, in each and every instance of ethnic democracy there is a connection, albeit of varying degrees, between religion and the state insofar as each country has an official religion..."
[212] Pp. 48-52. I am greatly indebted to the publisher, the Foundation for Jewish Publications, for permission to quote this material.

BIBLIOGRAPHY

Aish HaTorah. *Pathways to the Torah*, Jerusalem: Aish HaTorah Publications, 1988.
Amiel, Moshe A. *Ethics and Legality in Jewish Law*, Jerusalem: The Rabbi Amiel Library, 1992.
Arian, Asher. *Politics in Israel*, 2nd ed., Chatham, NJ: Chatham House, 1989.
Aviezer, Nathan. *In the Beginning: Biblical Creation and Science*, Hoboken, NJ: Ktav, 1990.
Baron, Salo W. *The Jewish Community, 3 vols.*, Philadelphia: Jewish Publication Society, 1948.
Baruk, Henri. *Tsedek*, Binghamton, Binghamton, NY: Swan House Publishing Co., 1972.
Bell, Daniel. *The End of Ideology*, rev. ed., New York: Free Press, 1961.
Ben-Dor, Gabriel, ed. *The Palestinians and the Middle East Conflict*, Ramat-Gan, Israel: Turtledove Publishing, 1978.
Ben-Gurion, David. *Memoirs*, New York: World Publishing, Co., 1970.
_____. *Israel: A Personal History*, Tel Aviv: Sabra Books, 1972.
Berdyaev, Nikolai. *Slavery and Freedom*, New York: Charles Scribner's Sons, 1944.
Berkovits, Eliezer. *God, Man and History*, New York: Jonathan David Publishers, 1965.
_____. *Not in Heaven: The Nature and Function of the Halakha*, Ktav, 1983.
Berman, Joshua. *The Temple: Its Symbolism and Meaning Then and Now*, Northvale, NJ: Jason Aronson, 1995.
Bloom, Allan. *The Closing of the American Mind*, New York: Simon Schuster, 1987.
Breuer, Mordechai. *The "Torah-Im-Derekh-Eretz" of Samson Raphael Hirsch*, Jerusalem/New York: Feldheim, 1970.
Cattan, Henry. *Palestine and International Law*, London: Longman, 1973.
Cohen, Aaron. *Israel and the Arab World*, London: W. H. Allen, 1970.
Cohen, Arnold. *An Introduction to Jewish Civil Law*, Jerusalem/New York: Feldheim, 1991.
Cox, Harvey. *Making Votes Count: Strategic Coordination in the World's Electoral Systems*, Cambridge University Press, 1997.
Donohue, John D. and John L. Esposito, eds. *Islam in Transition: Muslim Perspectives*, New York: Oxford University Press, 1982.
D'Souza, Dinesh. *Illiberal Education*, New York: Free Press, 1991.

Easton, Lloyd D. Guddat, Kurt H., eds. *Writings of the Young Marx on Philosophy and Society*, New York: Doubleday Anchor, 1967.

Eidelberg, Paul. *Judaic Man: Toward a Reconstruction of Western Civilization*, Middletown, NJ: Caslon Co., 1996.

_____. *Demophrenia: Israel and the Malaise of Democracy*, Lafayette, LA: Prescott Press, 1994.

_____. *Beyond the Secular Mind: A Judaic Response to the Problems of Modernity*, NY: Greenwood Press, 1989.

_____. *A Discourse on Statesmanship: The Design and Transformation of the American Polity*, Urbana/Chicago, IL: University of Illinois Press, 1974.

_____. *The Philosophy of the American Constitution: A Reinterpretation of the Intentions of the Founding Fathers*, New York: Free Press, 1968; University Press of America, 1986.

_____. Jerusalem vs. Athens: Toward a General Theory of Existence, New York: University Press of America,1983.

_____. *Sadat's Strategy*,Montreal: Dawn Books, 1979.

_____. *Beyond Détente: Toward an American Foreign Policy*, LaSalle, IL: Sherwood Sugden, 1977.

_____. *On the Silence of the Declaration of Independence*, Amherst, MA: University of Massachusets Press, 1976.

Eidelberg, Paul and Will Morrisey. *Our Culture "Left" or "Right": Littérateurs Confront Nihilism*, Lewiston, NY: Edwin Mellen Press, 1992.

Elon, Menachem. *Jewish Law*, B. Auerbach and Melvin J. Sykes, trans., 4 vols., Philadelphia/Jerusalem: Jewish Publication Society, 1994.

Feuer, Lewis S., ed. *Marx and Engels: Basic Writings on Politics Philosophy*, New York: Doubleday Anchor, 1959.

Gouldman, M. D. *Israel Nationality Law*, Jerusalem: Alfa Press, 1970.

von Grunebaum, G. E. *Modern Islam: The Search for Cultural Identity*, Berkeley: University of California Press, 1962.

Harkabi, Y. *Arab Attitudes to Israel*, Jerusalem: Keter Publishing House, 1973.

_____. *Arab Strategies and Israel's Response*, New York: Free Press, 1977.

Herzog, Isaac. *Judaism: Law and Ethics*, London: Soncino Press, 1974.

Heykal, Hasannin. *The Road to Ramadan*, New York: Quadrangle Press, 1975.

Hirsch, Samson Raphael. *The Pentateuch*, 6 vols., Gateshead: Judaica Press, 1982.

_____. *Judaism Eternal*, 2 vols., London: Soncino Press, 1956.
Hobbes, Thomas. *Leviathan*, Oxford: Basil Blackwell, 1956.
Jacobs, Louis. *The Talmudic Argument: A Study in Talmudic Reasoning and Methodology*, Cambridge: Cambridge University Press, 1986.
Kahana, Kopel. *The Case for Jewish Civil Law in the Jewish State*, London: Soncino Press, 1960.
Katsh, Abraham I. *The Biblical Heritage of American Democracy*, New York: KTAV Publishing House, 1977.
Katz, Moshe. *CompuTorah: On Hidden Codes in the Torah*, Jerusalem: privately published, 1996.
Katz, Shmuel. *The Hollow Peace*, Jerusalem: Dvir, 1981.
Keleman, Lawrence. *Permission to Believe: Four Rational Approaches to God's Existence*, Jerusalem: Targum/Feldheim, 1990.
Kissinger, Henry. *American Foreign Policy*, New York: W. W. Norton, 1974.
Klugman, Eliyahu M. *Rabbi Samson Raphael Hirsch*, Brooklyn, NY: Mesorah Publications, 1996.
Levy, Shlomo, et al. *Beliefs, Observations and Social Interaction Among Israeli Jews*, Jerusalem: Louis Guttman Israel Institute of Applied Social Research, 1993.
Lewis, C. S. *The Abolition of Man*, New York: Macmillan, 1947.
Machiavelli, Niccolo. *The Prince*.
Marx, Karl and Engels, Frederick. *The German Ideology*, New York: International Publishers, 1947.
Meislin, Bernard. *Jewish Law in American Tribunals*, New York: KTAV Publishing House, 1976.
Miller, John H., ed. *Curing World Poverty: The New Role of Property*, St. Louis, MO: Social Justice Review, 1994.
Montesquieu, Baron de. *Considerations sur les Causes de la Grandeur des Romains et de leur Decadence*, Paris, 1899.
Nasr, Seyyed Hossein. *Islam and the Plight of Modern Man*, London: Longman, 1975.
Nicholson, Harold. *Diplomacy*, London: Oxford University Press, 1970.
Nietzsche, Friedrich. *The Joyful Wisdom*, T. Common, trans., New York: Frederick Ungar Publishing Co., 1960.
_____. *The Will to Power*, New York: Random House, 1967.
Nisan, Mordechai. *Minorities in the Middle East*, Jefferson, NC: McFarland Co., 1991.
Peres, Shimon. *The New Middle East*, New York: Henry Holt, 1993.
_____. *David's Sling*, New York: Random House, 1970.

Peres, Yochanan. "Religious Adherence and Political Attitudes", Sociological Papers, Bar-Ilan University, Vol. 1, No. 2, Oct. 1992.
Quint, Emanuel B. and Hecht, Neil S. *Jewish Jurisprudence: Its Sources and Modern Application*, 2 vols., New York: Harwood Academic Publishers, 1982.
Rabin, Yitzhak. *The Rabin Memoirs*, London: Weidenfeld Nicolson, 1979.
Rabinowitz, Abraham H. *The Jewish Mind*, Jerusalem: Hillel Press, 1978.
Schechtman, Joseph B. *The Life and Times of Vladimir Jabotinsky*, 2 vols. Silver Spring, MD: Eshel Books, 1956.
Schroeder, Gerald L. *Genesis and the Big Bang: The Discovery of Harmony Between Modern Science and the Bible*, New York: Bantam Books, 1990.
Silberg, Moshe. *Talmudic Law and the Modern State*, B. Bokser, trans., New York: Burning Bush, 1973.
Slifkin, Nossom. *Seasons of Life: The Reflection of the Jewish Year in the Natural World*, Jerusalem: Targum Press, 1998.
Sorokin, Pitirim A. *The Crisis of Our Age*, New York: E. P. Dutton, 1942.
Spinoza, Benedict de. *Chief Works*, New York: Dover, 1951.
Stav, Arieh. *Peace – The Arabian Caricature: A Study of Anti-Semitic Imagery*, Jerusalem: Gefen Publishers, 1999.
_____. "The Israeli Death Wish: A Study in the Jewish Attitude Toward National Sovereignty", Ariel Center for Policy Research, Apr. 1999.
Strauss, Leo. *Liberalism Ancient and Modern*, New York: Basic Books, 1968.
_____. *The Political Philosophy of Hobbes*, Chicago: University of Chicago Press, 1952.
Taagepera, Rein and Matthew S. Shugart. *Seats and Votes: The Effects and Determinants of Electoral Systems*, New Haven: Yale University Press, 1989.
Tatz, Akiva. *Worldmask*, New York: Targum/Feldheim 1995.
_____. *Living Inspired*, New York: Targum/Feldheim, 1993.
Taylor, Henry. *The Statesman*, New York: Mentor Books, 1958.
Tibi, Bassam. *The Crisis of Modern Islam: A Preindustrial Culture in the Scientific-Technological Age*, Salt Lake City: University of Utah Press, 1988.
Tocqueville, Alexis de. *Democracy in America*, 2 vols., New York: Vintage Books, 1945.
Weinberg, Matis. *FrameWorks (Exodus)*, Boston: Foundation for Jewish Publications, 1999.

Whitehead, Alfred North. *Science and Philosophy*, New York: Philosophical Library, 1948.

Witztum, Doron *The Additional Dimension*, Jerusalem: privately published, 1989, Hebrew.

FOUNDATION FOR CONSTITUTIONAL DEMOCRACY

The **FOUNDATION FOR CONSTITUTIONAL DEMOCRACY**, incorporated in Israel and the USA, is an independent, non-profit, organization unaffiliated with any political party. Its primary goal is to promote Constitutional Democracy in Israel.

Most of Israel's major problems can be traced to its lack of a constitution. Of 75 countries having democratic elections for the lower (or only) branch of the legislature, Israel is the only one that does not have district (or regional) elections. Knesset Members owe their position, power, and perks not to the voters but to party leaders who (may) head cabinet ministries. Hence they cannot block unwise government measures without committing political suicide.

Since the cabinet consists of MKs whose position does not depend on constituency elections, the government can ignore public opinion with impunity, even on issues concerning the borders of the state. But thanks to a low electoral threshold, such is the multiplicity of parties in the cabinet that the government cannot pursue coherent and resolute national policies.

Accordingly, the **FOUNDATION** has designed a Constitution with institutional checks and balances and constituency elections. Because this Constitution assimilates democratic to Jewish principles and values, it should appeal to Israelis across the political spectrum.

To promote its Constitution, the **FOUNDATION** disseminates policy papers and political analyses, many of which are published in Hebrew- and Russian-language media.

Netanyahu, Benjamin, 112, 183, 191, 193-194
Nicholson, Harold, 178
Nietzsche, Friedrich, 55, 76, 109-110
Noahide Laws, 74-75, 202

Oral Law, 147-148, 153
Oslo, 161

Palestinian Authority, 183
Paramount Law, 31-32
Particularism, 71, 74
Parties, 11, 89
  Small, 91-93
Party-hopping, 88
Peace, 20, 43, 170
Peel Commission, 61-62, 168
Peres, Shimon, 96, 116, 160, 165, 171, 181, 240n104, 246,176
Personalized PR, 97
Plato, 44
PLO, 11, 13, 20, 56, 176, 179, 192
Pluralism, 80, 111
Politics, 36, 43
Post-Zionism, 13
Preferential Vote, 97, 101
Presidential Government, 112, 116, 120-122

Rabin, Yitzhak, 19, 31, 34, 55-56, 96, 116, 172, 179, 196
Racism, 56
Rambam, 40, 108, 110, 125, 138
  (See also Maimonides)
Relativism, 41, 45, 102, 131, 164
Religion, 39-40, 102, 108-109
Representative Democracy, 98, 100
Responsibility, 76-77
La Rochefoucauld, 105, 177
Roman Law, 141
Rousseau, Jean-Jacques, 44
Rule of Law, 210-214
Sadat, Anwar, 169-170, 185, 191, 197
Sanhedrin, 46, 50, 145

Shamir, Yitzhak, 116, 191, 240n100
Silberg, Moshe, 141-143
Socialism, 161, 165
Sovereignty, 36-37
Spinoza, Benedict de, 38-39, 43, 233n19
Split Ticket, 95
State, 36-38, 52
Statesmanship,
  Jewish (defined), 8-9, 105-108
Strauss, Leo, 24-25
Supreme Court
  American, 12, 146, 155
  Israeli, 12, 24, 37, 44, 62, 123, 126-128, 144, 146-147, 154, 158

Talmud,
  Babylonian, 123, 154
  Jerusalem, 46, 154
Taylor, Henry, 105
Tenure, 118-119
Theocracy, 49-51, 234n35
Tibi, Ahmed, 243n134
Tocqueville, Alexis de, 109
Torah, 10, 13, 22, 29, 41, 44-45, 50, 73, 100, 107-108, 144
  (see also Oral and Written Law)

Ultra-Secularists, 126-127
Unitary Executive, 112-114
Universalism, 71-74

War, 165, 170
Washington, George, 102, 108
Weimar Republic, 86
Weinberg, Matis, 227-229
What is a Jew? 75-77, 81
Who is a Jew? 77-80
Whitehead, Alfred North, 36, 44
Written Law, 147, 153

Zionism,
  Cultural, 25
  Political, 24
  Secular, 9, 13, 19
Zionists, 9

Foundations of Law Act, 134, 150, 154-155
Freedom, 32-33, 43-46, 52

Gavison, Ruth, 156-158
Ger, 73-74
Ger Toshav, 74-75
Germany, 97
Ge'ula (Redemption), 227-229
Goethe, Wolfgang, 152
Golan Heights, 172, 179-180, 238n88
Gouldman, M. D, 59, 67
Gur, Mordechai, 167
Guttman Institute, 71-72, 108

Halakha, 47-48, 76, 78
(see also Jewish Law)
Halevi, Judah, 40, 143
Hamilton, Alexander, 113-115, 119-120, 240n162
Harkabi, Yehoshafat, 188-189
Herzl, Theodor, 25, 51
Herzog, Isaac, 126
Hirsch, Samson Raphael, 39-40, 51, 100
Hobbes, Thomas, 160-161, 163-164
Homestead Act, 202-203
Honor, 47-48
Human dignity, 48, 144, 146
Humanism, 164, 193
Huntington, Samuel P., 198

Ibn Hazm, 177
Irish Constitution, 101, 103
Islam, 163, 186-189, 201
Islamic Modernists, 196, 204
Ivri, David, 167

Jefferson, Thomas, 19,
Jewish Beliefs and Practices, 71-72
Jewish Court of Arbitration, 148
Jewish Law, 47-48, 106-108, 112, 131, 137-138, 140, 145, 147, 153
Jewish Law Society, 149

Jewish People, 109-110
Jewish Statesman, 105-108, 198-199
Jewish Statesmanship, Prerequisites of, 195
Jihad, 188, 200-201
Jordan, 63, 167, 187
Judaism, 41, 45, 73, 202
Justice, 130-131, 145, 218

Kahana, Kopel, 138-140, 144, 147
Kant, Emanuel, 44-45
Kasher, Asa, 165
Kissinger, Henry, 182, 184
Knesset, 8, 58, 66, 83, 87-88, 99, 102, 154-155, 216
Krauss, Simcha, 136-138
Kara, Ayoub, 64-65

Labor Party, 10-11, 13, 65, 235n 56, 238n88, 240n100
Landau, Moshe, 58, 66
Land of Israel, 22, 29
Law of Return, 58, 66-67, 236n58
Laws of Noah,
(see Noahide Laws)
Lifenim mi-shurat ha-din, 49, 146
Likud, 11, 65, 192
Loyalty Oath, 69

Madison, James, 116-117, 213-214
Maimonides,
(see Rambam)
Majority rule, 42, 51, 233n25
Marx, Karl, 160-165, 181, 201
Meir, Golda, 29
Mill, John Stuart, 7, 207
Montesquieu, Baron de., 44, 111
Muslims, 63, 72, 164, 169, 171, 197

Nasr, Seyyed Hossein, 164
National Consciousness, 12
Nationalism, 21, 227-228
Nationality, 41, 67
Nationality Law, 74-75, 202
(See also Citizenship Law)

INDEX

Abdallah al-Tall, 159
Adams, John, 55, 76
Am vs. *Goy*, 21, 70
America, 37, 70
Arab Anti-Semitism, 134, 174, 186, 217, 232n18
Arab Demographic Problem, 9, 11, 12, 101
Arab MKs, 63-64
Arabs and Terrorism, 9, 55, 60-61, 65-69, 171, 183
Arafat, Yasser, 161, 179, 181, 184,
Ariel, Yaakov, 128-132, 135
Assad, Hafez, 179-180, 185
Assimilation, 131
Australia, 97

Bagehot, Walter, 123
Balfour Declaration, 26-28
Barak, Aaron, 127, 144, 150-152, 212, 241n111
Barak, Ehud, 171
Baron, Salo W., 133, 152-153
Baruk, Henri, 39
Bazak Yaakov, 124-128, 135
Basic Laws, 208-210
Begin, Menachem, 169, 191
Beilin, Yossi, 95
Bell, Daniel, 165
Ben-Gurion, David, 10, 20, 23, 66, 111
Berdyaev, Nikolai, 165
Berkovits, Eliezer, 234n35
Brazil, 118

Canada, 84
Capital punishment, 144-145
Chile, 84-86
Chosen People, 77
Christianity, 22, 41, 135, 170, 193,
Citizenship, 60
  Torah view of, 73
Citizenship Law, 32, 34, 56
  Reform of, 68
  (See also Nationality Law)
Cognitive Dissonance, 36-43

Cohen, Hermann, 110, 233n19
Constitution (American), 102
Constitution (Israel)
  Objections to, 207-208
  Proposed, 210-225
Conversion,
  (See Who is a Jew?)

Declaration of Independence
  American, 19, 33
  Israel, 20, 23-24, 26-27, 33-34, 62
Democracy,
  Classical or normative, 32-33, 52
  Contemporary or normless, 32, 33, 40-41, 47, 52, 66, 70, 89, 102
  General, 32, 36, 40 (defined), 42, 50, 52, 187-188
Dina d'malchuta dina, 129, 135-136, 153
Diplomacy,
  Martial vs. Democratic, 178-185
  Primer on, 194-196, 198-200
District Elections, 98-100, 238n86

Eben, Abba, 237n81
Economy, 203-204
Egalitarianism, 49, 66-67, 81
Egocentric Pluralism, 8, 40, 43-44, 111
Egypt, 167
Electoral College, 116-117
Electoral Rules, 83-87
Electoral Systems, 94-97
Electoral Threshold, 85, 89-91
Elon, Menachem, 135-136, 150, 154
Equality, 32-34, 46-49, 52, 56
English Law, 141-145
Ethics, 143

Family, 31, 37, 53, 202
Fear, 53, 62, 66, 202